TRANSPARENCY
and Secrecy Within the Catholic Church

*To our parents, who have taught us from childhood
to cultivate values of openness and discretion.*

TRANSPARENCY
and Secrecy Within the
Catholic Church

JORDI PUJOL SOLER
ROLANDO MONTES DE OCA

Midwest Theological Forum
Downers Grove, Illinois

Published in the United States of America by

MIDWEST THEOLOGICAL FORUM
4340 Cross Street, Suite 1
Downers Grove, IL 60515 USA
Tel: 630-541-8519 • Fax: 331-777-5819
www.theologicalforum.org

First Edition
Copyright © 2022 Midwest Theological Forum
ISBN 978-1-948139-81-6

Authors:	Rev. Prof. Jordi Pujol Soler, PhD
	Rev. Rolando Gibert Montes De Oca Valero
Original Title:	*Trasparenza e segreto nella Chiesa Cattolica* (Milan: Marcianum Press, 2022), 280 pp.
Translator:	Kira Howes
Contributing Editor:	Arlene Borg
Design and Production:	Stephen J. Chojnicki
Cover Design:	Marlene Burrell

Printed in the USA

Contents

PREFACE

THE PROBLEM WITH
THE PROBLEM OF SECRECY

by Russell Shaw

In setting out some years ago to write a book about the problem of secrecy in the Church,[1] I discovered at the start that Catholic theologians had little or nothing to say about it. When I consulted one prominent theologian about sources, he told me secrecy was a canonical issue, not a theological one, and I should look in canon law. When I looked in the *Code of Canon Law*, I found canons dealing with the confidentiality of Church records and things like that, but nothing about the abuse of secrecy in the Church. To be sure, moralists have written a great deal over the centuries about truth-telling and lying, but that is a different matter. And the abuse of secrecy is nowhere to be found on the theological radar screen.

Now, why is that? My guess is that it reflects the fact that the abuse of secrecy in the conduct of ecclesiastical affairs has come to be considered simply just part of the way things are done, almost as if secrecy arose from the very nature of the Church and the words "Go into all the world and preach the gospel"[2] had never been spoken. But they were spoken. As far as I know, Jesus did not say, "Go into all the world and keep quiet about what you are doing."Yet sometimes we have acted, and act now, almost as if they were. And against this background I am delighted that this book by Father Rolando Montes de Oca and Father Jordi Pujol breaks the silence and makes an important contribution to the discussion of transparency and secrecy.

---

1. R. SHAW, *Nothing To Hide: Secrecy, Communication, and Communion in the Catholic Church* (San Francisco: Ignatius Press, 2008).

2. Mk 16:15d.

The book I wrote — now, more than a decade ago — does not take an exclusively negative view of secrecy. As a matter of fact, it makes the case for secrecy and does it quite well. The seal of confession is the strongest example of strictly obligatory secrecy in the Church; current efforts in several countries to override this sacred imperative in the name of rooting out and punishing sex abuse, though perhaps understandable, are deeply alarming. There is also a serious obligation of secrecy in pastoral counseling situations. Furthermore, the Church has the same right to confidentiality to protect its legitimate financial and administrative interests that any other institution has, along with the obligation it shares with other groups to respect people's privacy rights.

Thus, the argument advanced in my book is not that the Church must make a total disclosure of everything. Rather, it is that the presumption in doing the Church's work should be in favor of openness and accountability, with the burden of proof in any particular case resting with those who favor secrecy.

It goes without saying that the Catholic Church is hardly the only institution in which secrecy is abused. This problem exists in government, the military, and the private sector — wherever the people in charge use secrecy to cover up wrongdoing and mistakes by themselves or their subordinates, or simply as a tool for exercising control over others, or just because they find it convenient not to have to explain what is going on to those who do not belong to the "in" group. Still, the fact that the abuse of secrecy is common among members of the leadership and management class in many institutional settings is important to understanding the same phenomenon as it is found in the Church.

At the same time, however, it is reasonable to ask whether there anything *special* about the abuse of secrecy in the Church. The answer, I believe, is both *yes* and *no*. It is *no* just to the extent that the same sort of abuse of secrecy is practiced in so many other contexts beside the religious one. Ethicist Sissela Bok expresses the problem in general in these strong terms:

> When linked, secrecy and political power are dangerous in the extreme. For all individuals, secrecy carries some risk of corruption and irrationality; if they dispose of greater than ordinary

power over others, and if this power is exercised in secret, with no accountability to those whom it affects, the invitation to abuse is great.... In the absence of accountability and safeguards, the presumption against secrecy when it is linked with power is therefore strong.[3]

What is special about the abuse of secrecy in the Church becomes clear when one asks oneself who exercise "power over others" in the ecclesial setting. Historically considered, the answer, both *de facto* and *de jure*, is clear: Within the Catholic Church, power over others is exercised by the members of the clerical hierarchy, as well as these days to some extent by their lay and religious collaborators. And this is to say that the abuse of secrecy in the Church is intimately bound up with clericalism.

Some years ago, I also wrote a book about that problem.[4] As with the book about secrecy, so also with the book about clericalism, I discovered that not much had been published about the subject. Of course, since the eruption of the scandal of clergy sex abuse and its concealment by bishops and religious superiors, that has changed, and more and more voices have been raised in condemnation of clericalism. The National Review Board, an entity established by the bishops of the United States to monitor their efforts to deal with the crisis, spoke for many in a report on the "causes and context" of the sex abuse scandal published in February 2004:

> Some witnesses likened the clerical culture to a feudal or a military culture and said that priests and bishops who "rocked the boat" were less likely to advance. Likewise, we were told, some bishops did not want to be associated with any problem for fear of criticism because problems arose on their watch. As a result, problems were left to fester.

And the report left no doubt about the link between clericalism and secrecy.

> In many instances, Church leaders valued confidentiality and a priest's right to privacy above the prevention of further harm

---

3. S. Bok, *Secrets: On the Ethics of Concealment and Revelation* (New York: Vintage Books, 1989), 126.
4. R. Shaw, *To Hunt, To Shoot, To Entertain: Clericalism and the Catholic Laity* (San Francisco: Ignatius Press, 1993).

to victims and the vindication of their rights. Both confidentiality and privacy are valuable.... But these values should not be allowed to trump the duty to keep children safe from harm.[5]

Needless to say, we have paid a very heavy price for ignoring that counsel. The case of former cardinal Theodore McCarrick is emblematic. Here was an instance, at a very high level in the hierarchy, where secrecy and clericalism worked in tandem to produce a disaster for the whole Church.

As that suggests, there is a special dimension to the abuse of secrecy in the Church in that it undermines the Church considered from the viewpoint of *communio*—that is, as a hierarchically structured communion or community of faith in which all the members are fundamentally equal in dignity and rights.

When I first became conscious of the abuse of secrecy in the Church as a serious problem, I saw the situation simply in pragmatic terms. As the person responsible for the media relations of the episcopal conference of the United States, I had become convinced that unnecessary secrecy on the part of the bishops was harmful to their own best interests by provoking continued tension and conflict between them and journalists. As time passed, however, I came to realize that the reasons for openness and accountability in the Church went far beyond merely improving their relations with reporters and facing up to the harm being done by secrecy to communion within the Church. A secretive ecclesial community is a handicapped ecclesial community; we are dealing here not merely with a problem in media relations but with a fundamental issue in ecclesiology, touching directly on the nature of the Church itself.

In any group or community, communication among the members is necessary for the group's health and good functioning, and that is certainly true of the Church. But what is at stake in the Church is something even larger. Back in 1971, the Pastoral Instruction on Social Communications, *Communio et Progressio*, published by what was then called the Pontifical Council on Social Communications, made the important point

5. National Review Board, "A Report on the Crisis in the Catholic Church in the United States," in *Origins* (March 11, 2004).

that members of the Church have "the right to all the information they need to play their active role in the life of the Church," a right that extends to both "the faithful as individuals and as organized groups."[6]

Plainly, of course, ecclesial communion has a vertical dimension: It begins in and is grounded in the relationship with God, and the primacy of this vertical dimension must always be recognized and respected. But ecclesial communion also has a *horizontal* dimension to which the statement of the Pontifical Council for Social Communications and other, similar statements by the Holy See point: It involves the human relationships among us who are members of the ecclesial community. The systematic abuse of secrecy and other offenses against open, honest communication in the conduct of Church affairs conflict with this basic principle of ecclesial communion by denying some members of the Church information that they need in order to be full, active, responsible members.

Recognition of this fact is far from universal even now. Progress is slow, but it is occurring, and this book contributes to it. I hope its message will be widely heard and taken to heart.

---

6. PONTIFICAL COUNCIL FOR SOCIAL COMMUNICATIONS (PCCS), Pastoral Instruction *Communio et Progressio* (May 23, 1971), 119–120, *www.vatican.va/roman_curia/ pontifical_councils/pccs/documents/rc_pc_pccs_doc_23051971_communio_en.html*.

INTRODUCTION

To have information is to have power, and for that reason, to classify something as secret is also to have power. Those who govern different civil, military, and religious institutions have always known this. Being transparent also leads to exposing one's vulnerability and thus makes one open to attack.

As people of our time and as members of the Church, we desire greater transparency in the Church and an end to absurd and pointless secrets. We have watched with horror the reports of cover-ups and lack of accountability on the part of cardinals, bishops, and religious superiors, and we would like these pages to be a *yes* to light, openness, and communication in all its glory.

Transparency is our battle cry, and in the process of writing this book we have discovered a treasure trove: Church messages that over time were forgotten — at least by us — and that call for openness, information, and even transparency. We also discovered that secrecy in the Church has a purpose, and we have understood what its place is. It has become clear to us that it is not appropriate to wage war in the field of Church communication but rather to build bridges and clear paths, listening and dialoguing with sincerity and compassion.

Although this study does not focus solely on sexual abuse, it was developed in a context that sees the presence of victims of sexual abuse by clergy and the Church's increasingly evident decision to end this crisis. Their stories and their pain echo as a cry from God, calling for the conversion of his Church. Precisely when we began this research in 2019 was when the international Meeting on the Protection of Minors in the Church was held, and there were two *Motu Proprios* from Pope Francis that influenced our work. For the Church to sympathize with (suffer with) the suffering of the victims, to listen to them, to welcome them, to respect them, and to make the changes necessary for putting an end to these tragedies, implies important questions related to communication. This work is part of a movement that cares about justice for people as well as the veracity of the facts and promotes communication that is increasingly consistent with the identity of the Church, which walks with those who suffer most.

While we were considering the need for transparency and secrecy and wondering about their spaces in Church communication, a priest friend was accused of pedophilia. He experienced the full force of *zero tolerance* policies. The press had access to all his data and published it indiscriminately. He had to go and live with a relative and find a lawyer on his own, while most of the priests, in order to "not get involved," refused to even greet him. In a private WhatsApp message, the accused priest complained that "although the prosecutor has not formalized the process or asked for a trial — seemingly for lack of evidence — the toughest thing is that the Church basically does not even listen to me and grants all favor to the alleged victim. There is little fairness in the process." This priest was not found guilty, and probably is not, but he has already been convicted in the court of public opinion. Transparency is necessary, but it must have some limits.

What are the limits of transparency and secrecy in Church communication? What are their purposes? Are transparency and secrecy related, or are they mutually exclusive? These are the issues that we seek to illuminate in the current research.

Transparency is not merely an attitude that implies *more communication*: Both transparency and secrecy are crucial in decisions of governance that affect the identity of the Church. It should therefore come as no surprise that we often look to ecclesiology. It is in the light of the Mystery of the Church that we understand how the metaphor of transparency — as contemporary society demands — may not be best suited to describing the communication of the Church, as it would compromise key elements of her identity and mission. The law, communications, and theology will help us grasp nuances and sketch out the contours.

A *culture of transparency* is necessary in all institutions that operate in the public sphere because it concerns the common interest and the public's right to truly know them. For these organizations, being transparent usually means having a unique discourse (internal and external). Transparency expresses honesty and human and social responsibility; it is based on the value of truth. Often acting in this way involves a deep process of transformation.

In the Galleria Borghese, one of Rome's most renowned museums, visitors can see one of Bernini's most personal works, which few know about. This is *La verità svelata dal tempo*, a marble sculpture completed between 1646 and 1652. In this work, the Truth is allegorically shown as a nude young woman who is unveiled by a figure that represents time. It is a work that Bernini never completed.

This masterpiece reflects the author's state of mind. His chief mentor died around that time, and meanwhile his rivals began to criticize him for his design of Saint Peter's Basilica. Many experts think that Bernini had created this sculpture not as a project to sell but for his own self-reflection. In fact, he also stated in his will that said sculpture was to remain in the family.[1]

The message he likely had in mind was that a reign of lies would not last forever: Time, in the end, reveals the truth. However, as Sarah McPhee says, the irony is that one of the effects of time is that it devours everything. In this sense, it is true that time unveils the truth, but it does not necessarily reveal it at the right time. The same is true of transparency and expanding the right to know. One might dream of a utopian democracy based on absolute transparency as a managerial solution, but the issue is deeper than that. Truth contains mystery and sanctity: It must be unveiled, but it can never be unveiled completely. As John D. Peters said, with absolute transparency modernity wants to "violate this mystery," as a definitive solution, but in reality the Truth cannot be exposed "in a nude and crude way," but must always be *unveiled*.[2] Readers will not find definitive solutions in these pages but rather some reasons to adhere to a *culture* of openness, of shared responsibility, and of organic communication, seeking to work to hold law and communication together.

---

1. Cf. J. PUJOL, "Transparency Is Not a Utopia but a Non-stop Process," in *Church, Communication & Culture* 2, no. 1 (2017), 115.

2. Ibid., 115–116.

The right to communication of the truth is not unconditional; that is, a right to know the truth cannot exist without limitations: The right we speak of here is that of seeing that the relationships between members of society (including within the Church) are established based on veracity. The latter is a fundamental requirement for the coexistence and the building of society, which is based on the value of mutual trust.

The structure of these pages follows the major themes of the book: the abuse of secrecy in the Church and the importance of protecting certain spaces of secrecy (Chapters 1 and 2), the incorporation of transparency into the Church with its nuances (Chapters 3, 5, and 6), the meaning of "zero tolerance" as a policy against abuse and the problem that it poses to the principle of the "presumption of innocence" (Chapters 4 and 7), the need for accountability on the part of the bishops (Chapter 8), and finally, the proposal for transformation and organic communication in the Church (Chapters 9 and 10). We conclude with an appendix that contains fifteen tips for "translucent communication": a model that combines the communicative approach with law and theology.

The book begins and ends with the contributions of two great people who are admired for their work in this area. Russell Shaw, who served as Secretary for Public Affairs at the United States Conference of Catholic Bishops, and who prophetically wrote fourteen years ago about the necessity for greater transparency and accountability in the Church, in his book: *Nothing to Hide: Secrecy, Communication, and Communion in the Catholic Church*. And SER Monsignor Charles J. Scicluna, Secretary of the Congregation for the Doctrine of the Faith and the main player in many of the reforms that we are seeing in the Church in recent years. His legal talents served Pope Benedict XVI and then Pope Francis. These two luminaries, each in his own field, show us that it is possible to work well in a climate of love for the Church, respecting and valuing the treasure of the theological tradition.

Also based on their example, this work aims to show the importance of a synergy between law and communication.

CHAPTER 1

THE ABUSE OF SECRECY IN THE CHURCH

> *He will surely rebuke you*
> *if in secret you show partiality.*
> *—Job 13:10*

Talking about secrecy in the Catholic Church often elicits conflicting reactions: there are those who defend it at all costs and those who instead reject it with no "ifs," "ands," or "buts."

Some believe that it is right to defend the institution, its spaces, and its rights, while others think that this is an unacceptable excess in an information society. Certainly, the Church is not a democracy and the "right to know" arises from citizens' claims against the constituted authority. The Church operates according to other parameters, which are predominantly spiritual, since she is mystery and the Sacrament of Salvation for all souls. For this reason, the Church must consider, in order to be faithful to her Founder (Jesus Christ) and her high purpose (the salvation of humanity), when to protect what is secret and when to provide information.

We shall focus on a case that may help us reach the most balanced and honest view, in the face of a goal that can never be considered definitively achieved.

In 2002, a team of journalists from the *Boston Globe* published a report on at least seventy clergymen who had sexually abused minors for decades. On the part of the Church hierarchy, the handling of this information had been maintained in the strictest secrecy.[1]

---

1. Among those accused of abuse have been priests, religious, catholic schoolteachers, etc. Since we are dealing with representatives of the Church, we have preferred to use the term "clergyman" or "cleric," as these are more general terms.

According to this report, the bishops and superiors in many cases procured the silence of victims and their families. They often required psychological treatment for the abusers before transferring them elsewhere. At the place of the transfer, however, no report was sent either on the incident or on the opinion of the psychologists or psychiatrists. The superiors or leaders and the faithful were unaware of the condition in which the new clergyman arrived; as a result, children were continuously put in harm's way and crimes were repeated, with the number of victims increasing, especially in the 1970s. Among the most deplorable cases is that of John Geoghan, who was accused by more than 100 people of having committed sexual abuse.[2]

The problem was not confined to Boston. The first case to make national news was verified in 1985 in Lafayette, Louisiana, where eleven children claimed to have been abused by their priest, Gilbert Gauthe. The trial showed that his superiors were aware of the issue with this clergyman, and they had made efforts to get him treated but had then gone on to transfer him — even though they had reason to believe he was still dangerous. They had even paid the victims to remain silent.

In response to the Gauthe case, Father Thomas P. Doyle, counsel for the canonical nunciature in Washington; F. Ray Mouton, defense counsel for Gauthe; and psychiatrist Michael R. Peterson wrote a ninety-three-page report calling for policies to address the cases of abusive priests. The report was, however, shelved without a response from the bishops' conference.

Meanwhile, the scandal was growing, and allegations of sexual abuse were popping up all over the country. The words of a 1987 article, distributed by Knight Ridder, sound like a true prophecy today: "The church's reluctance to address the problem is a time bomb waiting to detonate within American Catholicism."[3]

---

2. The Journalism School, *Reporting an Explosive Truth: Boston Globe and Sexual Abuse in the Catholic Church* (Columbia University: Case Consortium), ccnmtl.columbia.edu/projects/caseconsortium/casestudies/14/casestudy/files/global/14/Boston%20Globe%20and%20Sexual%20Abuse%20in%20the%20Catholic%20Church_wm.pdf.

3. Cf. Ibid.

In June of 1992 a group of American bishops, realizing that there was objectively a problem, formulated five principles,[4] the application of which led to a decrease in cases of abuse. Unfortunately, the autonomy of the local churches left the bishops free to decide whether or not to follow those guidelines; the implementation of the principles, therefore, varied widely.[5]

The mantle of silence that covered this scourge — and the total ignorance on the part of those responsible for communication — delayed and hindered more decisive action against abuses. At the level of communication, on the part of the lay press, the "dearth of hard facts created an information vacuum that the crisis of 2002 often would fill with sensationalism and exaggeration."[6] The absence of data and statistics, which was the result of excessive secrecy, prevented effective action at the level of communication. The perception of abuse was distorted because, although most of the events had occurred between twenty and thirty years earlier, they were perceived as current — happening now.

Another type of (indirect) victim was — and still is today — the vast majority of priests. Though they remain upright and faithful to their priesthood, they experience strong distrust because of these abominable crimes, and they must carry the heavy burden of suspicion. They are often forced to take preventative measures or engage in unusual or unnatural security behaviors. Finally, they are exposed to false accusations from which it is very difficult to defend themselves. Overall, the costs related to the credibility of the Catholic Church have been very high.

The breeding ground for these abuses has been a clerical environment (which is now less common) in which authority exercised with excessive force is met with excessive reverential

---

4. The five principles were a prompt response to allegations, dismissal of the priest in the case of a credible allegation, compliance with the law, reaching out to victims and families, and respecting the privacy of those involved. In 2002, reporting to the public authorities was added and marked as mandatory. Cf. UNITED STATES CONFERENCE OF CATHOLIC BISHOPS (USCCB), *Charter for the Protection of Children and Young People (Dallas Charter)* (Washington, DC, 2002), *www.bishop-accountability. org/resources/resource-files/churchdocs/DallasCharter.pdf.*

5. Cf. R. SHAW, *Nothing to Hide*, 90.

6. Cf. Ibid.

fear, where fidelity to God is confused with unconditional veneration toward the person of the superior, where the structure is pyramidal and closed. This is an environment in which it is especially difficult to deviate from the script or offer criticism.

GOALS OF TOP-SECRET POLICY

In Boston and in other US dioceses, senior clergy have sought to protect the good reputation of the clergymen who were guilty of sexual abuse of minors in order to safeguard the privacy of the victims and to preserve the standing of the Church — more specifically of the priesthood and consecrated life.

In part they kept silent to protect "the faith of the children," that is, to forestall the danger that the faith of individuals lacking sufficient formation would be diminished by discovering some of their pastors' corruption. As Shaw points out, using the "knowledge deficit" of the laity as an excuse to exclude them from an adult role in Church affairs becomes a kind of "self-fulfilling prophecy." This generates a vicious cycle: The less the laity are told, the more ignorant they become; the more ignorant they are, the less they are able to participate. At a certain point this vicious cycle must be broken.[7]

The policy of maximum secrecy imposed by the uppermost hierarchy has had the opposite outcome to what was desired. Moreover, it has produced other unwelcome effects, and it has in fact been an aggression, an unintentional attack on the identity and mission of the Church.

THE ABUSE OF SECRECY VIOLATES THE RIGHT OF THE FAITHFUL TO KNOW THE TRUTH

We speak of *the abuse of secrecy* because we are referring to a type of information that the laity had a right to have, particularly the parents and those responsible for these children — a right that the hierarchical superiors who accepted the abusers who

---

7. Cf. Ibid., 32.

changed locations after their first episode of child abuse also had.[8]

The secrecy surrounding the sexual abuse perpetrated by clerics and religious prevented their immediate superiors (vicars, parish priests, superiors of religious houses) and the lay faithful from accessing vital information. The assailant was sent to a new ecclesial destination without his immediate superiors' knowledge of his crime and without any diagnosis by psychiatrists. This incomprehensible *discretion* allowed abusers to have "normal" relationships with minors, who were unwisely exposed to the possibility of becoming potential new victims at the mercy of the temptation of the cleric, who was put in a position to commit new crimes.

Certainly, the fact that it was impossible to share information between dioceses, parishes, orders, and other religious structures was another barrier to prevention, correction of errors, and communication of experiences—all of which played into the hands of sexual abusers. In this sense, another deplorable fact was that different dioceses had the opportunity to "wash their hands," considering the crisis a problem only in Boston, and did not feel the need to engage, while the truth is that they were experiencing the same crisis and continued to cover it up.

This abuse of secrecy, in practice, expressed a preference for the good reputation of the assailant at the expense of the physical and psychological integrity of the minors involved. In extreme but real cases, the victims would even go so far as to kill themselves[9]

---

8. In addition to the problem that directly affects them, the laity, by their dignity as baptized, have the right to honest and respectful participation in information, to be part of the Church's internal dialogue and to be heard. Indeed, as was recognized years later, the hierarchy does not have the capacity to address and resolve this crisis without the valuable contribution of the lay faithful. "It is impossible to think of a conversion of our activity as a Church that does not include the active participation of all the members of God's People. Indeed, whenever we have tried to replace, or silence, or ignore, or reduce the People of God to small elites, we end up creating communities, projects, theological approaches, spiritualities and structures without roots, without memory, without faces, without bodies and ultimately, without lives." Cf. Pope FRANCIS, *Letter to the People of God* (August 20, 2018), *w2.vatican.va/content/francesco/en/letters/2018/documents/papa-francesco_20180820_lettera-popolo-didio.html*.

9. Cf. Pope FRANCIS, *Homily in the Chapel of the Domus Sanctæ Marthæ with a Group of Clergy Sex Abuse Victims* (July 7, 2014), *www.vatican.va/content/francesco/en/cotidie/2014/documents/papa-francesco-cotidie_20140707_vittime-abusi.html*.

because in this kind of ecclesial environment, nobody was likely to believe such an accusation. Thus, in addition to the trauma of the physical and psychological abuse, there was also an abuse of the *secrecy* imposed on the faithful, who had the right to know the truth. They were not offered the due information by ecclesial authority. This choice of secrecy is diametrically opposed to the choice that the Church's morals demand and is also a serious communication inconsistency.

The boundary for what "the faithful need to know" is not well-defined, and it never will be. Prudence requires evaluating the circumstances, but in no case does "prudence" mean "coming to terms with what is absolutely wrong," whether a vice or an illness. Preventing the faithful from knowing relevant information that concerns the common good of the community not only proved to be blatantly imprudent but also gravely disrespectful toward the dignity of the baptized. As Grisez said:

> All too often the faithful feel themselves to be, not brothers and sisters joined in intimate communion and full cooperators in carrying out the Church's mission, but citizens in a rather weak monarchic or aristocratic political society... whose inefficient clerical and lay bureaucracy often is impervious to advice and criticism.[10]

It treats them as eternal children, which is unjust discrimination because it limits them and excludes them from positions of leadership in the Church.

This only impoverishes the Church[11] and contradicts her truth. The Church is communion and is hierarchical in the manner of the Gospel. Since the Second Vatican Council, there has been talk of the exercise of pastoral authority in the Church as a service. And in effect it is. But as Shaw emphasizes:

> Honesty and openness are necessary if the exercise of authority is not to degenerate into paternalistic authoritarianism with

---

10. Cf. G. Grisez, *Living a Christian Life* (Quincy: Franciscan Press, 1993), 161.

11. Cf. Pontifical Council for Social Communications (PCCS), Pastoral Instruction *Ætatis Novæ* (February 22, 1992), in *AAS* 84 (2005), 447ff., no. 10, *www.vatican.va/roman_curia/pontifical_councils/pccs/documents/rc_pc_pccs_doc_22021992_aetatis_en.html*.

a smiling, "pastoral" face. Ending the abuse of secrecy for the sake of clerical manipulation and control is essential to that.[12]

To deny the faithful access to relevant information is to contradict the Magisterium with facts; it is to irresponsibly ignore the signs of the times and to distance the Church more and more from a society that values transparency, openness, and participation. Persisting in secrecy and denying the faithful the right to know means acting against the Church and weakening her to the point of compromising her ability to influence the world with a *prophetic message,* which is hers and which the world needs. The cover-up of crimes of sexual abuse (by the ecclesial authority) has often led to the Church being discredited on other matters, of which she is at the forefront, such as the defense of life and the promotion of social justice.[13]

The main scandal of abuse is that crimes were being covered up, not just that information was being withheld. These aspects are related but have different levels of gravity. The failure to apply the law is a grave injustice: It is one thing not to make information about a crime public; it is quite another—and much more serious—thing not to punish a crime. In the wake of Vatican II, "pastoral" has been the opposite of "doctrinal," and has meant the opposite of "penal." With the new Book VI of Criminal Law, we move from *puniri potest* to *punire debet.*[14]

THE ABUSE OF SECRECY GOES AGAINST JUSTICE

The fact that it was impossible to access information on the abuse of minors perpetrated by clerics was an obstacle to civil and canonical justice, which could not provide a timely and effective response that would prevent new offenses and hold perpetrators

---

12. R. SHAW, *Nothing to Hide,* 20.

13. Cf. B. CLARIOND, *Comunicar y Participar: La comunicación institucional en la Iglesia y su relación con la tutela y promoción del bien común* (Rome: Ateneo Pontificio Regina Apostolorum, 2018), 79.

14. Cf. J.P. KIMES, "Reclaiming 'Pastoral': *Pascite Gregem Dei* and Its Vision of Penal Law," in *The Jurist* 77 (2021), 269, 279–281.

accountable for their crimes.[15] The predators' experience of impunity, which was protected by secrecy, was not conducive to solving the crisis but exacerbated it. The secrecy surrounding these crimes served as a haven for predators.

There was another reason the abuse of secrecy did not help: When the abuses of minors and their cover-up were made public, the situation was left in the hands of the secular press, which often published statistics — sometimes exaggerated or manipulated — that had a very strong impact on public opinion.[16] At the same time, the lack of information prevented Church communicators from accessing data that would have allowed them to provide accurate information. The top leaders of the American Church, imprisoned by their own system of secrecy, were left powerless to respond. The public, Catholics, and society in general had no other choice than to accept what the media said as true. This *information vacuum* paved the way for a disastrous effect on public opinion and has facilitated the manipulation of information.[17]

Such an information vacuum has dealt a tremendous blow to the Church's credibility and has seriously undermined trust in the institution. Most dramatically, trust has broken down in the members closest (even institutionally) to these cases. These people are victims of dishonesty who have been lied to or denied a truth they had a right to know. The obsession with keeping everything hidden has caused those in charge to forget the importance of respecting and valuing these closest collaborators by sharing such facts with them. Providing relevant information so that everyone can contribute would be a victory for everyone, especially for the institution.

The climate of suspicion generated in public opinion has influenced the social perception of priests and religious, the vast

---

15. NATIONAL REVIEW BOARD, *A Report on the Crisis of the Catholic Church in the United States*: "In many instances, Church leaders valued confidentiality and a priest's right to privacy above the prevention of further harm to victims and the vindication of their rights. Both confidentiality and privacy are valuable. [...] But these values should not be allowed to trump the duty to keep children safe from harm or to investigate claims of sexual abuse against clerics and respond appropriately."

16. To expand on this topic, see R. SHAW, *Nothing to Hide*, 80–92.

17. Cf. R. SHAW, *Nothing to Hide*, 90.

majority of whom are not guilty of these crimes. In some places it was relatively common for priests, identified by their clerical garb, to be insulted or even subjected to physical violence because of it. When the Pennsylvania Report was published in the summer of 2018, some Catholic media outlets published the case of an innocent priest being physically assaulted by some who chanted, "*Questo è per tutti i bambini*" ("This is for all the children").[18]

The abuse of secrecy—as we have seen—is a strong ally of corruption. Both problems are closely linked to clericalism, which is a terrible interpretation of the hierarchical condition of the Church. Indeed, it denies the Church's understanding of herself: as communion. This is how Pope Francis spoke of it in his *Letter to the People of God* on August 20, 2018:

> This is clearly seen in a peculiar way of understanding the Church's authority, one common in many communities where sexual abuse and the abuse of power and conscience have occurred. Such is the case with clericalism. [...] Clericalism, whether fostered by priests themselves or by lay persons, leads to an excision in the ecclesial body that supports and helps to perpetuate many of the evils that we are condemning today. To say "no" to abuse is to say an emphatic "no" to all forms of clericalism.[19]

> Superiors covering for abusers...

> were acting reasonably by the standards of the clericalist culture to which they belonged. Wishing to be good servants of the Church, they served the clericalist system. And in the end this system of concealment and illusion betrayed them and the rest of the Church.[20]

Along with clericalism, Pope Emeritus Benedict XVI points to other *underlying causes* in the essay he wrote in 2019 on account of the February 21–24 meeting organized by Pope Francis with all the presidents of the world's episcopal conferences. First, he focuses on the social context of the issue: the growing "absence of God" from the public sphere and the sexual revolution of the

18. Cf. Redacción Aci Prensa, "*Al grito de 'Por todos los niños' atacan a sacerdote que no es culpable de abusos,*" in *ACI Prensa* (August 21, 2018), *www.aciprensa.com/noticias/al-grito-de-por-todos-los-ninos-atacan-a-sacerdote-que-no-es-culpable-de-abusos-20805.*

19. Pope Francis, *Letter to the People of God*, no. 2.

20. Cf. R. Shaw, *Nothing to Hide*, 16.

1960's, which affected the whole society, even the life of the Church and her ministers, with devastating effects; the collapse of Catholic moral theology and its doctrinal authority; the problem of the immoral climate within seminaries and the poor preparation and selection of candidates for the priesthood; the failure to apply penal canon law in the face of true and proper crimes in the name of "pastorality"; the guarantism that looked too much to the right of the accused without caring about the victims; and, finally, the insufficiency of the very regulations of the *Code of Canon Law* to implement the necessary measures.[21]

Within the framework described by Pope Emeritus Benedict XVI, a fact emerges: The goods in play have not been legally protected. According to what he suggests, the victims and the faith must also be legally protected, not just the accused. He insists on the fact that the abuse of minors and the cover-up on the part of authorities damages the faith both of the Church as a body and of individual members.[22] From this perspective, these crimes have been classified as *among the most serious*; that is why the competence to judge them was granted to the Congregation for the Doctrine of the Faith. The situation requires, first and foremost, *justice*: that is, establishing a penal process and actually punishing the crimes. "The severity of the punishment, however [discharge from the clerical state] also presupposes a clear proof of the offense."[23]

The renewal of the Church in this area necessarily begins with justice and truth. In this sense, confidentiality must be in harmony with the common good and human dignity.[24] Otherwise, it becomes a weapon against the very values that the authority was intended to protect and against the authority itself.

---

21. Cf. Pope BENEDICT XVI, "*La Chiesa e lo scandalo degli abusi sessuali,*" in *Klerusblatt* (April 11, 2019); in English, *www.catholicnewsagency.com/news/41013/full-text-of-benedict-xvi-essay-the-church-and-the-scandal-of-sexual-abuse.*

22. Ibid., no. II.2.

23. Ibid.

24. PCCS, *Communio et Progressio,* no. 121: "Secrecy should therefore be restricted to matters that involve the good name of individuals or that touch upon the rights of people whether singly or collectively."

ABUSE OF SECRECY DAMAGES THE AUTHORITY AND WEAKENS RELATIONSHIPS WITHIN THE CHURCH

Within the institution we can say that secrecy imposed by mere force of a badly exercised power weakens the cohesion of the organization and the credibility of its senior officials. The Church's failures to be truthful constitute a scandal and a betrayal of trust, which have damaged her credibility accordingly.[25]

It also weakens the institution in the eyes of its audiences, especially internally. For the internal audiences there is a distinction based on proximity, both at the level of responsibility and when it comes to the connection to the institution. Every person enjoys, to a greater or lesser extent, the right to receive truthful and relevant information from the authority. There is also the right to see that if something is *said* in words, then it is *actualized* in deeds, or at least, an attempt is made to actualize it.[26] Church institutions are required to ensure that governing decisions have "exemplary consistency with the teachings that the Church proclaims."[27]

The abuse of secrecy by the leader of an organization is unjust and disrespectful, which is why it undermines internal communication and trust.

> Secrecy, deception, stonewalling, spin, rejection of accountability, repudiation of shared responsibility and consultation — these are deadly foes of internal communication among members of any group. They subvert and eventually destroy community and 'horizontal' communion in the Church. [... They create] an us-versus-them mentality on both sides of the relationship.[28]

Trust is the response of the organization's members to its leaders when the leaders treat them with respect. The leaders demonstrate their respect for their collaborators when they

---

25. Cf. R. Shaw, T.L. Mammoser, F.J. Maniscalco, *Dealing with Media for the Church,* (Rome: EDUSC, 1999), 30–31.

26. Cf. Y. De la Cierva, *La Chiesa casa di vetro* (Rome: EDUSC, 2014), 128.

27. J.I. Arrieta, *Dimensione di governo: Prendere le decisioni, spiegare le proprie ragioni, in Teoria e pratica del giornalismo religioso. Come informare sulla Chiesa Cattolica: Fonti, logiche, storie, personaggi,* ed. G. Tridente (Rome: EDUSC, 2014), 250; translation ours.

28. R. Shaw, *Nothing to Hide,* 117.

consider them as ends in themselves and never as means to satisfy ambitions for power or even to achieve the legitimate purposes of the organization.

> Leaders demonstrate their respect by giving followers relevant information […] by including them in the making of decisions that affect them. […] [S]howing respect for people by including them in the flow of relevant information is the essence of transparency and trust.[29]

Since an organization is a set of interpersonal relationships,[30] if an excessive use of confidentiality weakens the relationships, then we must conclude that it threatens the institution itself.[31] This is true of any institution and *even more so* for the Church, which sees in service and communion several essential elements: They reflect the image of the triune God in whom she believes and in whose name she preaches.

ASYMMETRICAL RELATIONSHIPS WITHIN THE CHURCH

In the *Letter to the People of God*, which Pope Francis wrote on August 20, 2018, the Pope puts abuse of power, abuse of conscience, and sexual abuse on the same level, defining this as a "culture of abuse."

He puts at the center of the debate reflection on the "exercise of authority" and "health of interpersonal relationships" in the Church, guided by the hierarchical principle and the submission granted by the power of office, on which he had written to the Church in Chile.[32] The Pope warns of the danger of two forms of self-referentiality: clericalism and elitism, seen as "a peculiar way of understanding the Church's authority."[33]

---

29. W. Bennis, D.P. Goleman, J. O'Toole, *Transparency: How Leaders Create a Culture of Candor* (New York: John Wiley & Sons, Inc., 2008), ch. 2.

30. Cf. Y. De la Cierva, *La Chiesa casa di vetro*, 44.

31. Cf. Y. De la Cierva, "Comunicación Institucional en situación de crisis," in *Introducción a la Comunicación Institucional de la Iglesia*, ed. J.M. La Porte (Madrid: Palabra, 2012), 315–316.

32. Pope Francis, *Letter to the People of God in Chile* (May 31, 2018), www.catholicnewsagency.com/news/38567/full-text-of-pope-francis-letter-to-the-church-in-chile.

33. Pope Francis, *Letter to the People of God.*

In any human institution, relationships between the one who holds power and the individual are asymmetrical: It is inevitable. Generally, it is said that power has per se an *expansive* dynamic, that is, those who command tend to "not want checks, breaks, or limitations, and when such things are there, they consider them obstacles to their *mission of service*."[34] So it is also like this in the Church.

The *expansive dynamic of power* can also be verified in the Church, both at the local level for the individual priest and at the diocesan level for the bishop and his closest associates. Without adequate responsible awareness, one can fall into the self-deception of believing that one is thus serving the institution.

This power (*munus regendi*) is not in the people as it is in a democracy (there is no popular sovereignty in the Church) but in the pastors by virtue of the Sacrament.[35] It can be exercised with respect for canon law and personal dignity, animated by the desire to serve the common good of the Church. Or, unfortunately, it can be abused for personal gain, even of a self-referential or narcissistic kind.

In the initial formation of candidates for the priesthood, the *service* dimension of the priestly ministry is emphasized:

> Intrinsically linked to the sacramental nature of ecclesial ministry is its *character as service*. Entirely dependent on Christ who gives mission and authority, ministers are truly "slaves of Christ" (Rom 1:1), in the image of him who freely took "the form of a slave" (Phil 2:7) for us. Because the word and grace of which they are ministers are not their own, but are given to them by Christ for the sake of others, they must freely become the slaves of all.[36]

As Amedeo Cencini highlights, it is essential to transmit the message that the true authority of the priestly ministry passes through the identification with the authority of Christ the Good

---

34. Cf. Y. De la Cierva, *La Chiesa casa di vetro*, 205; translation ours.
35. Cf. Vatican Council II, Dogmatic Constitution on the Church *Lumen Gentium* (November 21, 1964), in *AAS* 57 (1965), no. 27. For more clarity and detail, cf. P. Goyret, *El Obispo, Pastor de la Iglesia. Estudio teológico del munus regendi en Lumen Gentium 27* (Pamplona: EUNSA, 1998).
36. *Catechism of the Catholic Church* (CCC) (Vatican City: LEV, 2002), no. 876.

Shepherd who welcomes, suffers with, and sympathizes with all, and in this way...

> prevents authority from being understood as power, or the illusion of power from becoming a form of corruption of an authentic *auctoritas*. Because in this way the identity of the minister would be distorted—he would go from being a servant interested in helping the other person "grow" to being a man of power who tends to possess and dominate, contradicting the Christian message.[37]

According to Cencini, if the authority of the ordained minister is not linked to the *compassion* of Jesus, model of the Good Shepherd, then "authority" can be confused with "authoritarianism"[38] and can easily fall into nonevangelical conceptions with the traits of narcissism or clericalism.

Clericalism leads one to think that "being marked with Holy Orders does not place one at the feet of one's neighbor (like Jesus in the Upper Room), but rather on a pedestal of power."[39] This is manifested, on one hand, in the instrumental use of the priestly role, exploiting or obtaining privileges in the sacred sphere or in the liturgical functions attributed to the lay faithful. On the other hand, it manifests itself in immature personalities, with...

> dreams and expectations, desires and illusions about one's ministerial future on the part of the young candidate. These are more or less unconscious, not infrequently unrealistic, and not

---

37. A. Cencini, S. Lassi (eds.), *La formazione iniziale in tempo di abusi, Servizio Nazionale per la tutela dei minori* (CEI, February 2021), 25; translation ours.

38. Ibid., 26; translation ours: "The authority is above all the coherent person, the first to practice what he asks of the other, and he is credible because he himself is convinced and feels committed to it; the authoritarian is the one who does not know how to justify what he is asking precisely because he does not experience it and therefore resorts to the violence of imposition. The authority is the one who welcomes the other, who wants to encourage his or her growth and free and responsible adherence to the good; an authoritarian is someone who is not so interested in the inner maturation and conviction of the other; he or she only needs to recognize his or her authority/power and at the same time demands what he or she calls 'obedience.' For this reason, those who are authoritative accept and encourage dialogue and sharing; those who are not, on the other hand, fear both, any confrontation, and common research. In short, authoritativeness is the natural expression of authority correctly understood; authoritarianism, on the other hand, is combined with power as a further deformation of true authority."

39. M. Semeraro, "*Discernere e formare per prevenire. Sugli abusi nella Chiesa*," in *La Rivista del Clero italiano* 10 (2018), 652; translation ours.

at all evangelical. The premises of a future abusive style is often already present in those unrealistic expectations.[40]

Recent studies have highlighted the role of relationships in the deep understanding of the human being, his sociality and anthropological structure, thanks also to the light of Trinitarian Revelation.[41] The Christian God is not an absurd contradiction, in his being one and triune at the same time, precisely because the identity of each Person is constituted by the relationship with the other two in such a way that God is not one despite being triune but is one precisely because he is triune. This is reflected in anthropology, putting the relational dimension, with the freedom that characterizes it, at the foundation of human psychological and social health. Evidently, the difference between the Creator and the creature is absolute: One cannot project the divine relationality *sic et simplicieter* in the categorial dimension. At the same time, for the creation in the image and likeness (cf. Gn 1:26–27), what is perfect in God cannot be equivocally given to human beings. Therefore, a gaze that is capable of reading relationships and a praxis that protects freedom touch on an element that is not only ethical and moral but even more so ontological, making the wound in this area terribly deep.

The Christian faith is a predominantly relational proposition and, in the life of the Church, each minister and each vocation includes within itself the aspect of relation.[42] The relationship with God is ontologically asymmetrical, while the asymmetry between members of the ecclesial community is accidental and derives from the established authority. Jesus Christ has explicitly made it known how he wants that authority to be exercised:

> If any one would be first, he must be last of all and servant of all. (Mk 9:35)

> If I then, your Lord and Teacher, have washed your feet, you also ought to wash one another's feet. (Jn 13:14)

---

40. A. Cencini, S. Lassi, *La formazione iniziale in tempo di abusi*, 28; translation ours.

41. Cf. P. Donati, A. Malo, G. Maspero (eds.), *Social Science, Philosophy and Theology in Dialogue: A Relational Perspective* (London: Routledge, 2019).

42. For a more in-depth analysis, cf. A. Clemenzia, *Sul luogo dell'ecclesiologia. Questioni epistemologiche* (Rome: Città Nuova, 2018).

Whoever would be great among you must be your servant. (Mt 20:26)

Here we have the "authentic" way of exercising authority as Jesus taught it to his disciples.[43]

The exercise of power in the Church (ordinary or delegated) is linked to the order and has a function that cannot be separated from the style of Jesus, from his words, and from his example as the Good Shepherd.

The abuse of authority causes a *disconnect* with the teachings of the Master. As Cencini explains:

> It arises from an erroneous interpretation, of a self-referential variety, of the role of authority that is part of this vocation, leading to a progressive process of corruption at an ideal and behavioral level. This process slowly transforms the authority into authoritarianism and then into power and the exercise of power, deforming what should be a service for the growth of the people entrusted to it into an instrument for its own affirmation, with the consequent enslavement of others.[44]

This takes the form of a multitude of toxic manifestations: the imposition of one's own viewpoint, the invasion of privacy, the generation of feelings of guilt, and dynamics aimed at creating dependence, for example by guaranteeing forms of gratification of privileges solely for the purpose of binding the other to oneself. For Bertomeu, the key factor is that "the greater the relational asymmetry, the greater the vulnerability."[45]

The abuse of hierarchical power can be seen in the ways of *administration*, but not only that: Where there is subordination, it can also enter into the spiritual sphere or that of conscience. This takes place when obedience at the external level combines with the realm of intimacy and of conscience (the internal forum): where desires and beliefs are elaborated and existential horizons of meaning are decided.[46] In particular, a spiritual abuse is . . .

---

43. Cf. G. GOULDING, "Towards a Theological and Synodal Response to the Abuse Crisis," in *New Blackfriars* 102, 1097 (2020), 99.

44. A. CENCINI, S. LASSI, *La formazione iniziale in tempo di abusi*, 53; translation ours.

45. Cf. J. BERTOMEU, "La respuesta de la Iglesia a la cultura del abuso," in *Vida Nueva* 3248 (November/December 2021), 26; translation ours.

46. Cf. N. GONZÁLEZ GAITANO, *El deber de respeto a la intimidad* (Pamplona: EUNSA, 1990), 26–27.

any relational manipulation of an emotional type, with arguments of religious-spiritual content ("in the name of God") that affects the person's sensitivity toward the divine. This manipulation contaminates and deforms the image of God in that person, disorients and damages his or her life of faith, and more generally, the person's relationship with his or her own inner world of values and convictions.[47]

Pope Francis [48] and recent publications (such as Cernuzio's book [49]) point to the specific problem of abuses of authority and power in female religious life. In particular, Pope Francis is very attentive to the way authority as service is exercised: "The separation between the internal and external forums [...] to the duration of mandates and the accumulation of powers."[50]

Father Cucci stated:

An analogous mode of clericalism in female communities seems to be the tendency to remain in power for as long as possible [...] imposing a single uniform mindset within the institution according to their own criteria, passing it off as God's will, and marginalizing or blaming those who think differently.[51]

Along with the misunderstanding of obedience and the exercise of authority as service, there is also racism and the call to abandon one's own interests and talents.[52] All forms of abuse that the Pope points out (abuse of power, of conscience, and sexual abuse), demonstrate a lack of "respect for the sacred and inalienable worth of each person and of his or her freedom."[53]

---

47. A. CENCINI, S. LASSI, *La formazione iniziale in tempo di abusi*, 54; translation ours.

48. Pope FRANCIS, *Address to Participants in the Plenary Assembly of the Congregation for Institutes of Consecrated Life and Societies of Apostolic Life* (Sala Clementina, Vatican City, December 11, 2021), *www.vatican.va/content/francesco/en/speeches/2021/december/documents/20211211-plenaria-civcsva.html*.

49. S. CERNUZIO, *Il velo del silenzio. Abusi, violenze, frustrazioni nella vita religiosa femminile* (Milan: Edizioni San Paolo, 2021); translation ours.

50. Pope FRANCIS, *Address to Participants in the Plenary Assembly of the Congregation for Institutes of Consecrated Life and Societies of Apostolic Life*.

51. S. CERNUZIO, *Il velo del silenzio*, 25.

52. Ibid., 41–42.

53. Pope FRANCIS, Post-synodal Apostolic Exhortation to Young People and to the Entire People of God *Christus Vivit* (March 25, 2019), no. 98, *www.vatican.va/content/francesco/en/apost_exhortations/documents/papa-francesco_esortazione-ap_20190325_christus-vivit.html*.

This phenomenon is especially relevant in relationships of spiritual direction, where what is sought is to "discern," to "do the will of God," to "make decisions and take responsibility," etc. In this context, the abuse of conscience takes the form of the appropriation of the will of the person being directed. We could define this intrusiveness as a...

> form of violation of the intimacy of others, which consists in leading the other person into one's own way of judging and one's own criteria of discernment, or of one's own moral (and penitential) sensibility.[54]

One of the challenges posed by the Pope in that 2018 letter is the "culture of care," which means, as Bertomeu puts it, to make "asymmetrical ecclesial relations healthy, generating freedom and inner peace."[55]

In many cases, this will involve spiritual directors avoiding protective attitudes and limiting the attachment on the part of the insecure persons when it is excessive. They should try not to dive into immediate solutions and insist on the need to discern, make decisions, and take risks, without fear of making mistakes. As Cito reiterates:

> The role of the one who accompanies is not to tell the person what to do, but rather to help him or her shed light on what he or she believes for him- or herself. To take the place of another's conscience is, precisely, an abuse of conscience.[56]

Thanks to God, the fruits of spiritual direction are evident in the life of the Church in all parts of the world, but improving the culture of care and fostering healthy asymmetrical interpersonal relationships is an ever-present challenge.

ASYMMETRICAL MALE-FEMALE RELATIONSHIPS

The *culture of care* and of *healthy asymmetrical relationships* also touches relationships between men and women, between ministers or consecrated persons in the Church. We are therefore referring to sexual asymmetry. The friendly relationship between

---

54. A. CENCINI, S. LASSI, *La formazione iniziale in tempo di abusi*, 56; translation ours.

55. J. Bertomeu, *La respuesta de la Iglesia a la cultura del abuso*, 26; translation ours.

56. D. CITO, "*Brevi annotazioni canonistiche sul concetto di abuso di potere e di coscienza*," in *Tredimensioni* 3 (2020), 309; translation ours.

Pope Saint John Paul II and Wanda Półtawska is one example,[57] among many, in a *culture of suspicion* in which the leaders of the Church live. Unfortunately, fantasy and gossip (or chatter, as Pope Francis says) often lead to malicious thinking and talking about relationships between men and women in the Church as if spiritual friendships could not exist.

A recent episode that shows this culture of suspicion was the case of the Archbishop of Paris, Monsignor Aupetit. Photographed by *Paris Match* magazine in the company of the theologian Laetitia Calmeyn a few hours after his resignation, he was immediately stigmatized: the photograph was published with the headline *"Exclusif: Monseigneur Aupetit, perdu par amour"*[58] ("Exclusive: Bishop Aupetit, Lost to Love"), a symptom of a culture overflowing with prejudice.

At that time, Pope Francis had accepted his resignation following a multi-faceted affair, which included the public revelation of inappropriate gestures and affection with a woman: events that took place in 2012. "An affair of which nobody seems to know all the details and whose truth it seems will remain unattainable, even if it has caused suffering in the Catholic world."[59]

Laetitia Calmeyn, responding to an interview with *La Croix* said in an ironic tone: "If it had been a man, a priest, at Archbishop Aupetit's side, would there have been the same treatment from the media?"[60] With these words, she was pointing out a paradox: On the one hand the Church is discerning—on an internal level—the right place to give women in the Church, and on the other, the secular world *casts the shadow of suspicion* over the relationship between consecrated persons (man-woman), likely projecting onto them *its own decadence* as a society, the

---

57. For a more in-depth analysis, cf. W. Półtawska, *Diario di un'amicizia. La famiglia Półtawska e Karol Wojtyła* (Milan: Edizioni San Paolo, 2010).

58. Rédaction Paris Match (December 8, 2021), on the cover of the print version, *www.parismatch.com/Actu/Societe/Exclusif-Monseigneur-Aupetit-perdu-par-amour-1775067*.

59. Redazione il Sismografo (December 12, 2021), *ilsismografo.blogspot.com/2021/12/francia-laetitia-calmeyn-se-fossi-stato.html*; translation ours.

60. C. Hoyeau (interview by), "*Laetitia Calmeyn : 'Si j'avais été un homme, la question de l'amitié avec Mgr Aupetit ne se serait pas posée,'*" in *La Croix* (December 12, 2021), *international.la-croix.com/news/religion/if-i-had-been-a-man-the-question-would-not-have-come-up/15355*.

victim of hypersexualized relationships, where a friendly relationship between a man and a woman seems almost impossible. "Where is the scandal today? Certainly not in friendship, but in the evil projected onto this friendship."[61]

Calmeyn's words show the suffering of those who are the victims of a news montage but also the pain experienced by a consecrated woman in the Church due to the lack of healthy asymmetrical relationships: "Should women in the Church be reduced to objects of suspicion, fantasy, an expression of jealousy or servility?"[62] And she suggests fraternity and friendship as ways to overcome clericalism and unhealthy relationships, reaffirming that it is possible "to live real relationships of communion."[63]

WOMEN IN THE CHURCH AND "WOKE" PRESSURE

The push initiated by Pope Saint John Paul II with *Mulieris Dignitatem* (1988) or the *Letter to Priests* on the importance of women in the life of the priest (1995), has continued with the catechesis of Popes Benedict XVI and Francis. The latter has also begun to nominate women (both lay and consecrated) to relevant posts in the Roman Curia, which are normally assigned to bishops. In any case, the role of women in the Church is a much richer and deeper topic.

We often lament the *resistance to change* in the Church. Yet, without sounding like a justification, history teaches us that the Church is slow but eventually "gets there."

The latter thought does not sit well with *woke culture*, a mostly female wave of mainly young, college-educated, upper-middle-class people, steeped in the rhetoric of systemic oppression (by a privileged white and male culture) and the need for

---

61. Ibid.
62. Ibid.
63. Ibid.

reprogramming for their empowerment[64] with a *disruptive* and iconoclastic style of activism that operates on the impersonality of crowds and is very active on social media. Anton argues that the *woke* narrative relies on two tools: a megaphone and a muzzle.[65]

The feminism of the 1970s protested women's lack of equal rights, the undervaluing of their opinions and abilities, and their confinement to motherhood and domestic care compared to men. Feminists of the 1970s and 1980s such as Gloria Steinem, Pauli Murray, and Ruth Bader Ginsburg (among others) aimed to center their strategy on the demand for abortion rights,[66] thinking that "free and easy access to abortion would empower women to achieve unsurpassed levels of autonomy, enabling them to take full advantage of the new freedoms and opportunities available to them."[67] The goal of making abortion a *right* was presented as the goal that could make women more free and finally allow them to grow and succeed. Bachiochi argues that, in the United States, this policy instead "has allowed women *to be taken advantage of more fully* in the workplace and in the bedroom instead."[68]

Currently, having overcome most of the discrimination against women—although there is still much work to be done on their access to positions of power—the issue focuses on why the work of *caring* for people falls disproportionately on them. Bachiochi responds in a very clear way:

> Rather than making room for dependents and the asymmetrical duties of care that inhere in both sex and caregiving, we have sought to remake women (and men) in the exalted image of the ever-competitive, rights-bearing, unencumbered, pleasure-

---

64. Among many examples of empowerment of "modern woman" characters in Netflix or HBO series, one could look at Rachel from the TV series *Friends*, who is presented to the audience after having just left her fiancé at the altar. The main message conveyed throughout the series is that she has created her own "family," which consists of lovable urban friendships, and is peppered with easy sex and witty banter. Cf. N. MERING, *Awake, Not Woke: A Christian Response to the Cult of Progressive Ideology* (Gastonia, NC: TAN Books, 2021), 137–138.

65. Cf. M. ANTON, *The Stakes: America at the Point of No Return* (Washington, DC: Regnery Publishing, 2020).

66. Cf. E. BACHIOCHI, *The Rights of Women: Reclaiming a Lost Vision* (Notre Dame, IN: Notre Dame University Press, 2021), 169–198.

67. Ibid., 303.

68. Ibid; emphasis ours.

maximizing, autonomous individual of Thomas Hobbes's imag-inings.[69]

The results can be clearly seen and — in fact — have betrayed women: Many of them have to take care of themselves, and sex (for both sexes) has been drained of meaning and reduced to a *sport*.[70]

While caring for people is neither valued nor supported, indi-vidualism continues to wreak havoc in the form of the exaltation of personal desires, the desire to be appreciated, and to succeed.

With the advent of gender theory and the subsequent irrel-evance of biological sex, the word "woman" has decayed, and feminism has gone out of style. In the name of *inclusion*, the complex and persuasive gender linguistics dominates the public sphere. The substitution of the word woman with "menstruat-ing person," "pregnant person," or "birthing person" has become the rhetorical key.[71] In this context, the new winning strategy is *wokism*.

All of this causes enormous dissatisfaction and frustration (in men as well as in women) because the reality is that we are noth-ing on our own. Isabel Sanchez shows with a mosaic of examples how validating and empowering those who *care for people* is a sign of civility.[72] This "culture of care," however, does not exclu-sively correspond to women. *Care robots* will help us with many functions, but they can never replace the care of people, which includes exclusively human elements such as symbolic language, freedom, and love.[73]

Our *dignity* requires family, community (school, church, etc.), work, and deep and meaningful relationships in order to grow. This whole set of ongoing transformations has a direct impact on the personal life of ministers and consecrated persons in the Church, especially women. And this comes at a time when the

---

69. Ibid., 303.

70. Ibid.

71. To learn about the intellectual roots and basic ideas of the woke culture, cf. N. Mering, *Awake, not Woke*.

72. Cf. I. Sánchez, *Mujeres brújula en un bosque de retos* (Madrid: Espasa, 2021), 134 ff.

73. Ibid., 139.

Church as a spiritual organization is discerning their role, in order to properly value them.

It would be illuminating to have a study that shows the permeation and influence of *woke culture* in the Church to better understand some modern situations (such as the decrease of female religious vocations) but above all to address the future. First of all, it would be to understand the evolution of women's involvement in crucial roles for the Church such as the pastoral-educational sphere: catechists, religious teachers, counselors, and pastoral leaders; and as managers of key offices of the Church: economic, communication, in ecclesiastical courts, administration, child protection, etc.[74] In the contemporary struggle the "culture of care" and "throwaway culture," to use Pope Francis's terms, women's leadership is clearly humanizing but still too invisible. The Church cannot do without *compass women*.[75]

---

74. To get an idea of the phenomenon in Italy, cf. M.E. GANDOLFI, "*Quante sono le donne nella Chiesa? Conoscere i dati per riconoscere una presenza*," in *Orientamenti Pastorali* 10 (2020), *www.centroorientamentopastorale.it/organismo/wp-content/uploads/2021/02/Gandolfi_102020.pdf*.

75. Cf. I. SÁNCHEZ, *Mujeres brújula en un bosque de retos*, 142–146.
[Editor's note: "Compass women" is a translation of the Spanish expression *mujeres brújula*. This roughly describes inspiring women who show meaningful leadership.]

CHAPTER 2

IS THERE A PLACE FOR CONFIDENTIALITY IN THE AGE OF INFORMATION AND TRANSPARENCY?

Secrecy should therefore be restricted to matters that involve the good name of individuals or that touch upon the rights of people whether singly or collectively.
— Communio et Progressio, no. 121

After having assessed the impact of *abuse of secrecy*, we must ask ourselves if secrecy is valuable and has a place in the life of the Church. In this journey, we consider it important to look at the norms of the Church and to listen to their reasons from a historical and juridical standpoint.

In December of 2019, Pope Francis modified some norms on the pontifical secret, abolishing secrecy (for some phases) in the cases of abuse of minors committed by clerics. Before speaking of the pontifical secret, however, it is worthwhile to try to understand what we are talking about.

From a communications standpoint, spaces for silence are always necessary in common life. An excess of information leads to misinformation.[1] Not only does silence exist, but it is extremely valuable: "The correct use of silence does not mean not speaking but saying things at the right time and keeping silent when necessary."[2]

shadows, and silences are also part of reality. When with them, the resulting view of reality is clearly

, *Informazione e Disinformazione, Armando Editore* (Rome, 1999), 31.
cnicas de comunicación oral (Madrid: Editorial Tecnos, 2012), 248;
rs.

distorted and manipulated because it is deprived of the necessary contrasts and perspective. The transparency of the lenses cannot be such as to leave them without the necessary gradation: The public must be offered a balanced view of the issues, giving everything the proper importance, the proper weight, and their due proportions.[3]

In the field of information, it sometimes seems that the formula is automatic: "The greater the amount of news, the greater the knowledge." But it is well known that an avalanche of information fosters a falsified presentation of reality in which what is abnormal and outlandish stands out, and this favors an amplified and simplistic perception of the phenomena being discussed. The compulsive search for what is shocking, emotive, and controversial and its presentation of facts in a trivial way increase misinformation[4] and promotes insensitivity and indifference.

However, not only is silence necessary to foster contrasts and serve the truth in the field of information, but in other areas of the lives of individuals and institutions, silence also occupies a healthy space. It is interesting how in canon law the Church recognizes this, presenting secrecy as a guarantor of other values: for example, good reputation, privacy, and the public good.[5]

PROFESSIONAL SECRECY, THE PONTIFICAL SECRET, AND THE SEAL OF CONFESSION

The long social and juridical tradition of maintaining official and professional secrecy by doctors, lawyers, civil servants, priests, and the like, proves the need for complete confidentiality in some human relationships.

The pontifical secret[6] is like the "peculiar *status*" decreed by the authority of the Church to legally protect certain matters that concern the personal good (the good reputation of the parties in

---

3. Cf. Ibid.

4. Ibid., 35–36.

5. Cf. CIC, can. 220.

6. Cf. J.M. LAUCIRICA, "*Secreto pontificio*," in *Diccionario general de derecho canónico*, ed. J. OTADUY–A. VIANA–J. SEDANO, vol. VII (Madrid: Thomson Reuters Aranzadi, 2013), 186–189.

the case) or the *bonum Ecclesiæ* of the community (ensuring the course of justice).[7]

From the earliest centuries of Christianity, the secrecy of confession has been considered absolute. The very language expresses this connotation with the definition of the *seal* of confession. The secrecy of confession has a fundamental value, and its doctrine remains unchanged even today. This *seal* is based on the fact that the confessor acts in the name of Christ and cannot reveal what the penitent intended to say to Christ.[8] The priest is not just any man, but he exercises a ministry that allows him to represent Christ (thanks to the Sacrament of Holy Orders), which he must exercise in communion with the Church.

In that moment, the priest serves as an instrument between the penitent and God. It is quite different when one is speaking to a priest "outside of Confession" compared to "in Confession." In the first case, the priest can and certainly must testify to the competent authorities against someone he knows to have committed a crime (of any kind). In the second case, rather, it is not possible, not because the Church intends to "cover up" the misdeed but because the penitent, on that specific occasion, has spoken with God and with the priest only because he was acting *in persona Christi*.[9] The priest is even required to forget everything that is said to him in confession.

Therefore at this juncture, secrecy only seeks two preserve two things: the greatness of the mystery of faith that accompanies it because it is God himself who hears the sins. The priest comes

---

7. Cf. M. VISIOLI, "*Confidenzialità e segreto pontificio,*" in *Periodica* 109 (2020), 448, 466.

8. Cf. *Code of Canon Law* (CIC) (January 25, 1983), in *AAS* LXXV pars II, can. 983 § 1: "For this reason, the defense of the sacramental seal by the confessor, if necessary *usque ad sanguinis effusionem*, represents not only an act of dutiful 'allegiance' towards the penitent, but much more: a necessary testimony—a 'martyrdom'— rendered directly to the uniqueness and salvific universality of Christ and the Church." Cf. CONGREGATION FOR THE DOCTRINE OF THE FAITH, Declaration on the Uniqueness and Salvific Universality of Jesus Christ and of the Church *Dominus Iesus* (August 6, 2000).

9. *In persona Christi* is a Latin locution that literally means "in the Person of Christ" or "as if it were Christ."

to know the sins of the penitent *non ut homo, sed ut Deus* ("not as man, but as God").[10]

And, on the other hand, respect for individuals' right to confidential communication is safeguarded. The Sacrament of Penance puts the penitent into contact with God and is a dialogue that takes place in the depths of conscience. The defense of the inviolability of one's conscience is part of what the sacramental secret guards.

The absolute prohibition imposed by sacramental secrecy is such that it prevents the priest from pronouncing the content of the confession with the penitent himself outside of the Sacrament "unless the penitent gives his or her explicit consent, and in any case it is better if he or she does not give it."[11] That is to say, it is a duty that cannot be questioned because one of the parties involved is God himself.

It is understandable that those who look at the matter "from the outside" and do not recognize the sacred bond of Confession struggle to understand this discourse. One may not think that there is something "inviolable" that even stands "above State law" and thus see this position as an improper and anachronistic abuse on the part of the Church.

The crux of the matter is to understand that there is a difference between the "legal plane" and the "plane of conscience."

Once the civil authorities have proven that a person is objectively guilty of a certain act, he or she will be condemned by a court of law. Human beings, however, can act and compel the guilty person only "from the outside": Nobody can change the conscience of the offender by force. We can put someone in prison, but who can "force" him or her to feel sorry for what has been done or compel one to say how he or she feels, deep down, about the offense committed?

---

10. Cf. M. Piacenza, *Presentazione della Nota sull'importanza del foro interno e l'inviolabilità del sigillo sacramentale* (June 29, 2019), *www.vatican.va/roman_curia/ tribunals/apost_penit/documents/rc_trib_appen_pro_20190629_forointerno- cardpiacenza_it.html*.

11. Pope St. John Paul II, Post-synodal Apostolic Exhortation on Reconciliation and Penance in the Mission of the Church Today *Reconciliatio e Paenitentia* (December 2, 1984), no.31, in *AAS* 77 (1985), 267, *www.vatican.va/content/john-paul-ii/en/apost_ exhortations/documents/hf_jp-ii_exh_02121984_reconciliatio-et-paenitentia.html*.

God, in confession, welcomes *this* part of us: He welcomes what is found in the conscience. And the conscience is an *impass-able sanctum* for anyone, including our friends, spouse, children, and parents. What is in our innermost self, in the deepest part of our soul, we manifest *only freely*, otherwise it remains hidden. It is a space that is only ours and God's.

No one can come between God and the human conscience, except to play the role of simple "intermediary" (which is precisely what the priest does, by mandate of Jesus himself, during Confession). That is why the content of every single confession must remain "hidden," regardless of the sins reported.

We should clarify another issue regarding this topic: By the very spiritual nature of the act of confession that implores God's forgiveness and mercy, the confessor cannot impose on the penitent the obligation to incriminate him- or herself to the civil justice system as a condition to receive absolution because of the natural principle *nemo tenetur se detegere* ("no one is held to self-incrimination"). Some have read into this a certain collusion with evil, as a ruse that escalates the cover-up, as if forgiveness granted in the black box of *Confession* authorizes someone to offend again.[12]

The Royal Commission of Australia stated this to the Australian Bishops' Conference, asking them to formally request the following from the Vatican:

> If a person confesses during the sacrament of reconciliation to perpetrating child sexual abuse, absolution can and should be withheld until they report themselves to civil authorities.[13]

The Holy See replied:

> Concerning absolution, the confessor must determine that the faithful who confess their sins are truly sorry for them and that they have a purpose of amendment (cf. CIC, can. 959). Since repentance is, in fact, at the heart of this sacrament, absolu-

---

12. Cf. L. Morris-Marr, "Priest Who Confessed to Abuse 1500 Times 'Proves Need for Change,'" in *The New Daily* (June 14, 2018). *thenewdaily.com.au/news/national/2018/06/14/confession-child-abuse-royal-commission/*.

13. Royal Commission, *Institutional Responses to Child Sexual Abuse: The Final Report*, vol. 16, Book 1, no. 77 (2017), *www.childabuseroyalcommission.gov.au/final-report*. All volumes available in pdf format on the Royal Commission's website. Available in print in some public libraries in Australia.

tion can be withheld only if the confessor concludes that the penitent lacks the necessary contrition (cf. CIC, can. 980). Absolution then, cannot be made conditional on future actions in the external forum.[14]

Confession is a "tribunal for the soul," and God's forgiveness is instantaneous, if the person is truly repentant. Sincere repentance will be followed by a commitment to turn oneself in, but such civil implications are not for the priest to verify.

Of course, understanding what is strictly related to the spiritual and civil sphere cannot be simple in our culture, which tends more and more to defend secularism and to see the civil laws as also moral laws.

When the Sauvé Report on sexual abuse in France was presented in October of 2021, Minister of the Interior Gérald Darmanin summoned the President of the French Episcopal Conference (CEF) Monsignor Moulins-Beaufort, reminding him that "priests cannot be considered above the law," since "rien n'est plus fort que les lois de la République" ("nothing counts more than the law of the Republic"). This statement was preceded by the report of the Independent Commission on Abuse in the Catholic Church (CIASE), which included forty-five recommendations, two of which called for the abolition of the secrecy of confession (nos. 8 and 43),[15] suggesting that confessors should not be able to evade, on account of the secrecy of Confession, their obligations under the [French] penal code to report cases of sexual violence toward a child or vulnerable person to the competent authorities. They speak of it, however, as an exception and say that they do not want to generally distort the value of secrecy in Confession.

In 2019, the California State Senate approved Bill 360 by a large majority. The bill, proposed by Senator Jerry Hill, urged priests to violate the secrecy of Confession if they became aware of abuse against minors in the confessions of other priests or Church officials.

14. Holy See, *Letter N. 484.110* (February 26, 2020), Recommendation 16.26, pp. 7–8, *www.catholic.org.au/images/Observations_of_the_Holy_See_to_the_Recommendations_of_the_Royal_Commission.pdf.*

15. Cf. Independent Commission on Sexual Abuse in the Catholic Church (CIASE), *Final Report "Sexual Violence in the Catholic Church France 1950–2020," www.ciase.fr/medias/Ciase-Summary-of-the-Final-Report-5-october-2021.pdf.*

The measure drew 140,000 letters in protest [16] as well as a multitude of demonstrations supporting "civil disobedience" by bishops and priests. This reaction was also supported by leaders of the Orthodox Church, Baptists, Pentecostals, Anglicans, Lutherans, Muslims, Jews, and Mormons. Along with social pressure, a legal report from the Committee on Public Safety [17] warned that the law went against the religious freedom defended in the US Constitution, making it impossible to implement. Faced with this prospect, Senator Hill recused himself the day before an oversight session, stating that he had not completely scrapped the bill but merely put it "on hold," declaring that it "had not been withdrawn."

The political and legislative initiatives of the lay authorities (Australian, French, and Californian, among others) to force this inviolability — both of the penitent and of the confessor — by creating a *mandatory duty to report* sexual abuse of minors, undermine the religious freedom of these persons (cf. Article 18 of the UN *Universal Declaration of Human Rights*), and threaten the legitimate autonomy of the Church. Anticlerical secularism does not allow for the understanding that Confession takes place in a space that is not political, but spiritual. And the priest is required to defend this bond at all costs.

Brian Lucas masterfully addresses the conflict between the civil imperative of the mandate and the divine mandate to safeguard sacramental secrecy in Australia,[18] offering the classic response of the Church's social doctrine:

> The citizen is obliged in conscience not to follow the directives of civil authorities when they are contrary to the demands of the moral order, to the fundamental rights of persons or the teachings of the Gospel. *Refusing obedience* to civil authorities, when their demands are contrary to those of an upright conscience, finds its justification in the distinction between serving God and serving the political community. "Render therefore to Caesar the things that are Caesar's, and to God the things that

---

16. Cf. *www.fcdflegal.org/victory-for-religious-liberty-california-seal-of-confession-bill-scrapped/*.

17. Cf. *leginfo.legislature.ca.gov/faces/billAnalysisClient.xhtml?bill_id=201920200SB360*.

18. Cf. B. Lucas, "The Seal of the Confessional and a Conflict of Duty," in *Church, Communication, and Culture* 6, no. 1 (2021), 99–118.

are God's" (Mt 22:21). "We must obey God rather than men" (Acts 5:29).[19]

And he ends with this other appeal:

Where citizens are oppressed by a public authority overstepping its competence, they should not protest against those things which are objectively required for the common good; but it is legitimate for them to defend their own rights and the rights of their fellow citizens against the abuse of this authority, while keeping within those limits drawn by the natural law and the Gospels.[20]

The law recognizes that the court must prove guilt, not force the accused to confess. Having made these remarks on the Sacrament of Forgiveness, we reiterate that the Church is on the side of justice and truth: She does not intend to foster grave social plagues (although we recognize that in some places this has happened). Each jurisdiction has its own sphere and its own rules for the exercise of power.

Pope Francis decisively expressed the commitment that the Church must make to put an end to the problem of pedophilia:

May the protection of minors increasingly become an ordinary priority in the Church's educational activity; may it be the promotion of an open, reliable and authoritative service, firmly opposed to every form of domination, violation of intimacy, and *complicit silence*.[21]

Defending confessional secrecy, therefore, does not mean "supporting crimes." It means distinguishing "the human plane" from a "divine plane," keeping alive the commitment to do everything possible so that the person, repentant in heart before God, also remedies his or her errors from the social, community, and civil standpoints.

We could make a similar argument even if the person going to confession has suffered rather than caused a serious evil. Let

---

19. CCC, no. 2242.

20. VATICAN COUNCIL II, Pastoral Constitution on the Church in the Modern World *Gaudium et Spes* (December 7, 1965), 74, in *AAS* 58 (1966), 1096.

21. Pope FRANCIS, Appeal at the *Conference "Promoting Child Safeguarding in the Time of COVID-19 and Beyond,"* organized by the Pope John XXIII Community with Azione Cattolica Italiana and the Centro Sportivo Italiano, in collaboration with the Centro per la Vittimologia e la Sicurezza [Center for Victimology and Security] of the University of Bologna, held in the Sala San Pio X in Rome, (November 4, 2021).

us take the case of a woman who complains of having been beaten by her husband.

> Should there be a penitent who has been a victim of the evil of others, it will be the concern of the confessor to instruct him regarding his rights as well as about the practical juridical instruments to refer to in order to report the fact in a civil and/or ecclesiastical forum to invoke justice.[22]

SECRECY PROTECTS THE RIGHT TO PRIVACY AND TO A GOOD REPUTATION

Secrecy has a bad reputation, but when it is related to the rights of individuals, we all understand that discretion, reservedness, and confidentiality are acceptable. Since 1983 the Church has formally recognized this: "No one is permitted to harm illegitimately the good reputation which a person possesses nor to injure the right of any person to protect his or her own privacy."[23]

Resting on the foundation of this right to reputation and privacy, there are other canons that protect these private goods in legal processes. The canonical norm requires that attorney-client privilege protect privacy in litigious judicial processes. Judges and assistants...

> whenever the nature of the case or the proofs is such that disclosure of the acts or proofs, will endanger the reputation of others [...] give rise to scandal or some other disadvantage....[24]

Regarding penal proceedings, Title I of the Motu Proprio *Vos Estis Lux Mundi*, when it speaks of the reception of reports of abuse on the part of the clergy, religious, and consecrated persons, establishes the necessity of protecting the information in such a way as to guarantee its "safety, integrity, and confidentiality."[25] As regards reporting itself, it also indicates: "The good name and

---

22. M. PIACENZA, "Note of the Apostolic Penitentiary on the Importance of the Internal Forum and the Inviolability of the Sacramental Seal" (June 29, 2019), *www.vatican. va/roman_curia/tribunals/apost_penit/documents/rc_trib_appen_pro_20190629_ forointerno_en.html*.

23. CIC, can. 220.

24. CIC, can. 1455 § 3.

25. Pope FRANCIS, Motu Proprio *Vos Estis Lux Mundi*, art. 2 § 2, *www.vatican.va/content/ francesco/en/motu_proprio/documents/papa-francesco-motu-proprio-20190507_vos-estis-lux-mundi.html*.

the privacy of the persons involved, as well as the confidentiality of their personal data, shall be protected."[26]

In canon law, particular norms have been developed regarding secrecy in the area of the privacy of seminarians and candidates for religious life:[27] for example, the level of confidentiality of conversations about spiritual direction, on the use of medical or psychological information in the selection and formation of candidates for Holy Orders, and the protection of personal information.

Similarly, the confidentiality of information about candidates to the priesthood and religious vows, the preparatory acts for the appointment of a bishop, information concerning the dismissal of a religious from his or her institution, and the like, are all required.[28]

SOME TYPES OF SECRETS THAT PROTECT THE PUBLIC GOOD OF THE CHURCH

Other aspects that require custody in silence are the freedom and autonomy of the institution in the process of self-government. Along these lines, the secretary of the conclave seeks to preserve the election of the Successor of Peter from any kind of external pressure. Another example is the case of the pontifical secret imposed in the selection process of candidates for the episcopate and in the election of a new bishop himself.[29] On one hand, the process is free from pressure, and those who find themselves choosing are in this sense freer; on the other hand, the good reputation of the candidates, especially those who are not elected, remains protected.

---

26. Ibid, art. 5 § 2.

27. Cf. CONGREGATION FOR CATHOLIC EDUCATION, *Guidelines for the Use of Psychology in the Admission and Formation of Candidates for the Priesthood* (June 29, 2008; EV 25 / 2011, 1239–1289), no. 6; CONGREGATION FOR THE CLERGY, *The Gift of the Priestly Vocation: Ratio Fundamentalis Institutionis Sacerdotalis*, nos. 191–196 (December 8, 2016), *www.clerus.va/content/clerus/en/notizie/new11.html*.

28. For a more in-depth analysis, cf. M. VISIOLI, "*Confidenzialità e segreto pontificio*," in *Periodica* 109 (2020), 447–491; U. RHODE, "*Trasparenza e segreto nel Diritto Canonico*," in *Periodica* 107 (2018), no. 3, 465–492.

29. Cf. CCC 377 § 2–3.

As in other civil and public institutions, confidentiality in the Church is so important that penalties are prescribed for those who reveal secrets that needed to be protected, with a penalty that varies according to the secret violated.

Silence understood as "secret" or "reservation" has its natural and even legal place in the life of the Church, as a "promised" secret, linked to the various offices. A specific case of the secrecy of office is the *pontifical secret*, which is necessary for the exercise of certain functions in the Apostolic See. The subjection to the pontifical secret is by reason of the matter or office and is formalized under oath. The *General Regulations of the Roman Curia* explains it as so:

> At the time of appointment or employment, everyone must make a profession of faith and take an oath of fidelity and observance of the secrecy of office before the Head of Department or the Senior Prelate, with the formulas given in the Appendix.[30]

And further down in article 36:

> All are obliged to strictly observe official secrecy. They may not, therefore, give to anyone who does not have the right to do so information relating to acts or news of which they have become aware because of their work.[31]

And in articles 72.5 and 76.3, the "violation of secrecy *ex officio*" can be grounds for suspension or dismissal from work.[32]

As Rhode explains, in current law there is a wide variety of norms (universal, local, specific, concordat) that relate to the protection of secrecy: norms that require an oath of secrecy, norms that establish penalties for those who violate secrecy, norms on the preservation in secrecy of documents and other material in archives, norms that grant the right to silence, particularly with regard to matters covered by the so-called attorney-client

---

30. *General Regulations of the Roman Curia* (Washington, DC: United States Catholic Conference, 1968), art. 18 § 2.

31. Ibid., art. 36 § 1.

32. Secretary of State, *Regolamento Generale della Curia Romana* (April 30, 1999), in *AAS* 91 (1999), 629–699.

privilege, and norms agreed to with the States on the protection of the attorney-client privilege and ecclesiastical archives in civil law.[33]

As Rhode points out, the duty to keep a secret can be justified on two kinds of grounds. On one hand, secrecy may depend on the *type of communication*: We see, for example, the seal of the Sacrament of Confession, the confidentiality of spiritual direction, or the different levels of secrecy of the advisory bodies.

Secondly, the obligation to secrecy may derive from the *content of the information itself*. Protected contents primarily include those belonging to the privacy of individuals, among which we see the necessary confidentiality of the penal proceeding. The *Code of Canon Law* contemplates several secret contents concerning the public good of the Church: the preparatory acts for the appointment of bishops and the creation of cardinals, the procedures of canonization, the secrecy required for the election of the Roman Pontiff, etc.

Laws, in addition to explicitly determining some cases, can also give general guidance on respecting confidentiality, the application of which requires the good sense of authority. Sometimes it will be *legal* to maintain silence, but after an evaluation of the circumstances, it may be found immoral. The function of laws is limited.

We reiterate many times in these pages, and from different perspectives, that the Church's starting attitude toward information must be one of openness, not secrecy. As Del Pozzo affirms, secrecy "has a character that is exceptional and residual, motivated, or circumscribed."[34]

Secrecy as *pretext* is something else: It is the corruption of confidentiality. That is why the Church seems to live a paradox: She guards confidentiality in certain spaces, but she denies it when transparency is more desirable. The problem is in understanding transparency as something "limited" because otherwise it inevitably leads to a series of attitudes that offend human

---

33. Cf. U. Rhode, *La trasparenza e il segreto nel diritto canonico*, 465–492.

34. M. Del Pozzo, *Lo statuto giuridico fondamentale del fedele* (Rome: EDUSC, 2018), 148; translation ours.

dignity and the common good. And silences, secrets, or reservations have reason to exist only in the service of the common good. Likewise, as we have seen, imposing silence without the necessary reference to human dignity and to the common good generates grave abuses. So far, the Church has sinned more in the latter way than by excessive transparency. Presumably, that is the reason Pope Francis ordered the removal of the pontifical secret (for some procedural phases) in cases of child sexual abuse.

ABOLITION OF THE PONTIFICAL SECRET FOR CASES OF ABUSE

Archbishop Charles J. Scicluna, Adjunct Secretary of the Congregation for the Doctrine of the Faith, has been one of the central figures in the Vatican when it comes to the Church's fight to combat sexual abuse committed by clergy. He was commissioned by Joseph Ratzinger [later Pope Benedict XVI] to conduct the investigations into the case of Father Maciel in Mexico and then, by Pope Francis's order, the investigations on the cases of abuse in Chile, together with Monsignor Jordi Bertomeu.

Scicluna frames this decision as another piece of the reform process that the Church began with Pope Saint John Paul II—and continued with Popes Benedict XVI and Francis—regarding the sexual abuse of minors by clerics. It is a reform process that includes many different kinds of actions: measures that affect the organizational structure of the Church; legal measures (that affect punishments or trials); and actions of inculturation, prevention, and internal awareness such as the meeting that took place with the Episcopal Conferences in Rome in February 2019.

In recent years Pope Francis has overseen the passage of a mosaic of legal reforms on abuse cases, including *As a Loving Mother* (2016) and *Vos Estis Lux Mundi* (2019), which establish certain consequences for negligence or cover-ups by bishops and religious superiors. Another provision is the reform of Book VI of the *Code of Canon Law*, and of the *Vademecum* with guidelines for the action of diocesan tribunals and of bishops in cases of abuse, as well as the updating and modifications of the "Norms on the Delicts Reserved to the Congregation of the Doctrine of the Faith" (promulgated by Pope Saint John Paul II in 2001 and updated by Pope Benedict XVI in 2010), to adapt them, albeit in summary, to the new Book VI and to the measures approved in 2016 and 2019.

Pope Francis has approved the abolition of the pontifical secret (for three particular instances: accusation, trials, and decision) for the cases of abuse of a minor,[35] with the Instruction *On the Confidentiality of Legal Proceedings* (December 17, 2019). Excluded from the category of the "pontifical secret" are crimes of sexual abuse committed by clerics or consecrated persons against minors and vulnerable persons and crimes of child pornography that have young people (under the age of eighteen) as their object, as well as any conduct of Church authorities that attempted to silence or cover up such crimes.

The abolition of the pontifical secret in cases of sexual abuse of a minor by a cleric is not a penal matter but rather a procedural matter since it involves the complaint and some communications that concern the process. As Scicluna explained:

> The victim did not have the possibility of knowing the sentence that followed his or her complaint because it was under the pontifical secret. Other communications were also hindered because the pontifical secret is a very high level of secrecy in the confidentiality system of canon law.[36]

Matteo Visioli, the former Undersecretary of the Congregation for the Doctrine of the Faith, stated:

> An unintentional climate of hostility has been created between authorities that, despite having their own independent systems, have the same objective at heart: namely, the ascertainment of the truth, the prosecution of crimes, and the restoration of justice. In this sense, the notion of "secrecy"—rather than being understood as protection of the value of intimacy, confidential-

---

35. In December 2019, two *Rescripta ex Audientia SS.mi* were approved (December 3 and 6, 2019), one modifying articles 6, 13, and 14 of the Norms reserved to the CDF promulgated with the 2010 Motu Proprio *Sacramentorum Sanctitatis Tutela*, and the second promulgating a new Instruction that removes some phases of the penal process of abuse cases from the pontifical secret. Both were published by *L'Osservatore Romano* 288, no. 4 (December 18, 2019), 4–5.

36. A. TORNIELLI, *Scicluna: "Scelta epocale che toglie ostacoli e impedimenti"* in *Vatican News* (December 17, 2019), *www.vaticannews.va/it/vaticano/news/2019-12/scicluna-scelta-epocale-che-toglie-ostacoli-impedimenti.html*; translation ours.

ity, and good reputation—has often been interpreted as cover-up, obstructionism, or concealment of the truth.[37]

The documents of the proceeding are not in the public domain, but now that the pontifical secret is eliminated, the documentation enjoys a confidentiality appropriate to this type of information: It is treated as it would be in a criminal trial. As Scicluna said in an interview: "The institutional obstacle" is thus removed.[38] "The Pope has put an end to this by unambiguously declaring that the pontifical secret must not be invoked to avoid justice."[39]

With this change, the Church lifts a major barrier and shows an attitude of greater collaboration with the civil authorities since the diocese or religious congregations that know the case are no longer bound by this secrecy. They can collaborate by delivering a copy of the documentation to the civil authorities in the three stages of the procedure listed by the new Instruction promulgated by Pope Francis (denunciation, trials, and decision).

Even with these changes, the privacy of individuals, the good reputation of those involved, and the dignity of each person continue to be safeguarded. To some extent, confidentiality is always required in the penal sector, and this is still guaranteed.

Confidentiality, which must protect the good name of the individuals involved, is now assured by the *secrecy of office* established by canon 471 § 2 of the *Code of Canon Law*. This change in canon law eliminates any internal obstacles that may stand between the ecclesial authorities and the victim, and it allows for a better (external) collaboration between the ecclesial authority and the State.

However, Visioli shows that, in fact, "the norm on PS [the pontifical secret] is practically absent from the normative texts of

---

37. M. Visioli, *"Istruzioni sulla riservatezza delle cause. Considerazioni a margine del Rescriptum ex Audientia SS.MI del 6 dicembre 2019,"* in *Ius Ecclesiæ* 32, no. 3 (2020), 730; translation ours.

38. A. Tornielli, *Scicluna: "Scelta epocale che toglie ostacoli e impedimenti";* translation ours.

39. C.J. Scicluna, *"Vos estis lux mundi. Avances y desafíos de su recepción,"* in *La Revista Católica* 1207 (2020), 77; translation ours.

reference for the life of the Church," and he considers it urgent to have...

> a development of the institution of PS, establishing with a greater level of detail the boundaries, content, subjects, form, extenuating circumstances and exceptions, competent authorities, and consequences of its violation with the procedure to be followed for its ascertainment and eventual prosecution.[40]

A new norm on the pontifical secret would help restore the credibility of the Church also because, as Visioli points out, "there are no convictions for such a delict."[41]

Linda Ghisoni has reiterated similar ideas at the meeting held at the Vatican in 2019:

> It will be necessary to review the current norms on the pontifical secret so that it protects the values it is intended to protect: namely, the dignity of the people involved, the good reputation of each individual, and the good of the Church, but at the same time allows for the development of a climate of greater transparency and trust, avoiding the idea that secrecy is used to hide problems rather than to protect the goods involved.[42]

---

40. M. Visioli, *Confidenzialità e segreto pontificio*, 486; translation ours.

41. Ibid., 488; translation ours.

42. L. Ghisoni, *Communio: Agire insieme*, Presentation in the *Meeting "The Protection of Minors in the Church"* in *Vatican.va*, (February 22, 2019), no. 3.5, *www.vatican. va/resources/resources_lindaghisoni-protezioneminori_20190222_it.html*; translation ours.

CHAPTER 3

THE CHURCH'S "YES" TO TRANSPARENCY

You will know the truth,
and the truth will make you free.
— John 8:32

Transparency has gone from being a mere property of physical bodies to becoming a commonly used metaphor in the spheres of economics, government, and communications — ultimately, of society. To say that an administrative act has not been transparent sounds like an accusation of corruption; a manager who does not act with transparency "is definitely hiding something," and unfortunately there is no shortage of examples even in the Catholic Church.

In 2011, the Bishop of Limburg (Germany) changed the status of the ecclesial body "Bischöflicher Stuhl" (Episcopal seat), abolishing the supervisory and control functions that this body exercised. He did so in secret and did not publish the new statute, which established the Apostolic See as the exclusive supervisory body without informing it of that fact. In this way it was *de facto* free from all control.

The bishop began construction on a new residence with money from the Opera di San Giorgio foundation. Instead of entrusting the project's supervision to the respective office of the diocesan Curia, he entrusted it exclusively to a small circle of people. The invoices were paid by an external company, to which the ecclesiastical body reimbursed its expenses. For all documents, a special secret archive was created in a building outside the diocesan Curia that only a few people could access. The protection of the secret took place perfectly. No one could criticize the project with accurate information.

Subsequently, the Holy See asked the German Bishops' Conference to establish an inquiry commission. The commission's report, which revealed many details and in particular brought out the secret maneuvers of the bishop, was published on the website of the bishops' conference. This transparency was considered necessary for reestablishing a relationship of trust with the faithful and with the public. For the same purpose, in the following years almost all dioceses in Germany published the financial statements of their respective ecclesiastical bodies.

The "Tebartz-van Elst case" caused one of the most serious crises in the history of the Church in Germany because it was proven that the bishop fraudulently diverted funds from a bishop's foundation dedicated to the poor to the financing of his personal residence. The project cost 31 million euros. The money was fraudulently diverted, but the bishop's secrets (with few exceptions) were not technically illegal.[1] Yet it was clearly an example of bad governance and immorality.

The German Bishops' Conference chose to adopt an attitude of total transparency, publishing information from all the dioceses, to try to alleviate the sense of distrust that this case produced in the faithful and public opinion. That transparency was not required by civil or canon law: It was a choice of governance.

It is not possible for canon lawmakers to foresee all the cases and circumstances in which it will be necessary to act with transparency or to maintain secrecy. In many cases, laws can only give some general guidelines, but their application then requires good discernment on the part of the competent authority.

Transparency has more and more esteem in the collective imagination—sometimes too much. Its esteem is supported by the demands of truth and justice, which are entirely necessary for society, but we can ask ourselves if transparency is *always*

---

1. The newspaper *Spiegel* first revealed the prelate's less than ideal habits: Cf. M.U. Müller, P. Wensierski, "Bishop's Extravagant Behavior Triggers Uproar," in *Spiegel* (August 3, 2012), *www.spiegel.de/international/germany/german-bishop-of-limburg-triggers-uproar-with-luxurious-lifestyle-a-851707.html*; Months later it revealed other attitudes shrouded in secrecy: "*Kosten für Bischofssitz könnten auf 40 Millionen Euro steigen,*" in *Spiegel* (October 12, 2013), *www.spiegel.de/panorama/gesellschaft/tebartz-van-elst-kosten-fuer-bischofssitz-steigen-um-weitere-millionen-a-927556.html*.

the most appropriate response, if it always leads to a solution in every case, or if instead of solutions it will generate (or has already generated) new problems.

In this world that continuously demands transparency stands the Church, known for the colors of her Gothic stained-glass windows, the light of her libraries, the darkness of her Romanesque style, and the black of her cassocks. Even in the corridors of the Vatican, in seminar rooms, and in some parishes, people have begun to talk about transparency because it is linked to some values that have a lot to do with the Church's identity: more than it might seem at first glance.

These values include openness, the flow of relevant information, the right to inform and to be informed, accountability, shared responsibility, freedom of expression, public opinion, etc. All of these are oriented toward the common good and human dignity: objectives that the Church cannot renounce without betraying herself.

It is therefore not surprising that the Church is embracing this modern-day call for transparency. Even back in 2005, Pope Saint John Paul II said: "Communication both within the Church community, and between the Church and the world at large, requires *openness*."[2] Shortly thereafter Pope Benedict XVI used that same word to address the crisis of sexual abuse when he wrote to the Bishops of Ireland: "Only decisive action carried out with complete honesty and *transparency* will restore the respect and good will of the Irish people towards the Church"[3]

For his part, Pope Francis said in a letter addressed to priests:

> If in the past, omission may itself have been a kind of response, today we desire conversion, *transparency*, sincerity, and solidarity with victims to become our concrete way of moving forward.

---

2. Pope St. John Paul II, Apostolic Letter to Those Responsible for Communications *The Rapid Development* (January 24, 2005), no. 12, *www.vatican.va/content/john-paul-ii/en/apost_letters/2005/documents/hf_jp-ii_apl_20050124_il-rapido-sviluppo. html*; emphasis ours.

3. Pope Benedict XVI, *Pastoral Letter to the Catholics of Ireland* (October 19, 2010), *www.vatican.va/content/benedict-xvi/en/letters/2010/documents/hf_ben-xvi_ let_20100319_church-ireland.html*; emphasis ours.

This in turn will help make us all the more attentive to every form of human suffering.[4]

Beyond the prophetic voices of the Magisterium, this "joining the demands for transparency" has not been easy or quick for the Church (as for many other institutions); indeed, it is a process that involves resistance, successes, excesses, and crises. In short, we are in the midst of a journey of cultural transformation, which if accomplished well, will make the Church in her governance and communication ever more similar to her essence and truth, to what she is called to live.

Therefore, before delving deeper into the long paths along which this cultural transformation is unfolding, before asking ourselves what the scope and limits of transparency are, it is appropriate to highlight some dimensions of the Church's identity. They will help us understand the "whys" and the "hows" of transparency and secrecy and will give us the insights we need to analyze some stories from which we still have much to learn.

THE CHURCH EXISTS TO COMMUNICATE

The Church was born with the task of proclaiming the Word of God, Christ, to all nations.[5] A baptized person cannot *not* proclaim the Word of Salvation that he or she has received; he or she is aware that it is addressed to every woman and every man, and that each of us needs it, even those who do not know it.

The essence of the Church is to communicate the Good News.

> The Church is not just an organization *of* constituted communication, as all organizations are. The Church is constituted *for* communication. [...] For the Church, communicating is not only a right but also a duty.[6]

In fact, the Church throughout history has been very active in spreading her message and has done so in many ways: through art (painting, sculpture, architecture, and music) and the various

---

4. Pope FRANCIS: *Letter to Priests on the 160th Anniversary of the Death of the Holy Curé of Ars* (August 4, 2019), *www.vatican.va/content/francesco/en/letters/2019/documents/papa-francesco_20190804_lettera-presbiteri.html*; emphasis ours.

5. Cf. Mk 16:15.

6. Y. DE LA CIERVA, *La Chiesa casa di vetro*, 46; translation ours.

information technologies (books, press, radio, cinema, television, Internet, and social media).

This essentially communicative nature of spreading salvation implies that...

> the Church has her own agenda: She is not contented with society as it is, but she wants to change it using legitimate means, convincing rather than conquering. As [Saint] John Paul II said, "The Gospel does not impose, it proposes."[7]

In this sense, the Church tirelessly defends essential values such as the dignity of each person (of the unborn, the elderly, the disabled, the migrant, etc.), freedom and social responsibility, the social importance of the family, etc.

In the Church, the communicative dimension is not only spiritual since she is an agent like so many others in the public sphere. This means that she must give information about herself and, as we will see later, she must also communicate the negative aspects.

> The Church strives and will strive more and more to be a "glass house" where everyone can see what is happening and how it fulfills her mission in fidelity to Christ and the Gospel message.[8]

THE CHURCH IS COMMUNION

The Church is the People of God in which all are "equally faithful": both ordained ministers and lay people. The dignity of the members is common; there is no inequality in Christ or in the Church.

> By the will of Christ some are made teachers, pastors and dispensers of mysteries on behalf of others, yet all share a true equality with regard to the dignity and to the activity common to all the faithful for the building up of the Body of Christ. For the distinction which the Lord made between sacred ministers and the rest of the People of God bears within it a certain

---

7. Ibid., 48; translation ours.

8. Pope St. JOHN PAUL II, *Discorso ai giornalisti riuniti in vaticano per celebrare il Giubileo della Redenzione* (January 27, 1984), no. 4, *www.vatican.va/content/john-paul-ii/it/speeches/1984/january/documents/hf_jp-ii_spe_19840127_giornalisti.html*; translation ours.

union, since pastors and the other faithful are bound to each other by a mutual need.[9]

Already in the first millennium, the Church understood herself as communion, which implies "equal dignity" and "community in relations." This concept was also recovered by the Second Vatican Council, which speaks of communion in the Church as a gift received from God: a gift that must be lived out with deep responsibility.[10]

> In the Christian faith, the unity and brotherhood of man are the chief aims of all communication and these find their source and model in the central mystery of the eternal communion between the Father, Son and Holy Spirit who live a single divine life.[11]

In fact, although communication cannot be reduced to the visible structure of the Church, it includes and constitutes it, so that the Church is called to manifest in all her dimensions, including the visible ones, the communion that she is and is called to live in fullness.

"This reality involves any organizational structure and helps prevent any power struggle or selfish pursuit of private interests."[12] "The Church is a communion, not a political democracy; therefore openness and accountability are even more important in the Church than they are in a democracy."[13]

THE CHURCH IS HIERARCHICAL

The Church's hierarchical constitution is another dimension of her identity and mission, and it significantly influences the way she practices transparency and secrecy.

> In the Church, the first and fundamental aspect is to be members through incorporation into Christ. [...] Only after that will

---

9. VATICAN COUNCIL II, Dogmatic Constitution of the Church *Lumen Gentium* (November 21, 1964), in *AAS* 57 (1965), 5 ff, no. 32.

10. Cf. R. BLÁZQUEZ, *La Iglesia del Concilio Vaticano II* (Salamanca: Seguimi, 1988), 59.

11. PCCS, *Communio et Progressio*, no. 8.

12. A. RÍOS, "*La comunicazione interna al servizio del Chiesa diocesana*," licentiate thesis in *Institutional Communication*, pro manuscripto (Rome: Pontifical University of Santa Croce [PUSC], 2014), 13; translation ours.

13. Cf. R. SHAW, *Nothing to Hide*, 9.

we be able to speak of hierarchy as authority put into place by Christ as the Head and at the service of God's people.[14]

The Church is a people born of God, whom God himself chooses and establishes, placing various ministries at the forefront. These institutions of the Lord must serve all God's people in Christ's name by virtue of his authority and power. Christ himself chose the Apostles (cf. Jn 15:16) and sent them in the same way he had been sent by the Father (cf. Jn 20:26). He wanted his successors, the bishops, to be apostles of his Church until the end of time, and he established Peter at the head of them as the perpetual and visible principle of faith and communion.[15] For this reason the hierarchical structure in the Church is a sacred authority, which comes directly from Christ; that is, she is not governed by the style of this world's authority, but rather authority is exercised within the fraternity and in the service of human beings.[16] This service excludes any pursuit of human glory and any kind of populism that leads to bending to people's whims; it seeks to faithfully transmit the Word of God, to sanctify, and to seek unity, correcting what is necessary, exhorting, and commanding.[17]

The fact that *she is not a political democracy* and that power in the Church lies with the pastors by virtue of the Sacrament cannot be an alibi.

> If the Church wants to be credible in the contemporary world, then she cannot continue to be content to merely state, "The Church is not a democracy," in order to absolve herself from criticism. [… It is] necessary, however, for the Church to be able to clearly define the objective criteria of her operational choices, which is an indispensable condition for an effective dialogue with other juridical systems.[18]

Institutional communication can also facilitate this process internally, enhancing coresponsibility in the edification of the Church as indicated by canon 204 of the *Code of Canon Law*.

---

14. J.A. Sayés, *La Iglesia de Cristo. Curso de Eclesiología* (Madrid: Palabra, 1999), 305; translation ours.

15. Cf. Vatican Council II, *Lumen Gentium*, no. 18.

16. Cf. R. Blázquez, "*Ministerio y poder en la Iglesia*," in *Communio* 6 (1984), 222, no. 3.

17. J.A. Sayés, *La Iglesia de Cristo*, 309.

18. É. Kouveglo, "*I fedeli laici e l'esercizio della potestà nella Chiesa. Status quæstionis e ricerca di una chiave funzionale di lettura*," in *Apollinaris* 90, no. 1 (2017), 208; translation ours.

Later in these pages, we will suggest criteria and operational choices, taking our cue from Kouveglo.

THE CHURCH HAS A MAGISTERIUM

On the other hand, the Church exhorts, teaches, reflects, and corrects, remaining faithful to what she has received. In the words of Von Balthasar: "What is in us is greater than us."[19] The Magisterium of the Church was born and has — since her origins — the mission of transmitting and interpreting in an authentic — sometimes infallible — way the truth of the Revelation of Jesus Christ. Knowledge of the truth tends to grow over the centuries: This requires a dynamic interpretation of certain challenges and signs of the times, which demand a coherent response from the Church without her denying what she has always believed.[20]

In that sense, Pope Francis said:

In her ongoing discernment, the Church can also come to see that certain customs not directly connected to the heart of the Gospel are no longer properly understood and appreciated.[21]

And he exhorted: "We should not be afraid to re-examine them." He clarified:

The Church has norms or precepts which may have been quite effective in their time, but no longer have the same usefulness for directing and shaping people's lives.[22]

This is not to be confused with *an erroneous statement of the disembodied Gospel,* which would itself be a contradiction; in fact, "A faith that does not become culture is a faith that is not fully accepted, not fully thought out, and not faithfully lived."[23]

---

19. H.U. Von Balthasar, *Il Chicco di grano* (Milan: Jaca Book, 1994), 134; translation ours.

20. G. Calabrese, et al., "*Magistero,*" in *Dizionario di Ecclesiologia* (Madrid: LAC, 2016), 834.

21. Pope Francis, Apostolic Exhortation on the Proclamation of the Gospel in Today's World *Evangelii Gaudium* (November 24, 2013), no. 43, in *AAS* 105 (2013), *www. vatican.va/content/francesco/en/apost_exhortations/documents/papa-francesco_ esortazione-ap_20131124_evangelii-gaudium.html.*

22. Ibid.

23. Pope St. John Paul II, *Discorso ai partecipanti al Congresso Nazionale del Movimento di "Impegno Culturale"* (January 16, 1982), *www.vatican.va/content/john-paul-ii/it/ speeches/1982/january/documents/hf_jp-ii_spe_19820116_impegno-culturale.html;* translation ours.

During the whole life of the Church and thus also in the way of protecting confidentiality and managing transparency, the Church is called to strive to live in truth and charity. For the Church, "To defend the truth, to articulate it with humility and conviction, and to bear witness to it in life are therefore exacting and indispensable forms of charity."[24] Service to the truth requires openness to discovering it and recognizing it.

> This mission of truth is something that the Church can never renounce. Her social doctrine is a particular dimension of this proclamation: it is a service to the truth which sets us free. Open to the truth, from whichever branch of knowledge it comes, the Church's social doctrine receives it. [...][25]

THE TERM "EFFECTIVENESS" HAS A DIFFERENT MEANING FOR THE CHURCH

The real identity of the Church and her mission, albeit with her riches and its limitations, must be the compass that points to when and how to speak or remain silent. In this sense, we should remember that in the Church, by her very nature, the criteria of effectiveness have a connotation and objectives that are totally different from those normally found in the business world, where there is often an imposed model. In an organization whose mission is the salvation of souls and whose goal is eternal life (which is why the Church exists), attitudes that contradict these truths are highly jarring.

If by *effectiveness* we mean sound management and *good governance*, then the latter is a principle that can be ascribed to the essence of the Church: It concerns the *munus regendi*, which, like everything in the Church, is ordered to the *salus animarum*.

> The need for transparency and the explicit explanation of certain criteria for choosing or guiding is increasingly felt as a manifestation of good governance. It is not a matter of making everything clearly visible (a sort of "open-door" management) but of manifesting what concerns the possible intervention of the community or a qualified personal interest.[26]

---

24. Pope BENEDICT XVI, Encyclical Letter on Integral Human Development in Charity and Truth *Caritas in Veritate* (June 29, 2009), in *AAS* 101 (2009), 641 ff., no. 1.

25. Ibid., no. 9.

26. M. DEL POZZO, *Lo statuto giuridico fondamentale del fedele*, 148; translation ours.

We can conclude that the management of transparency and secrecy in Church communications has to do with the fundamental principles of the identity of the Church herself; in this sense, she either proclaims or contradicts her essence, fidelity to her mission, and her prospects.

WHY SPEAK OF TRANSPARENCY IN THE CHURCH?

Beyond the fact that transparency is a "fashionable" metaphor, a sort of discovery that nobody seems to be able to do without, transparency is connected to a series of concepts and practices that closely relate to the identity and mission of the Church and are manifested in her daily activity.

We are talking about accountability, openness, flows of relevant information, the right and duty to inform and be informed, and dialogue and participation within the Church.

Transparency is a concept that is closely related to accountability, a practice that has been appreciated and established by the Church from the very origins of Christianity. The first reference to responsibility is found in the *Didache* (ch. II), where it is made clear that those who receive alms without needing them must account for why. This ensures that the Church does not receive goods for her own sake but for the mission, for her higher purpose.[27]

Other documents from the early centuries of Christianity such as the *Didascalia*, the *Traditio Apostolica*, and the *Constitutiones Apostolorum* point to the bishop as the steward of goods for charitable purposes and for the support of ministers. These documents agree on the fact that the bishop must see that goods arrive where they are truly intended to go and must be accountable to God. Accountability has naturally been present in the doctrine and in the legislation of the Church and "has been a paradigm and a model of rigor on many occasions in ancient and

---

27. La Didaché (I, 5) makes it clear that those who accept alms without needing them must account for why they receive them. Cf. D. Zabildea, *La rendición de cuentas en el ordenamiento canónico: transparencia y misión* (Pamplona: Eunsa, 2018), 23.

recent history."[28] From the earliest times, accountability has been considered "a tool for carrying out the mission of the Church."[29]

A CHURCH IN WHICH THERE IS FREEDOM OF INFORMATION, OPENNESS, PARTICIPATION, AND DIALOGUE: VATICAN II

The Second Vatican Council and the doctrine that originated from this great event have led to a strong and clear "yes" to openness and communication. However, implementing these principles, as we will see below, has been difficult. It has been necessary to contrast the strong inertia of past centuries, in which the Church, like other institutions, has preferred secrecy. One should not think that the Church tends to be more closed than the societies in which she lives; she has often seen her autonomy and even the content of her faith threatened. In addition, pastors have also been men with temporal power, who, in addition to their pastoral commission, defended political, economic, and military interests.

Vatican II attracted hundreds of journalists. This time, as had happened during Vatican I, secrecy was imposed, followed by "leaks,"[30] and journalists often relied on alternative sources.[31] Openness, in practice, has been a long process. The lively journalistic activity during this important event "marked a point of no return in the opening of the Church, with significant consequences for the following decades."[32]

Certainly openness, freedom of information, participation, and dialogue are part of the life of the Church; they express her essence, and in this sense the Church says "yes" to transparency. Let us look at how some of the documents of Vatican II reveal just that.

---

28. D. ZABILDEA, *La rendición de cuentas en el ordenamiento canónico*, 30; translation ours.

29. Ibid., 16–17; translation ours.

30. Cf. E. BARAGLI, "*Segreto ed informazione nella Chiesa*," in *La Civiltà Cattolica* 124 (1973), 350, no. 2.

31. Cf. B. BARTOLONI, *Le orecchie del Vaticano* (Florence: Mauro Pagliai Editore, 2012), 35.

32. M. TOSATTI, "*Chiesa e informazione: Storia di un rapporto*," in *Teoria e pratica del giornalismo religioso. Come informare sulla Chiesa Cattolica: Fonti, logiche, storie, personaggi*, G. TRIDENTE, ed. (Rome: EDUSC, 2014), 43–44; translation ours.

FREEDOM OF INFORMATION

The decree *Inter Mirifica* affirms the right to seek out and disseminate news "in accord with the circumstances in each case, about matters concerning individuals or the community."[33] This right is reaffirmed by the Pastoral Instruction *Communio et Progressio* and calls practices contrary to the freedom of information "inadmissible"; among them is a distorted way of presenting facts or ideas with the intent to manipulate:

> Some types of propaganda are inadmissable. These include those that harm the public interest or allow of no public reply. Any propaganda that deliberately misrepresents the real situation, or that distorts men's minds with half-truths, selective reporting or serious omissions, that diminishes man's legitimate freedom of decision.[34]

It highlights, "Freedom of opinion and the right to be informed go hand in hand."[35]

The document *Ethics in Communications* warns against the use of the media as "instruments for control and domination" and states that one should not be "practicing unnecessary secrecy and otherwise offending against truth."[36] The Magisterium insists on every individual's right to freedom of information, clarifying that it is not an absolute right: It must be considered in relation to access to information and public opinion, taking into account what the common good demands. As Pope Saint John XXIII previously pointed out:

> Man has a natural right to be respected. [...] He has a right to freedom in investigating the truth, and—within the limits of the moral order and the common good—to freedom of speech

---

33. Vatican Council II, Decree on the Media of Social Communications *Inter Mirifica* (December 4, 1963), in *AAS* 56 (1964), 145 ff., no. 5.

34. PCCS, *Communio et Progressio*, no. 30.

35. Ibid., no. 33.

36. PCCS, *Ethics in Communications*, no. 18 (June 4, 2000), *www.vatican.va/roman_curia/pontifical_councils/pccs/documents/rc_pc_pccs_doc_20000530_ethics-communications_en.html*.

and publication. [...] He has the right, also, to be accurately informed about public events.[37]

PARTICIPATION AND DIALOGUE IN THE CHURCH

Communio et Progressio points out that, for an active participation of the faithful in the dialogue around the Church, it is necessary to have "a steady two-way flow of information between the ecclesiastical authorities at all levels and the faithful as individuals and as organized groups."[38] This flow of information in both directions and around the world promotes the formation of correct public opinion.[39]

Ætatis Novæ says it clearly:

Among the members of the community of people who make up the Church, there is a radical equality in dignity and mission that arises from Baptism and underlies the hierarchical structure and diversity of office and function, and this equality necessarily will express itself in an honest and respectful sharing of information and opinions.[40]

In this spirit of participation and dialogue, we understand the accountability toward the faithful, which is connected to their state as baptized persons. "Accountability is a practical consequence and a legal manifestation of the very nature of the Church."[41] This organic relationship between identity, mission, information, and dialogue in the Church gives us a fundamental criterion for understanding the role of confidentiality and transparency in the Church.

---

37. Pope St.John XXIII, Encyclical Letter on Establishing Universal Peace in Truth, Justice, Charity, and Liberty *Pacem in Terris* (April 11, 1963), in *AAS* 55 (1963), 260, no.7, *www.vatican.va/content/john-xxiii/en/encyclicals/documents/hf_j-xxiii_enc_11041963_pacem.html*; cf. PCCS, *Communio et Progressio*, nos.33–35.

38. PCCS, *Communio et Progressio*, no.120.

39. Back in 1950 Ven. Pius XII had warned that "the Church, after all, is a living body, and she would be missing something in her life if she were missing public opinion": Ven. Pius XII, *Discorso di Papa Pio XII ai giornalisti cattolici riuniti a Roma per il loro IV Congresso Internazionale* (February 17, 1950), in *AAS* 42 (February 17, 1950), *www.vatican.va/content/pius-xii/it/speeches/1950/documents/hf_p-xii_spe_19500217_la-presse.html*; translation ours.

40. PCCS, *Ætatis Novæ*, no.10.

41. D. Zalbidea, *La Rendición de cuentas en el ordenamiento canónico*, 82; translation ours.

Transparency, supported by all these values and by the good practices that we have considered, albeit in summary, is not an *absolute*, and the temptation to embrace it indiscriminately leads, as we said, to new abuses with the resulting victims.

CHAPTER 4

TRANSPARENCY: ALL OR NOTHING

He who goes about gossiping reveals secrets;
therefore do not associate with one who speaks foolishly.
— Proverbs 20:19

The word "transparency" derives from the Latin *transparentem* and is comprised of two distinct terms: *trans*, which means "through, beyond, across," and *parere*, which means "to come into view, to appear." The original meaning was "show light through," but it later took on a figurative connotation, and today it means "easily seen through."[1]

Transparency is etymologically and semantically associated with vision and originally belongs to the language of physics: It refers to the "property of a material object to allow light to pass through it without distortion, making the object beyond it entirely visible."[2] The opposite concept to transparency is opacity, which means blocking the passage of light.

The concept of transparency has evolved with respect to its etymological meaning of "seeing the light through," to the point that it can now be applied to *governance* as well. Being transparent, in this field, means to allow others "to see the truth of an act or a fact without any alteration." In this sense, the opposite of transparency is not the "physical opacity" of some material but rather secrecy. Secrecy is the will to *conceal* one's actions, while transparency refers to the intention to *reveal* them.

In the case of *governance*, transparency can be seen as a positive aspect in the decision-making process because it allows

---

1. Cf. M.A. AGUILAR, *The Communicative Values of Transparency in the New Financial System of the Diocese of Calbayog*, licentiate thesis (PUSC, 2018), 6.
2. R.T. YOUNG, *The Obligation of Transparency in the Administration of Temporal Goods of the Church in Canon 1287 § 2*, doctoral thesis (PUSC, 2016), 13.

one to fight corruption. Transparency is then connected to the availability of information about the institution: The more the institution is open and facilitates the public in obtaining information, the greater the transparency. Transparency is also considered a value in politics: Indeed, it allows for the evaluation of organizational actions and programs.[3]

Some consider transparency an instrumental value (as a means to reach an ulterior end), but others see it as an end in itself. Transparency as an instrumental value, according to D. Heald, should be linked to concepts such as effectiveness, trust, accountability, autonomy and control, confidentiality, privacy and anonymity, fairness, and legitimacy.[4] R. Young, rather, makes a shorter list: accountability, participation and collaboration, communication, trust, and credibility.[5]

As we can see, the concept of transparency is closely linked to the notion of openness, which garners approval across today's diverse ideological spectrum. The culture of transparency did not originate with the Internet, but it obviously changes the dimensions of the culture of transparency and increases claims to the "right to know."[6]

Luciano Floridi explains that the transparency of an organization or State can be understood in two different ways. One can say "Open Government" if the State respects its citizens' right to know and monitor the work of the government. The second meaning that transparency can take on is the one Floridi proposes when he speaks of the "Gentile Government":

> The State can be transparent in the same sense in which a technology (e.g., an interface) is: invisible not because it is not there but because it delivers its services so efficiently, effectively, and reliably that its presence is imperceptible. When something works at its best, behind the scenes as it were, to make sure that we can operate as easily as possible, then we

---

3. C. BALL, "What Is Transparency?" in Public Integrity 11 (2009), no. 4, 293–308.

4. Cf. D. HEALD, Transparency as an Instrumental Value, in Transparency: The Key to Better Governance? C. HOOD and D. HEALD, ed. (New York: Oxford University Press, 2006), 59–60.

5. R.T. YOUNG, The Obligation of Transparency, 14.

6. Cf. M. SCHUDSON, The Rise of the Right to Know. Politics and the Culture of Transparency, 1945–1975 (Cambridge, MA: Harvard University Press, 2015), ch. 2.

have a transparent system. This second sense of transparency should not be seen as a surreptitious way of introducing, with a different terminology, the concept of "Small State" or "Small Governance." On the contrary, in this second sense, the State is as transparent and as vital as the oxygen that we breathe. It strives to be the ideal butler. There is no standard terminology for this kind of transparent State that becomes perceivable only when it is absent.[7]

The notion of openness has different origins and meanings, which fundamentally concern three areas: politics, the economy, and information technology.

The philosopher Henri Bergson theorized the idea of an "open society" in his work *The Two Sources of Morality and Religion* (1935). The concept of openness, with the resulting contrast between a closed society and an open society, would then be reprised by Karl Popper in his book *The Open Society and Its Enemies* (1962). Popper developed his theory in the sphere of political philosophy, while Friedrich Hayek did so in reference to economics. The two influenced one another. Both thought that a society (or a market) cannot be organized from the center: Competition and the possibility of choice are crucial to ensure freedom.[8]

The notion of openness is connected to the governing of political institutions and the economy, as we said earlier, but it is also closely related to the software world and has developed strongly in the network culture. In the information world the battle for openness is not against "closed forms of knowledge," as Popper claimed; what he criticized were "closed infrastructures." In this regard, a debate has arisen about the openness of operating systems and the freedom of software.

This debate began in the United States and saw the formation of two groups. First, we find the *Free Software Movement*, which arose in the 1980s, and was comprised of MIT programmers (among whom Richard Stallman particularly distinguished himself) who left the university to create "free software," defining

---

7. L. FLORIDI (ed.), *The Onlife Manifesto: Being Human in a Hyperconnected Era* (New York-London: SpringerOpen, 2015), 62.

8. Cf. N. WEAVER, *Wikipedia and the Politics of Openness* (Chicago: University of Chicago Press, 2015), 15, 19.

it as "open" in terms of copyright. For-profit appropriations were forbidden, but people were completely free to use, modify, and distribute the software. The late 1990s, however, saw the rise of the *Open Source Initiative,* led by programmers Eric Raymond and Linus Torvalds (the father of the Linux operating system). They deliberately use the expression "open source" instead of the word "free": In this way, they emphasize the fact that technical excellence cannot be free, but the programs should provide a code open to modification. They contrast two modes of production: the cathedral and the bazaar. The cathedral is produced exclusively, centrally, and by specialists, while "bazaar" development, which is much more utopian, is open to all kinds of contributions and is much more indeterminate.[9]

"Open" initiatives (which, as mentioned, are different from "free") are very common in the scientific and educational worlds: See, for example, *Massive Open Online Courses* (MOOCs) placed on the portals of universities or research centers, or "open access" scientific journals that make all their contents available on the Web, focusing on the dissemination of science and inverting the normal relationship between those who pay and those who get paid; in this case, readers (i.e., those who consume) do not pay, and those who want to distribute (i.e., those who produce) do pay. Many of the open initiatives focus on online participation and collaboration (wikis), a well-known example of which is Wikipedia.[10]

There are those who absolutize this openness, such as the *Open Everything* movement, who see openness as "applicable to many areas of life."[11] In this case, the concept of openness becomes a banner for activists who want to radically transform society. According to Tkarcz, these "network culture" movements do not just remain in the software world but are under great

---

9. Ibid., 20–24.

10. For more information, cf. *www.familyandmedia.eu/internet-e-social-network/ wikipedia-e-davvero-la-nuova-enciclopedia-post-moderna/.*

11. N. WEAVER, *Wikipedia and the Politics of Openness,* 27.

political pressure to change the economy, education, social communication, the way politics is practiced, and the like.[12]

Google is a company that more than others has made openness an institutional value and quality. Jonathan Rosemberg (former Vice President of Products at Google) wrote *The Meaning of Open*,[13] and defined openness as quality of the system. A few years later he proposed it as one of the necessary qualities for organizations that want to have a future, especially in the fields of education, healthcare, science, government, and transportation.[14]

There are many in favor of openness among classical liberals as well as progressives, libertarians and Marxists, utopians, and different kinds of activists, depending on their area of interest or discussion. The notion of "open" is linked to concepts like transparency, competition, cooperation, and participation.

The main criticisms of the concept of *openness* [15] are as follows:

1. It is a concept developed primarily in a reactive way: we focus on the *enemies* of the principle and not on the virtues of openness itself.

2. Open societies do not admit any determination, nor is there any room to assert incontestable or absolute truths.

3. Open societies propose a new individualism with no limiting constraints (e.g., family ties).

4. The open system also causes "closures," as the 2008 economic crisis showed or as is seen with the lack of transparency of nondisclosure agreements of technology companies with their employees.

---

12. Cf. N. Tkacz, *Wikipedia and the Politics of Openness* (Chicago: University of Chicago Press, 2015), *press.uchicago.edu/ucp/books/book/chicago/W/bo19085555.html*.

13. Cf. J. Rosenberg, "The Meaning of Open," in *Google: Official Blog* (December 21, 2009), *googleblog.blogspot.com/2009/12/meaning-of-open.html*.

14. Cf. J. Rosenberg, "The Future Is Open," in *Think Open* (October 2012), *www.thinkwithgoogle.com/_qs/documents/157/the-future-is-open_articles.pdf*.

15. Cf. G. Lovink, "Academic Nostalgia for a Utopian Open and Free Society Thanks to the Web," in *Networks Wihout a Cause. A Critique of Social Media* (Cambridge: Polity Press, 2011), *familyandmedia.eu/internet-e-social-network/nostalgia-accademica-di-una-utopistica-societa-aperta-e-libera-grazie-al-web/*.

5. When an organization or a project becomes categorized as "open," sometimes openness is considered sufficient, as if nothing else is needed.[16]

THE CHURCH AS AN ORGANIZATION IN THE PUBLIC SPHERE

The Church as a visible organization is a *truth-telling institution*; in this sense transparency is a value to be promoted in the Church's style of governance and administration. On the contrary, secrecy and opacity appear as a failure of internal and external communication: "There is no authority without truth."[17]

However, why would I disclose a negative fact that would otherwise not be in the public domain? For honesty, because communication is based on trust. "Honesty is necessary for building credibility and trust before, during, and after a crisis."[18] In fact, in many cases opacity is unnecessary because "the public will find out the information in other ways."[19] As De la Cierva reiterates, the lack of openness and of willingness to inform is perceived as intent to hide because "something bad is being done,"[20] and this generates suspicion. Therefore, candor and openness of information need to be especially addressed when there is a crisis. Hiding relevant facts or responding untruthfully is bad, and distortion of the truth is punished because there is a link between truth and justice. Communicators on behalf of the Church cannot take "ethical corners in the service of religion."[21] "[Trust] is irretrievably lost if the error is voluntary, and a lie is always a voluntary error."[22]

So is there an obligation to always tell the whole truth in the public arena? Church communicators certainly do not have to draw media attention to confess all the bad news of the organization they represent. According to Soria, there are, however, two

---

16. Cf. Ibid., 33–37.

17. Y. DE LA CIERVA, *La Chiesa casa di vetro*, 98; translation ours.

18. Ibid.; translation ours.

19. Ibid.; translation ours.

20. Ibid.; translation ours.

21. R. SHAW, *Dealing with Media for the Church*, 32.

22. Y. DE LA CIERVA, *La Chiesa casa di vetro*, 99; translation ours.

attitudes that can be demanded: honesty in presenting the facts when asked and taking the initiative to inform when the facts impact the interests of the public with whom the organization relates.[23] As you can see, there is no single answer, but it is a matter of prudence.

It must be said that transparency is not the same as truth. According to Byung-Chul Han, *transparency* has a powerful element of exhibition,[24] while the notion of *openness* speaks more to sincerity or frankness. For this reason, yet again, we distance ourselves from the absolute notion of transparency, and we add the nuance of being an institution of truth and high trustworthiness.

As Pope Saint John Paul II explained in a very illustrative way:

> Just as every house has special rooms, which at first are not open to all guests, so, too, for dialogue within the Church, rooms are needed for talks to be conducted with due confidentiality. This has nothing to do with secrecy but rather with mutual respect for the benefit of the matter under consideration.[25]

On one hand, the structure of the Church is hierarchical by divine constitution; on the other, the definition of the Church as the "People of God" cannot be understood in the logic of *power*. The *ecclesiology of communion*[26] must be understood in all its richness: There are vertical and horizontal relationships, a local and universal organic structure, and an activity of its faithful and ministers in the world of the visible and of the invisible (of the Spirit). These ecclesiological traits allow for a correct understanding of the different notions. The hierarchical nature of the Church cannot change, while the *just forms of governance* change with the historical circumstances.

Communion in the Church can only be carried out through relationships of trust between members of the Church according to the principles of transparency and shared responsibility. In other words, those in office must share information, accept criticism, and be responsible in their mandate to serve the Church.

---

23. C. Soria, *El laberinto informativo. Una salida ética* (Pamplona: EUNSA, 1997), 76.

24. Cf. B-C. Han, *La sociedad de la trasparencia*, 12.

25. Pope St. John Paul II, *Discorso ai vescovi austriaci in visita ad limina apostolorum* (June 21, 1988); cited in De la Cierva, *Chiesa casa di vetro*, 215–216; translation ours.

26. Vatican Council II, *Lumen Gentium*, no. 32.

In fact, Pope Francis's commitment to transparency from the beginning of his pontificate has been evident, especially in the economic-financial sphere[27] and on the matter of sexual abuse. From an organizational standpoint, a rethinking of the Holy See's information system is being pursued.[28] However, making the principle of transparency "internal culture" in the Church's style of governance and communication is not possible with only laws or norms regulating processes; it is necessary to create this *culture*. Communication is a great ally of the Law in this mission.

In the Church, the right to information as a fundamental right of the faithful has not yet been formalized. As Professor Schouppe emphasizes, it is urgent to fill this gap[29] in two senses: On one hand there is the faithful's right to information, to "be informed in a general way on the ecclesial government, at both the central and local levels."[30] As Mendoza reiterates:

> The Catholic Church is therefore developing in an environment where people want to receive more information and know more details about the internal processes of electing leaders

---

27. Pope Francis, Chirograph (July 18, 2013) that establishes the Pontifical Commission for Reference on the Study and Guidance of the Organisation of the Economic-Administrative Structure of the Holy See (COSEA); Motu Proprio *Fidelis Dispensator et Prudens* (February 24, 2014), which creates three new bodies (Council for the Economy, Secretariat for the Economy, and Office of the Auditor General) to separate the management from the patrimony, from the bodies of oversight and supervision. To make this separation effective, the Pope signed the Motu Proprio *I beni temporali* (July 4, 2016). For procurement, purchasing, and spending controls, on June 1, 2020, he approved, "On Transparency, Control, and Competition in the Procedures for Awarding Public Contracts of the Holy See and Vatican City State." This formalized the adoption of the internationally used principle of transparency.

28. On June 27, 2015, the Dicastery for Communication was established within the Roman Curia, with the commitment to reorganize and integrate all of the realities of the information system of the Apostolic See that have developed throughout history: Sala Stampa, Radio Vaticana, Tipografia Vaticana, Servizio Internet, TV Vaticana, Fotografia e Libreria Editrice Vaticana, PCCS.

29. Cf. J.-P. Schouppe, "*Diritti fondamentali dei fedeli in rapporto alla partecipazione al governo dei beni temporali,*" in *Ius Ecclesiæ* 26 (2014), 397–414.

30. Ibid., 412; translation ours.

of the institution, institutional decision making, management of fiscal resources, etc.[31]

On the other hand, there is the right to information understood as freedom of the news media to communicate on the Church. The latter requires the Church to have an attitude toward communication characterized by openness and proactiveness.

We read in the *Code of Canon Law* that the faithful "are free to make known [...] their needs, especially spiritual ones, and their desires,"[32] and according to their background, professional competence, and standing, they have "the right and even at times the duty to manifest to the sacred pastors their opinion on matters which pertain to the good of the Church."[33] The Pastoral Instruction *Ætatis Novæ* (1992) highlights the importance of the right to dialogue and information within the Church, as affirmed by *Communio et Progressio*,[34] and the need to *find effective ways* to promote and protect this right.

> Among the members of the community of persons who make up the Church, there is a radical equality in dignity and mission which arises from baptism and underlies hierarchical structure and diversity of office and function; and this equality necessarily will express itself in an honest and respectful sharing of information and opinions.[35]

Sheltering the faithful from scandal or considering them men and women who are not prepared to know the truth is

---

31. C. MENDOZA, "*Trasparenza (principio di)*," in *Glossary* (CASE Stewardship), *casestewardship.org/glossario/trasparenza/*; translation ours: "The principle of transparency should make it possible, in any case, to respect the fundamental spiritual mission of the Church, which is not a business in which financial information must be fully up-to-date, and which is not a political association in which the reporting of decisions is a responsibility to the voters. The social expectation of an ever-growing amount of information can be, however, satisfied by 'operational transparency,' which is a good opportunity to show the public the many pastoral and evangelizing works of the Church: thousands of children educated in poor countries, thousands of sick people cared for by religious throughout the world, millions of Eucharistic celebrations and Sacraments, etc. The principle of transparency, in addition to presenting 'the numbers of the Church,' would allow us to put back at the center her task of proclaiming the Gospel without falling into obligations that do not correspond to the spiritual mission of the ecclesial institution."

32. Cf. CIC, can. 212 §2, in *AAS* 75, no. 2 (1983), 34.

33. Cf. Ibid.

34. Cf. PCCS, *Communio et Progressio*, 634–636.

35. PCCS, *Ætatis Novæ*, 10.

a big mistake — one that is still damaging the Church. Shared responsibility between pastors and lay people (even in dealing with problems) is the path that Church teachings indicate. This requires greater transparency among the responsible parties.

THE NOTION OF TRANSPARENCY AS CEASELESS COMMUNICATION

Returning to the notion of transparency we mentioned at the beginning, there are many different ways of understanding it. One way to categorize transparency is to distinguish between transparency as *compliance* and transparency as a communication exercise.[36] Some authors like Mendoza frame transparency within the Church as a value associated with the concept of stewardship,[37] that is, as a "culture of collaboration and participation."[38] Here, the approach to transparency we are referring to is the one concerning the exercise of communication. Therefore, ideas on communication applying to institutions that operate in high-risk contexts and that are reliable by virtue of their role and dimensions are useful.

In High Reliability Organizations (HROs)[39] like the Church, one must *communicate ceaselessly* as an operating style. "When it goes silent, that's unexpected, that's trouble, and that's bad news."[40] "Information which reports failure is particularly welcomed as it allows organizations to detect weaknesses before they escalate into full-blown crises."[41]

This *ceaseless communication* should not be done at random: Each and every person must be aware, without exceptions. As

---

36. Cf. A. HENRIQUES, *Corporate Truth: The Limits to Transparency* (London: Earthscan, 2007), 99.

37. Cf. J. MIÑAMBRES, "*Corresponsabilità [Stewardship]*," in *Glossary* (CASE Stewardship), *casestewardship.org/glossario/*.

38. C. MENDOZA, "What Kind of Transparency for the Church? Proposing Operational Transparency for Processes, Solutions, and Decisions in the Catholic Church," in *Church, Communication & Culture* 5, no. 2 (2020), 211.

39. Cf. K. SANDERS, "British Government Communication During the 2020 COVID-19 Pandemic: Learning from High Reliability Organizations," in *Church, Communication & Culture* 5, no. 3 (2020), 356–377.

40. K.E. WEICK, K.M. SUTCLIFFE, *Managing the Unexpected: Sustained Performance in a Complex World* (Hoboken, NJ: John Wiley & Sons, 2015), 60.

41. K. SANDERS, *British Government Communication During the 2020 COVID-19 Pandemic*, 359.

Claudia Ciocca explains, this means communicating (a) on one's own initiative, (b) what is relevant, (c) to the relevant audiences, (d) with a specific purpose.[42]

a) Communication can be initiated on *one's own initiative* or be (legally) mandatory. In the context of internal communication, one might pose the following question: Why be transparent when you do not have to be? To create a culture of transparency toward the outside world, I must first incorporate it internally as a principle and strategy and then promote and respect the procedures that derive from it. At the structural level, transparency means having a system of checks and balances that is based on the separation of powers. From the strategic standpoint, it means involving the whole institution (operations, culture, tools, and personnel); this strategy implies a change of mentality. In other words, as Claudia Ciocca argues, transparency is not a formal strategy but a relational one "because it affects power dynamics, conditioning behavior patterns and attitudes."[43]

b) The information must be *relevant*, which is why it is a matter of providing the right information (not just any information) in a manner that is punctual and precise with regard to timing, following the appropriate channels or procedures. These criteria of transparency must be accompanied by the proper tools if they are to be implemented: appropriate systems of information technology and competent personnel.

c) These *audiences* are internal (priests and lay people who work in the Curia, clerics and lay people at the local level, etc.) and external (civil society, the media, etc.). The way issues are communicated must be appropriate to the audience and the context. There are "explosive contexts" that require special prudence.

d) The *purpose* of transparency (like ceaseless communication between coresponsible subjects) finds its roots in the social doctrine of the Church: the common good, the dignity of

---

42. C. Ciocca, *Webinar: Transparency and Governance in the Church* (May 5, 2020), *www.pusc.it/article/webinar-transparency-and-governance-church*.

43. Ibid.

the human person, solidarity, and subsidiarity. From the functional standpoint, one must follow "a ranking"; that is, there is information linked to a person's position (not everyone has to know everything). At the same time, to implement this change it is important to identify the information to be shared in order to establish an open and sincere internal debate so that it is not a waste of time. In this way, transparency can be an internal catalyst for engagement, that is, shared responsibility, a sense of belonging, and trust.

In tune with the music of these pages, which call for more openness and accountability, it is worth reiterating that there are organizational experts who point to a *dark side of transparency*[44] — that is, some negative effects that they observe from the implementation of transparency at the corporate level:

> Excessive sharing of information creates problems of information overload and can legitimize endless debate and second-guessing of senior executive decisions. High levels of visibility can reduce creativity as people fear the watchful eye of their superiors. And the open sharing of information on individual performance and pay levels, often invoked as a way of promoting trust and collective responsibility, can backfire.[45]

This paradox shows us how transparency is essentially good, but at the same time, research such as that of McKinsey reveals that *it is not always good*. According to them, in many cases the sharing of information has not improved the decision-making process but has even reduced its effectiveness due to an emerging accountability gap, "where information is in the hands of people who may not use it wisely."[46] Transparency is important, but it requires the ability to weigh it appropriately.

Carrying forward a culture of transparency and ceaseless communication within the Church, we find, on one hand, obstacles and internal resistance because this change in mindset is a slow and arduous process. And on the other hand, ceaseless

---

44. J. BIRKINSHAW, D. CABLE, "The Dark Side of Transparency," in *The McKinsey Quarterly* (February 1, 2017), *www.mckinsey.com/business-functions/people-and-organizational-performance/our-insights/the-dark-side-of-transparency*.

45. Ibid.

46. Ibid.

communication does not mean "sharing everything." Those who govern need the prudence to know when to speak and when to remain silent. Transparency can generate problems in power relations within the structure. All these costs are part of the transformative process we are proposing—in these pages—for a model of organic communication for the Church.

CHAPTER 5

"ZERO TOLERANCE" HAS A BOOMERANG EFFECT

*He who justifies the wicked
and he who condemns the righteous
are both alike an abomination to the* LORD.
—*Proverbs 17:15*

The vigilante moral style of some users (especially activists) on social media is reminiscent of *public shaming* practices promoted by vigilante zealots who enforce rules with no constituted legal authority. *The Scarlet Letter*, an American novel written in 1850 by Nathaniel Hawthorne, tells the story of a woman in seventeenth-century Puritan New England who after committing adultery is condemned to wear a scarlet letter "A" (which stands for "Adulteress") on her chest and must stand on the scaffold to be reviled by the whole village. She gives birth to a daughter but refuses to reveal the identity of the father.

Hawthorne describes in his novel how *public shaming* was used as a *weapon* in Puritanical cultures to punish those who violated the community's rules. The message to those who broke the law was, "We trample you down [...] because the spectacle of your agony may discourage others of similar unlawful inclinations."[1] Within this moral framework, there is no space for reconciliation or for starting a new life. That person is permanently identified with his or her transgression.

One of the problems with these social media *zealots* is that they get confused very easily, as happened with Kyle P. Quinn, the victim of an identification error. This professor was incorrectly identified in an online photograph as a participant in a white supremacist rally in Charlottesville. Although he had no

---

1. N. HAWTHORNE, *The Scarlet Letter* (New York: Barnes & Noble Classics, 2003), 177. Cf. J. HAWTHORNE, "The Scarlet Letter by Nathaniel Hawthorne Reviewed," in *The Atlantic* (April 1886), 17.

connection to the events, a viral storm of condemnation was unleashed against him, followed by dismissal.[2] Within just a few hours there were calls for him to be expelled from his position at the university; fortunately, he arrived in time to explain the misidentification (by the accusers) to his bosses before they made that unilateral decision. Something similar is happening with criticism of *Black Lives Matter*. There is a long list of people who have lost their jobs or been suspended for criticizing or questioning this movement. This kind of *justice* is based on an ethical agenda that is worth focusing on for a bit.

Rabbi Jonathan Sacks, drawing on a postwar work by Ruth Benedict distinguishing the American *guilt culture* from the Japanese *shame culture*,[3] distinguished the Ethic of *Justice* (based on objective morality), in which actions are just or unjust, from the Ethic of *Reputation* (of public shame), where people are good or bad relative to a standard of social morality.[4] The ethic of justice is based on restitution, and the immediate consequence is *guilt*, while the ethic of social reputation is based on honor and leads to external condemnation. In the paradigm of justice, ethical judgment would lead to saying, "You committed a bad act," or, "You are in the wrong," while in a shame paradigm, one says, "You are a bad person."

In the first case, the moral principle of judgment is objective (just or unjust), whereas in the second it is more arbitrary and emotional (the person is good or bad), depending on the standard of the social perceptions. The consequences that follow are not trivial. In public shaming practices, wrongdoers are simply "taught a lesson" as those shaming them are seeking revenge rather than just punishment.

---

2. For a more complete look, cf. "Professor wrongly labelled as racist in Charlottesville," in *BBC* (August 15, 2017), *www.bbc.com/news/world-us-canada-40935419*.

3. Cf. R. Benedict, *The Chrysanthemum and the Sword* (Boston: Houghton Mifflin, 1946).

4. J. Sacks developed this idea earlier in the section of his website, "Thought for the Day" (November 4, 2014), *www.rabbisacks.org/archive/the-difference-between-shame-and-guilt-cultures/*; he took up the subject again because of the publication of the book J. Sacks, *Morality: Restoring the Common Good in Divided Times* (New York: Hodder & Stoughton, 2020), 206–212.

As Sacks reminds us, in line with the Christian tradition, the Bible makes an extremely significant distinction between the sin and the sinner. What is wrong is the act, not the person.[5] In a shame culture, however, there is identification between the wrong acts and the person him- or herself, as we mentioned in Chapter 1 with woke culture and cancel culture. A person's good name can be publicly destroyed in the digital ecosystem (think of Google's record), and once the person has been denigrated and degraded in public, his or her work, social relationships, and reputation are ruined. The return of *revenge* with social media is for Sacks an enormous "social regression."[6]

The social media ecosystem highlights what lies in the human soul (the good and the bad), which emerges thanks to this tool. The responsibility lies with individuals, and only secondarily with the channels they use to express themselves. Obviously, these platforms are not solely responsible for content shared by users (text, photos, and videos). However, it has been proven that the design of algorithms is not neutral and that technology companies take the initiative to promote and filter content, profile users, and create bubbles of people, depending on their tastes, opinions, or interests, and each one is recorded as metadata depending on online activity.[7] In any case, blaming technology or primarily blaming social media in an effort to explain such a complex phenomenon would miss the mark.[8] As Dans stated

> The real culprits are not bots and fake accounts managed in the Balkans or Russia, but our collective naivety. [... Education] should be about developing the skills to search for and qualify information online.[9]

---

5. Cf. J. SACKS, *Morality*, 215.

6. Ibid., 216.

7. Cf. J. PUJOL, "*Chi dobbiamo incolpare per la crisi delle* Fake News? *Tre fattori in gioco sulla verità online,*" in *Medic* 26, no. 1 (2018), 1–9.

8. Cf. N. GONZÁLEZ GAITANO, "More Than a Media System Failure? Reason, Faith, and Mercy as Comprehensive Paradigms for Communication," in *Church, Communication & Culture* 2, no. 1 (2017), 1–7.

9. E. DANS, "Why Textbooks and Education Are to Blame for Fake News," in *Forbes* (March 9, 2018).

A 2018 study conducted at MIT and published in its scientific journal *Science*[10] shows how on Twitter false news is spread twenty times faster than news that is true. In addition to the speed of the spread, the other relevant fact is that those responsible for this phenomenon are not bots but people. The authors conclude that robots...

> accelerated the spread of both true and false news, [and] it affected their spread roughly equally. This suggests that false news spreads farther, faster, deeper, and more broadly than the truth because humans, not robots, are more likely to spread it.[11]

As González Gaitano argues, blaming technology, making it a scapegoat, is a quick remedy for a process that is actually much more complex.[12]

Justice on social media and in the networked public sphere poses three important problems: (a) The punishment for "wrongs" committed is disproportionate; (b) there is no due process: People are punished without being heard; and (c) there is no restitution in the case of misinformation. Online shaming is not regulated by the legal system: Instead of being reliably punished by a public authority, unlimited public pillorying takes place. This is no longer the procedural and impartial, deliberative and neutral justice that is typical of a liberal democratic society.[13]

In the world of social media, like the colonial Puritan communities of 1700, "the Internet is quickly becoming a powerful norm-enforcement tool,"[14] a public platform that punishes people through "online shaming" because according to secular,

---

10. The study conducted by the Media Lab of the Massachusetts Institute of Technology (MIT) analyzed the differential diffusion of all news, both true and false, verified and published on Twitter from 2006 to 2017. The data includes about 126,000 stories *tweeted* by about 3 million people more than 4.5 million times. The news was categorized as true or false based on the information of six independent organizations (*Snopes.com*, *Politifact.com*, and other independent fact-checking institutions) that checked 95–98% of the categorizations. Cf. S. Vosoughi, et al., "The Spread of True and False News Online," in *Science*, vol. 359, no. 6380 (March 9, 2018), 1146–1151.

11. Cf. S. Vosoughi, et al., *The Spread of True and False News Online*.

12. Cf. N. González Gaitano, *More Than a Media System Failure?* 3.

13. For a deeper analysis of the process and consequences of public shaming, cf. J. Ronson, *So You've Been Publicly Shamed* (London: Picador, 2015), 63 ff.

14. D.J. Solove, *The Future of Reputation: Gossip, Rumor, and Privacy on the Internet* (New Haven & London: Yale University Press, 2007), 86.

civic, unwritten rule, some ideas are "bigoted" or "problematic." We see these kinds of reactions (that is, of intolerance) toward representatives of the Church, priests, and bishops, in the public sphere.

At the same time, the speed of social media storms and the power of perception in the public media sphere add pressure on leaders, who do not want to be seen as complicit in the sins of the past. This quickness is not "decisiveness" but haste, and it does not pair well with the discernment and prudence that good governance and justice require. In this sense, it is ironic that some sectors of the Church have made "zero tolerance" their anthem. As we shall see below, "zero tolerance" in the Church (unlike the Puritan attitude mentioned earlier) should imply that (criminal) acts are not in any way endorsed and are dealt with appropriately in accordance with justice, but because of human freedom and social degradation, they can never be completely avoided.

IS THE CHURCH IN FAVOR OF ZERO TOLERANCE?

In 2002, Pope Saint John Paul II told US cardinals and bishops in the Vatican: "There is no place in the priesthood and religious life for those who would harm the young."[15] For one thing, the Pope was confirming the path to follow in the fight against abuse, begun by US bishops in 1992, with the policy of the Five Principles: (1) a prompt response to allegations, (2) dismissal of the priest if there is a credible allegation, (3) compliance with the law, (4) reaching out to victims and families, and (5) transparency (but respect for the privacy of those involved). This practice, agreed to in 1992 by the US Bishops' Conference, initially required free adherence on the part of the bishops and ten years later became common policy and mandatory for all US dioceses in 2002 with the *Dallas Charter*.[16]

On the other hand, Pope Saint John Paul II intended to send a clear message to the whole Church on the importance of the

---

15. Pope St. JOHN PAUL II, "Address to the Cardinals of the United States," (April 23, 2002), *www.vatican.va/content/john-paul-ii/en/speeches/2002/april/documents/hf_jp-ii_spe_20020423_usa-cardinals.html*.

16. USCCB, *Charter for the Protection of Children and Young People (Dallas Charter)*.

new law, *Sacramentorum Sanctitatis Tutela*,[17] enacted on April 30, 2001, precisely to stop abuse.

This 2002 speech gave rise to the slogan "zero tolerance," which expresses great determination but in fact did not arise from a phrase pronounced literally by the Roman Pontiff.

Since then, the Church has attributed her commitment to fight abuse with a zero-tolerance policy. Pope Francis has been the first Pope to use this expression literally, on several occasions.[18]

"Zero tolerance" is an expression used to refer, in a drastic and strict way, to the level of flexibility [zero] that will be applied to certain behaviors. As can be understood, this is not a legal concept but an expression with strong communicative impact.

From the ethical and juridical standpoint, the principle of zero tolerance would be more like the legalistic conduct we have just discussed than like the canonical juridical tradition. Church law seeks to "repair the scandal, restore justice, reform the offender."[19] Thus, doing justice is not a matter of strictness or magnanimity. In this sense, the expression "zero tolerance" can be an equivocal slogan because as Baura says, *rigor iuris* is not opposed to *dispensatio misericordiæ*.[20]

Justice in the Church seeks not only to restore justice and repair the scandal caused but also to obtain the conversion of

---

17. Pope St. John Paul II, Apostolic Letter by Which Are Promulgated Norms on More Grave Delicts Reserved to the Congregation for the Doctrine of the Faith *Sacramentorum Sanctitatis Tutela* (April 30, 2001), *www.vatican.va/content/john-paul-ii/en/motu_proprio/documents/hf_jp-ii_motu-proprio_20020110_sacramentorum-sanctitatis-tutela.html*.

18. Cf. Pope Francis, *Interview with Journalists During the Return Flight from the Holy Land* (May 26, 2014), *www.vatican.va/content/francesco/en/speeches/2014/may/documents/papa-francesco_20140526_terra-santa-conferenza-stampa.html*; *Address to the Members of the Pontifical Commission for the Protection of Minors* (September 21, 2017), *www.vatican.va/content/francesco/en/speeches/2022/april/documents/20220429-pontcommissione-tutelaminori.html*; *Letter to the People of God* (August 20, 2018), *www.vatican.va/content/francesco/en/letters/2018/documents/papa-francesco_20180820_lettera-popolo-didio.html*.

19. CIC, can. 1341.

20. Cf. E. Baura, "*L'attività sanzionatoria della Chiesa: note sull'operatività della finalità della pena*," in *Ephemerides Iuris Canonici* 2 (2019), 613.

the prisoner. These three elements of punishment pertain to the ultimate goal of the Church, which is *salus animarum*.[21]

There are several cases that show how "zero tolerance" can become a misunderstood slogan — or worse — a boomerang.

In 2011, a court in the Czech Republic found Father Adam Stanisław Kuszaj, a Polish Salvatorian religious missionary in the Czech diocese of Ostrawa-Opava, guilty of sexual abuse. The accusation had been filed by a former altar server, who claimed to have been abused by Kuszaj in 2009, when he was only sixteen years old. Under these circumstances Kuszaj was discharged from the clerical state.

Kuszaj was sentenced to two years in prison, which was reduced to six months for good behavior, and was thereafter prohibited from approaching or interacting with minors under the age of eighteen. Once released, Adam Stanisław, who had been removed from his congregation and now had no financial means to support himself, began to work like any other person, but he bore the weight of public opinion, which labeled him a pedophile.

After eight years, the tribunal of the city of Jesenik acquitted the Polish priest, revealing something sensational. In the appeal process, the plaintiff's friends had given false testimony. The former altar server had decided to take revenge on the priest by fabricating an accusation just because the cleric had refused to give him money. This revelation coincided with that of the experts, who described the alleged victim's statements as not credible.

In the face of the acquittal by the civil court, it is also expected that the ecclesiastical sentence will be retracted. Father Adam Stanisław Kuszaj has declared that after those "nine lost years" he would like to return to the priestly ministry: "It is my dream, and I want to fulfill it."

Despite being referred to in the context of the "Meeting on the Protection of Minors in the Church" organized by the

---

21. Cf. J. PUJOL, "*El contexto eclesiológico y los principios que guiaron la revisión del Libro VI del CIC,*" in *Ius Canonicum* 61, no. 122 (2021), 865–885.

Holy See, the story of Father Kuszaj's acquittal remained in the background, almost without relevance; the story was lost in the regional news, highlighted only by some Catholic media.

Unfortunately, this is not an isolated incident. We shall cite three examples: In 2016, the American magazine *Newsweek* published an extensive report that revealed a series of falsehoods by a former Philadelphia altar server, Daniel Gallagher, better known as "Billy Doe," which led to the conviction and imprisonment of three priests and a teacher in the Archdiocese of Philadelphia. They had been falsely accused of sexual abuse perpetrated against the boy. Father Avery and Shero [a former teacher] were incarcerated, and Father Engelhardt died in prison in November of 2014 after being denied a heart operation that would have saved his life. Daniel Gallagher had been awarded a nearly US$5 million settlement.[22]

We also see the case of Colombian priest José Isaac Ramírez, who was released after having served three years in prison. He had been falsely accused of abusing a child under fourteen years of age.[23] Finally, we can think of Father Eugene Boland, who was falsely charged in 2010 with five counts of indecent assault of a minor.[24]

Transparency, when it is manifested in the practice of "zero tolerance" and in the solidarity offered to alleged victims no matter what, comes into conflict with the right to presumption of innocence until proven guilty and with the right to a good reputation. In other words, "innocence" and "reputation" are on different levels: *Reputation* is the way one appears to public opinion and follows the rules of communication, whereas *innocence*, or being not guilty, is a juridical reality and follows the rules

---

22. Cf. D. López Marina, "*Develan falso caso de abusos sexuales que acabó con un sacerdote muerto en prisión*," in *ACI Prensa* (February 2, 2016), *www.aciprensa.com/noticias/develan-falso-caso-de-abusos-sexuales-que-acabo-con-un-sacerdote-muerto-en-prision-35151*.

23. Cf. Redacción Aci Prensa, "*Luego de tres años de prisión liberan a sacerdote falsamente acusado de abusos en Colombia*," in *ACI Prensa* (October 15, 2015), *www.aciprensa.com/noticias/luego-de-tres-anos-de-prision-liberan-a-sacerdote-falsamente-acusado-de-abusos-en-colombia-48776*.

24. Cf. Redacción Aci Prensa, "*Declaran inocente a sacerdote acusado falsamente de abusos en Irlanda*," in *ACI Prensa* (March 13, 2014), *www.aciprensa.com/noticias/declaran-inocente-a-sacerdote-acusado-falsamente-de-abusos-en-irlanda-36857*.

of a proper legal proceeding. The Barbarin case, which will be presented in the next chapter, shows that the two paths may not coincide.

The irresponsible handling of some pedophilia cases along with modern society's continuous demand for transparency have generated a tension and a *climate of suspicion* toward clerics, which obscures the truth and generates new victims, albeit of a different kind.

Often in these cases, putting the principle of "zero tolerance" into practice has led to expulsion from the clerical state and to the spread of negative and false profiles of religious people in the collective imagination.

"Zero tolerance" has been a necessary reaction on the part of a Church who has found herself having to correct past excesses of tolerance and secrecy. It is necessary to understand the underlying intention: to eliminate cover-ups and complicit behavior in order to get at the root of the problem and to heal.[25] Unlimited transparency, however, does not lead to justice and does not serve truth: It is a simple but mistaken understanding of "zero tolerance," a kind of "legalism" or even "spectacular justice."[26]

UNLIMITED TRANSPARENCY AS ABUSE OF POWER

Unlimited transparency is put into place by those who have power over the accused and by the media. It is a decision that is intended to show just intolerance for presumed crimes, but it risks exposing someone who is not actually guilty. It is therefore an attack on the presumption of innocence to which each person has a right, aggravated by a lack of charity: the bond that should

---

25. "The holy People of God looks to us, and expects from us not simple and predictable condemnations, but concrete and effective measures to be undertaken": Pope FRANCIS, Introduction to the Meeting *"The Protection of Minors in the Church"* (February 21, 2019), *www.vatican.va/content/francesco/en/speeches/2019/february/documents/papa-francesco_20190221_incontro-protezioneminori-apertura.html.*

26. "The Church does not like spectacular justice": G. CARDINALE, *Interview of Msgr. Charles Scicluna on the Strictness of the Church in Cases of Pedophilia* (March 13, 2010), *www.vatican.va/resources/resources_mons-scicluna-2010_it.html;* translation ours.

unite those who make up part of an institution that defines itself as "communion."

The most obvious reason for protecting the principle of the presumption of innocence is that it concerns an essential tool for protecting the innocent from unjust conviction. Conviction of a criminal offense brings a variety of negative consequences: punishment, censure, and social stigma. Conviction and punishment send a specific message: This person is a criminal since he or she violated the standards of conduct expected of members of the community to which he or she belongs. Associated with censure is the stigma suffered by those who have been convicted of a crime. Stigma may have consequences for the way a person is treated by his or her community, formally or informally. There must be a valid justification before these consequences can be imposed on an individual.[27]

It is interesting to note that the requirement of proof for conviction entered civil law because it already existed in canon law. According to Stumer, at the Fourth Ecumencial Council of the Lateran (1215), canon lawyers (based on sources in Roman law), came to the conclusion that guilt had to be *proven* and not *presumed*.[28] Later, this principle became a maxim of English law, immortalized by Blackstone: "It is better that ten guilty persons escape than that one innocent suffer."[29] This maxim recognizes the grave injustice of condemning an innocent person and the need for evidence in prosecution.

Publishing data, including the names of the accused, knowing that this will lead to them being perceived as guilty and that they will be judged as such by public opinion, poses the problem of fidelity to the truth, which must take into account not only the "spoken truth," but also the "perceived truth." In some countries, such as the United States, where after the great media exposure of the *Pennsylvania Report* in August 2018, the attorney general

---

27. Cf. A. Stumer, *La presunción de inocencia. Perspectiva desde el Derecho Probatorio y los derechos humanos* (Madrid: Marcial Pons Ediciones Jurídicas y Sociales, 2018), 50–51.

28. Ibid., 22–23.

29. W. Blackstone, *Commentaries on the Laws of England*, Book IV (Oxford: Clarendon Press, 1769), 352.

of Nebraska asked three dioceses in its territory to publish the names of people in the Church who had been accused of sexual abuse since 1978. The Bishop of Omaha was one of those who joined the petition and published the names of thirty-eight priests and deacons who had *"substantiated allegations"* of abuse in the diocese. One of them was Andrew Syring, who was asked by the bishop in October of 2018 to leave his parish. The priest obeyed, but he sued the diocese for defamation.[30]

According to the norms of canon law, if a priest is accused of abuse, then the bishop must first conduct a preliminary investigation to see if the accusation is credible and to inform the Congregation for the Doctrine of the Faith about it. During that investigation, the identity of the priest must remain confidential, but in reality, these investigations are often made public. What happens is that, from the time of the accusation and with the imposition of some precautionary measures, the priest bears the burden of proof, that is, he has to prove his innocence. The universal legal principle is that "everyone is innocent until proven guilty,"[31] but in these cases, suspicion already weighs on the priest or religious (even before the truth of the accusation is proven).

A similar case involved Father Eduard Perrone of the diocese of Detroit. He was suspended from his ministry in the diocese after having been accused of abuse of a minor for an incident that had allegedly occurred forty years earlier.

Father Perrone sued the detective who made the rape report on which the archdiocese's decision was based. The detective's office offered him an out-of-court settlement of US $125,000 to avoid going to court. A few months later, a group of twenty parishioners sued the archdiocese claiming that they suffered emotionally from the unjust suspension of their pastor (Father Perrone). This case highlights the tension between the zero-tolerance policy (as a show of force to regain credibility) and the

---

30. Cf. M. NACINOVICH, "Priest's Defamation Suits Are the Latest Wrinkle in Sex-Abuse Fallout," in *National Catholic Reporter* (November 25, 2020), *www.ncronline.org/news/accountability/priests-defamation-suits-are-latest-wrinkle-sex-abuse-fallout*.

31. So it was also inserted in the new version of Book VI of the *Code of Canon Law*: "When an external violation has occurred, imputability is presumed unless it is otherwise apparent" (can. 1321 § 3).

injustice toward and isolation of a priest who falls victim to false accusations.[32]

If one bears in mind that the Church's authority is understood in terms of *service* and trust, then there is also an abuse of power and strong clericalism behind unlimited transparency. In different US dioceses *transparency has been abused* with the widespread and questionable practice of publishing the names, resumes, photographs, personal files, and sometimes even mailing addresses of priests accused of pedophilia (even those already dead) and their condition before the law (summoned, accused, or convicted). They even offer information that has nothing to do with the alleged crime and that is of no public interest. This is an abuse in full regalia,[33] exercised by superiors who boast of "zero tolerance"—which they use to shield themselves at the expense of their duty to seek the truth, their obligation to preserve the good reputation of their subordinates, and their duty to grow communion in the community or in the priesthood.

This *unlimited transparency* with which some superiors shield themselves and incorrectly think they have solved the problem has a negative impact on the institution's reputation. Public opinion is formed not only by objective facts but mainly by perceptions: "The way the public sees the situation becomes *the reality*."[34] Following this logic, the publication of the allegation about one member *generates opinions* about the entire body.[35]

TRANSPARENCY WITHOUT LIMITS UNDERMINES JUSTICE AND COMMUNION

An accused clergyman who is expelled from his community and consigned to the court of public opinion, even if he wishes to return to the priesthood, may bear irreversible wounds. Unlimited transparency destroys good reputations, but it also damages relationships of trust in a religious family or a diocese. It is difficult to continue to "feel like a family" in an institution that has taken the

---

32. Ibid.

33. Cf. D.G. ASTIGUETA, "*Trasparenza e segreto. Aspetti della prassi penalistica,*" in *Periodica de Re Canonica* 107, no.3 (2018), 523–526.

34. R. COHN, *The PR Crisis Bible* (New York: St.Martin's Press, 2000), 33.

35. Cf.Y. DE LA CIERVA, *La Chiesa casa di vetro*, 82–83.

accusation at face value, dismissed the accused from the clerical state, and has publicized—and even spread—slander.

The wounding of trust can strike not only those directly affected by the slander but also other members of the community since it generates insecurity and weakens their sense of belonging. If there is a lack of trust, then all ambiguous behaviors are viewed as suspect and all conduct is, by definition, ambiguous![36] Unlimited transparency generates a negative sensation: With the support of "transparent" leaders, any member, at any time, can be unjustly accused and condemned to bear at least one slander for life.

The bishop of Fort Wayne-South Bend, Indiana, fell victim to this double-edged sword of transparency-suspicion, in keeping with the zero-tolerance model. After the outrage that took place in Pennsylvania in August of 2018 (when inquiring about abuses that had occurred in Pennsylvania's six dioceses), news came out that Bishop Kevin C. Rhoades had been accused of harassment—probably of a sexual nature—when he was bishop in a previous location (Diocese of Harrisburg, Pennsylvania).[37]

Several reckless judgments overlapped in this matter and are worth looking at briefly. First, there was no formal accusation. It involved a family member (of the alleged victim) who said that the bishop had gone to Puerto Rico on a trip with his cousin (according to him, at the age of thirteen or fourteen) and thought that there was a "strange relationship" between the bishop and his cousin (called J.T. to maintain anonymity), which itself was not true. There was no "strange relationship"; they had gone on a trip together. Secondly, J.T. was not a minor when the bishop first met him in the county jail at his mother's request. Third, the journalist speculated that the alleged harassment is "possibly sexual," an assumption that has no basis beyond his imagination and prejudices (not even the family member from whom the rumor originated had specified this).

---

36. Cf. W. Bennis, D.P. Goleman, et al., *Transparencia*, ch. 2.

37. I. DeJesus, "Former Harrisburg Bishop Kevin Rhoades Is Accused of Misconduct, Possibly of a Sexual Nature; Bishop Denies," in *PennLive* (PA Media group) (September 6, 2018), *www.pennlive.com/news/2018/09/kevin_rhoades_accused_bishop_h.html*.

A week after the publication of the news, the bishop was cleared of any wrongdoing:

> This has been a case of a public airing of mere speculation of impropriety with no foundation. In this case, the leaking of what turned out to be an unfounded report did unnecessary harm. This has done a disservice to actual victims of sexual abuse. It has also caused significant and unnecessary harm to Bishop Rhoades.[38]

Another newspaper reported that the accusation was false [39] after the harm had already been done. This irresponsible accusation in the media has unjustly hurt the reputation of the bishop and of the Catholic community.

Cases like that of Monsignor Rhodes will be increasingly common in the Church; they are the result of a *culture of suspicion* and the consequence of a distorted understanding of transparency and zero tolerance. In this sense, the Pope's words on why he immediately accepted the resignation of the Archbishop of Paris, Monsignor Aupetit, center on unacceptable media pressure:

> But when the gossip grows, grows, grows, and takes away the reputation of the person. He will not be able to lead because he has lost the reputation, not because of his sin, which is sin — like Peter's, like mine like yours — but because of the gossip of the people responsible for reporting things, a man who has lost his reputation so publicly cannot govern. And this is an injustice and that is why I accepted Aupetit's resignation, not on the altar of truth, but on the altar of hypocrisy.[40]

The Pope's explanations touch on several different themes. We shall see their context better later. However, as regards the topic we are discussing now, the last words of the Pope reveal that in the Aupetit case the reputation damaged by the media

---

38. F. Chardo, *Bishop Kevin Rhoades Cleared of Any Wrongdoing Following Referral by Diocese, Dauphin County District Attorney's Office* (September 13, 2013), *dauphin. crimewatchpa.com/da/310/post/bishop-kevin-rhoades-cleared-any-wrongdoing- following-referral-diocese*.

39. Cf. IndyStar, *Fort Wayne Bishop Cleared of Wrongdoing in Pennsylvania Investigation* (September 13, 2018), in *IndyStar, eu.indystar.com/story/news/crime/2018/09/13/ catholic-church-bishop-fort-wayne-cleared-wrongdoing-after-probe/1288974002/*.

40. Pope Francis, *Pope Francis' In-flight Press Conference from Greece* (December 6, 2021), *www.catholicnewsagency.com/news/249798/full-text-pope-francis-in-flight- press-conference-from-greece*.

prevailed: This is a very dangerous precedent also for communion in the Church.

ABSOLUTE TRANSPARENCY IS INHUMANE AND DISTORTS THE TRUTH

Transparency without limits distorts the reality of things because it is not possible to live always and totally exposed. Having spaces of solitude, silence, and intimacy is a necessity that is part of the life of every human being and takes on unique relevance in the existence of those who have consecrated themselves to God, who is Mystery.

This natural space of the human being has been recognized as a fundamental right to "privacy," to the inviolability of one's "house"; and in the tradition of the US, privacy has been formulated with an eloquent expression: "the right to be left alone."

Thus, as Byung-Chul Han said: "The imperative of transparency makes everything that is not subject to visibility suspect. This is what their violence consists of."[41] Although it is just to presume innocence, the ambition of transparency without limits in the age of "zero tolerance" seeks out culprits and spreads suspicion like a witch hunt.

The media forcefully demands transparency without limits, and it often prefers simulacrums, where the truth is replaced by verisimilitude and events and people are simplified, eliminating the human mystery so that it is easy to report on and to manage, so that it is "operable."[42] Galdón compares this to a *media circus*:

> In order for the house to be packed each day, it is convenient that there is no shortage of rations of morbid and bloody news; moreover, the stories must develop antagonisms between good guys and bad guys (progressives and retrogrades, according to the script); and it must constantly remind us of the plight of the latter, who happen to be the people, ideas, or institutions that cannot come into play as representatives of different subjects or scripts.[43]

---

41. B-C. HAN, *La sociedad de la trasparencia*, 31; translation ours

42. Cf. Ibid., 48.

43. G. GALDÓN, *Informazione e Disinformazione*, 48; translation ours.

That is why it is unsurprising that the proven innocence of Father Kuszaj was given hardly any media space and was immediately forgotten.

Unlimited transparency does not take into account the truth of the Church, either within the community itself (because it damages the relationships of trust that are essential for it) or from the outside because...

> there is sin in the Church and evil. But even today there is the Holy Church, which is indestructible. Today there are many people who humbly believe, suffer and love, in whom the real God, the loving God, shows Himself to us. Today God also has His witnesses (*martyres*) in the world.[44]

The pretense of a transparency without limits causes this multitude of good Christians, though greater in importance and number, to be minimized, nullified, and to go unnoticed at the media level.

Unlimited transparency is a tool that is capable of hiding relevant information and, in the erroneous desire to adapt communication in the Church to the demands of the world, ends up dissolving her truth and her prophetic capacity.[45]

---

44. Pope BENEDICT XVI, "The Church and the Scandal of Sexual Abuse," in *ACIPrensa* (April 14, 2017), no. III.3, *www.catholicnewsagency.com/news/41013/full-text-of-benedict-xvi-essay-the-church-and-the-scandal-of-sexual-abuse.*

45. Prophethood is not compatible with an identity that is dissolved and confused by excessive transparency. "The Church's identity is based on both her presence and her difference in relation to the world": R. BLÁZQUEZ, *La Chiesa. Mistero, Comunione, Missione* (Salamanca: Seguimi, 2017), 116; translation ours.

CHAPTER 6

THE PRESUMPTION OF INNOCENCE CANNOT BE "THE ELEPHANT IN THE ROOM"

We may take a jealous care of our reputation,
but not idolize it.
— Saint Francis de Sales

According to internal-use statistics of the Congregation for the Doctrine of the Faith and as described by Jordi Bertomeu,[1] from 2001 to 2020 there have been 9000 reports of sexual abuse committed by clergy against minors or vulnerable people. One should consider, however, that there are about 466,000 priests in the whole world (diocesan and religious) in addition to deacons and bishops. The geographic distribution of priests accused of abuse is as follows: 33% are Hispanophones, 23% are Anglophones, 9% are Lusophones, and 6% are Francophones. A sign that the Church is growing in sensitivity to this problem is that...

> over 40% of accusations that reach the CDF are dismissed or resolved with non-criminal disciplinary measures because they are simple imprudence or ambiguous behavior, not true and proper crimes.[2]

As for false accusations against priests or religious, unofficial estimates indicate that they account for 5% of total accusations. In countries such as the United States where studies are done annually, the percentage of new accusations received that were "unsubstantiated or determined to be false" averaged 11.7%

---

1. Cf. J. BERTOMEU, *"La respuesta de la Iglesia a la cultura del abuso,"* in *Vida Nueva* 3248 (November/December 2021), 21–32; translation ours.

2. Ibid., 23; translation ours.

for the years 2006–2011.[3] In the 2018 Report, of the 840 new accusations received, 26% were unable to be proven, 9% were unfounded, and 2% were "obviously false."[4]

Given that now not only clerics but also lay people and those in consecrated life can be punished in the Church for these delicts (cf. CIC, can. 1398 § 2), it will be necessary to see how the accusations will evolve. It would be interesting if they were compared to similar accusations in the civil sphere, where the percentage of false accusations of parents, teachers, etc., that we calculate are much higher.

The numbers of false reports of clerics are not huge (estimated to be 5%), but when real people are at stake, with their own stories and feelings, the numbers no longer matter, and we realize that they, too, are actually victims. The Church has long felt pressure from social and media to improve her response to the abuse crisis after decades of *failing* in that effort. This pressure makes it difficult to talk about the presumption of innocence without being misunderstood.

JOURNALISM AND JUSTICE: A BIZARRE RAPPORT

In March of 2018, Cardinal Philippe Barbarin was accused again — for a case that had already been closed — of having covered up for an abusive priest. After a first-degree conviction in February 2019, the cardinal appealed to defend his innocence and put his situation in the hands of the Pope. Pope Francis rejected the dismissal in the name of presumption of innocence. On his return flight from Morocco on March 31, 2019, when questioned about Barbarin, he explained his position more fully, saying, "If a case is open, there is the presumption of innocence. The person may not be innocent, but is presumed to be so."[5]

---

3. USCCB, *2011 Annual Report: Findings and Recommendations* (April 2012), 39, *www. usccb.org/issues-and-action/child-and-youth-protection/upload/2011-annual-report. pdf.*

4. USCCB, *2018 Annual Report: Findings and Recommendations* (June 2019), 35, *www. usccb.org/issues-and-action/child-and-youth-protection/child-abuse-prevention/ upload/2018-CYP-Annual-Report.pdf.*

5. Pope FRANCIS, *Press Conference on the Return Flight from Rabat to Rome* (March 31, 2019), *www.vatican.va/content/francesco/en/speeches/2019/march/documents/papa-francesco_20190331_marocco-voloritorno.html.*

The Pope's defense of the presumption of innocence was widely criticized by the media because, according to them, it betrayed the "zero-tolerance" policy and contradicted the climate that the Pope had created in his February of 2019 meeting with the presidents of the world's bishops' conferences.

Returning to the case of Barbarin, at that time (2018) Pope Francis had well in mind the harm caused by false accusations and the destructive effect of media condemnation. On his return flight from Ireland in August of 2018, he recounted a story about false accusations against priests, which expresses his feeling very well. The speech is a bit long, but it is worth quoting here.

> Three years ago, more or less, the issue of so-called paedophile priests came up in Granada—a small group of seven, eight or ten priests, who were accused of abuse of minors and of holding parties, orgies and such things. I received the accusation directly in a letter sent by a twenty-three year old man, who claimed to have been abused; he gave names and details. [...] I replied: "Go to the Archbishop, the Archbishop will know what you should do." The Archbishop did everything he was supposed to do, the matter even went to the civil court. There were two trials. The local media began to talk, and talk.... Three days later the words "paedophile priests," and similar expressions, appeared all over the parish, and so there was a sense that these priests were criminals. Seven of them were interviewed, and nothing was found; in three cases the investigation went ahead, they remained in custody for five days, two days, and one day—Father Roman, who was the parish priest—for seven days. For almost three years they suffered the hatred and insults of everyone: they were criminalized, they weren't able to go out, and they suffered humiliations during the jury's attempt to prove the young man's accusations, which I do not dare to repeat here. After three years and more, the jury declared the priests innocent, all of them innocent [...] and the accuser guilty. Because they had seen that that young man had quite an imagination; he was very intelligent and was working in a Catholic school, and thus had a certain prestige which gave the impression that he was telling the truth. He was sentenced to pay the costs and all that, and they were innocent. These men were condemned by the media rather than by the justice system. For this reason, your work is very sensitive: you have to follow things; you have to speak about things, but always with this legal presumption of innocence, and not the legal

presumption of guilt! And there is a difference between a reporter, who provides information about a case without deciding
the matter beforehand, and the detective, who plays Sherlock
Holmes, with the presumption that everyone is guilty. [...] They
are two different roles. But reporters must always start from
the presumption of innocence, stating their own impressions,
doubts, ... but without condemning. This case that occurred in
Granada is, for me, an example that will do us all good, in our
[respective] professions.[6]

Pope Francis has also included himself in his reflections, as
the Supreme Judge in the Church. As we shall see, time has
shown how right he was to defend the value of the presumption
of innocence, both with Pell and with Barbarin.

On January 30, 2020, the Court of Appeal of Lyon acquitted
Cardinal Barbarin. On April 7, 2020, the High Court of Canberra
acquitted Cardinal Pell of the crime of sexual abuse for which
he had been serving his prison sentence for more than a year.
In both cases, the scandal caused by the conviction (which was
later deemed unjust) did not get the same media coverage as
the final sentence, that is, the proclamation of their innocence.
The damage was already done: Many people knew about the
conviction, but not as many then knew about the outcome of
the investigation and that there had been a complete acquittal.

These cases confirm that if the Pope defends the presumption of innocence, it is not a form of corporatism but is done to
safeguard justice.

The presumption of innocence is at the foundation of justice.
We agree to put our own judgments and opinions on hold until
the accused has received a fair trial. Without that presumption,
justice is unattainable.[7]

Following the "presumption of innocence" in canon law is not
saying that someone is held to be a *saint* until they are proven
delinquent. The point of the issue is the burden of proof; a penalty cannot be applied until there is definitive legal certainty of

6. Pope FRANCIS, *Press Conference on the Return Flight from Dublin to Rome* (August 26,
2018), *www.vatican.va/content/francesco/en/speeches/2018/august/documents/papa-
francesco_20180826_irlanda-voloritorno.html*.

7. J.I. DOMINGUEZ-LOPEZ, "The Presumption of Innocence," in *The Tablet* (February 5,
2020), *thetablet.org/the-presumption-of-innocence/*.

fact and of guilt. However, certain clues and elements of guilt that come to light during the course of the investigation are taken into account, for example to limit ministry or apply precautionary measures. The State is much tougher than the Church on this aspect: For example, it provides for pre-trial imprisonment or punishment after the first sentence.

Sometimes, those who practice journalism stand as judges and err, carried away by their prejudices. Certainly, however, on other occasions, journalism allows deception to be exposed and justice to be done. In the case of Cardinal Pell, it was the journalist Andrew Bolt—the face of Sky TV—who made a major breakthrough in the case. Faced with a highly toxic environment, polarized into two extremes of *haters* and *supporters*, the journalist—who was certainly not pro-Pell—decided to dedicate his program *The Bolt Report* to this matter.[8]

He thus went step-by-step though the journey of what Pell and the alleged victims did, following their testimonies and the various minutes of the proceeding, the timing, and the filming of locations and distances. The conclusion was clear: "Not only is it unlikely that Cardinal Pell committed the crime, it is literally impossible."[9]

The conclusion was very similar to that of the Richard Jewell case at the 1996 Olympics in Atlanta. Jewell was a security guard: He prevented the deaths of hundreds of people by foiling an attack during the Olympics. For three days he was anointed a hero, but a breakthrough in the investigation marked him as the only suspect. It eventually became clear that the true culprit was not him, but because of those false assumptions, his life fell apart overnight. Within a week of the bomb explosion, according to the timeline that the FBI was able to track, it was impossible for Jewell to have called emergency services from a public phone. This evidence was underreported, however, because they could

---

8. *www.youtube.com/watch?v=Ze5jHaDB4pk*.

9. *www.tempi.it/ho-la-prova-cronometrica-dellinnocenza-del-cardinale-george-pell/*; translation ours.

not afford to have an attack without a perpetrator since the whole world was watching Atlanta.[10]

Going back to the facts, places, and times of the allegation is a key exercise in journalistic curiosity and professionalism in inquiry to get at the truth. Journalism can abuse its privileged position before public opinion, but it can also reveal the truth and help justice prevail. Such was the case in Poland, when journalists[11] offered the evidence necessary for the action of Church authorities to resume the path of justice. The investigations of Poland's Sebastian Karczewski and the independent daily newspaper *Gazeta Wyborcza* — described by experts as "avowedly anti-Catholic" — were helpful in revealing the chain of lies.

The protagonists of this story are, on one hand, Marek Lisiński, the famous alleged victim whose hand Pope Francis kissed asking forgiveness and whose photo made its way around the world, and on the other, the accused priest, Father Zdzisław Witkowski, punished with a ban on exercising priestly ministry and found guilty by his diocesan bishop and by the Congregation for the Doctrine of the Faith in the Vatican.

Lisiński's story was credible and dated back to the years 1980–1981 when he was an altar boy in his hometown and was allegedly sexually abused by Father Witkowski. A truly moving drama, but a false one.

The journalistic investigation brought to light the fact that in 2007 Lisiński obtained a loan from the priest that was worth almost €5000 for the treatment of his wife suffering from cancer. Later, when the priest discovered that there was no illness, he asked for the money back. In 2008, Lisiński promised to return the money but replied with a threat: "If you don't calm down, Father, I know how to entrap you."

---

10. For further information on the case, cf. A. KENT, K. SALWEN, *Il caso Richard Jewell. La storia di un uomo in cerca di giustizia* (Milan: Mondadori, 2020); M. BRENNER, "American Nightmare: The Ballad of Richard Jewell," in *Vanity Fair* (February 1997), *archive.vanityfair.com/article/share/1fd2d7ae-10d8-474b-9bf1-d1558af697be*.

11. For the case described and analyzed here, we have taken the information from the article by W. REDZIOCH, "*Polonia: colpire la Chiesa con le false accuse sulla questione degli abusi,*" in *Acistampa* (June 19, 2019), *www.acistampa.com/story/polonia-colpire-la-chiesa-con-le-false-acuse-sulla-questione-degli-abusi-11699*.

In 2010, after having studied on the Internet how to stage a credible accusation and demand reparations from the Church, Lisiński wrote a letter to the Bishop of Płock, the diocese where everything had allegedly taken place, but the experts of the ecclesiastical tribunal determined that there were no grounds for moving forward with this allegation, an opinion that the psychologist in charge corroborated.

However, the climate surrounding abuse has changed. In 2013, after a film about clergy sexual abuse was screened in Poland, a strong media campaign was launched that pointed to the Church as a den of pedophiles, and the "Have No Fear" foundation was created to support victims in their accusations and claims demanding compensation. Lisiński quickly became the president of this foundation.

In this context, the journalist Karczewski says that the bishop wanted to appear as an example of "zero tolerance," showing a decisively combative attitude against abuse. The *story* of Father Witkowski, Lisiński's alleged assailant, presented the perfect opportunity.

In the midst of the "witch hunt" unleashed against priests, nobody wanted to investigate Witkowski's case. The bishop, for his part, did not listen to the many witnesses in favor of the priest but imposed sanctions against the alleged abuser, including a ban on priestly ministry for three years. These sanctions were later confirmed by the Congregation for the Doctrine of the Faith. This decision by the Holy See was, according to the journalistic investigation, based on inaccurate reports sent by the bishop.

However, Lisiński's story, as alleged victim, does not end there: Letters were sent to the chancellor of the Curia in which he asked for "financial support" of almost € 35,000, and shortly afterward compensation for a total of € 47,000.

An email sent to the organist of Father Witkowski's parish was also discovered. It asked for € 35,000 from the Curia and concluded with the expression, "There is a lot that can be charged.... The priest of the curia is so frightened he will do anything to convince me not to go to the press, but you remain silent."

Finally, when Lisiński obtained from the bishop the copy of the Vatican decree against the priest, he went straight to court asking the Church for €235,000 as a reward for withdrawing the accusation.

It is interesting to note that Father Witkowski sought to file an accusation against Lisiński, but the then-chancellor — on behalf of the bishop — demanded that the priest immediately withdraw the accusation against Lisiński, an indication with which Witkowski complied in a spirit of obedience.

UNDER THE BANNER OF TRANSPARENCY AND ZERO TOLERANCE

The case we just described shows a long chain of errors committed in the belief that "transparent" procedures were being carried out in the spirit of "zero tolerance."

It was easy for the false victim, simply searching on the Internet, to figure out how to mount a credible story so that he could ask for money. This happened in 2010. Today it would be even easier to carry out such a plan because many credible stories of sexual abuse are public and because it is well known that any priest risks severe punishment if there is a "credible allegation" against him.

The accusation was initially rejected due to the lack of evidence, but in the clamor of the new cases and the climate of opinion that was generated, the accusation became credible, and the data, although the same as in the beginning, was considered sufficient. The arbitrariness with which the concept of sufficiency of data is evaluated leaves a bitter taste in one's mouth. It is clear that a media campaign and an environment marked by crimes makes a criminal out of even someone who was not before.

According to the journalist, the bishop's intervention was not exemplary: He preferred not to investigate, he did not listen to the priest or the faithful, and he sent inaccurate news to Rome. The journalist showed that the bishop forbade the accused priest to *take legal action*. This stringency on the part of the bishop almost seemed to give him *authority* because it aligns with the attitude of *zero tolerance*, but the Church always seeks justice and truth.

For Father Witkowski there was no right to presumption of innocence or to a hearing. Moreover, we do not know if there was a public apology. He was condemned by the unbridled ambition of his false victim and by the poor judgment of his bishop.

Addressing and effectively resolving the problem of sexual abuse of minors in the Church is an overriding necessity; punishing abusers is just. But it is clear that transparency and "zero tolerance" can become empty mottos, foreign to the legal tradition of the Church. Managing media pressure is part of the task of ecclesiastical authority. Allowing oneself to be carried away by this logic, in addition to exhibiting antievangelical behavior, does not put us on the side of the victims but generates new victims and further destroys the Church's credibility because it acts against her identity and her truth.

A FLOOD OF NEGLIGENCE AND IRREGULARITIES IN THE PROCESS

An investigative report by Moisés Alvarado for the magazine *Séptimo Sentido* (La Prensa Group from El Salvador) gave a highly detailed account of the case of the Salvadorean priest Antonio Molina, who was wrongfully convicted and expelled from the clerical state by a 2016 decree by the Pope, on charges of having raped his accuser Isaí Ernesto Mendoza when Mendoza was a teenager and part of the group of altar servers.[12] The description of the case coincided with many others, impressed upon the collective imagination: a priest who had abused a minor.

Antonio Molina defended his innocence from the beginning and denounced the many irregularities in the process, including two especially significant ones. On one hand, the statements read that the accused priest...

---

12. Cf. M. ALVARADO, "*Antonio Molina: el exsacerdote salvadoreño al que el papa Francisco destituyó por un caso no probado de violación y amenazas,*" in *Séptimo Sentido* (February 18, 2018), 7s.laprensagrafica.com/antonio-molina-exsacerdote-salvadoreno-al-papa-francisco-destituyo-caso-no-probado-violacion-amenazas/.

does not know the complainant and that it is possible that [the complainant] has never resided in Pachimalco, something that the Archdiocese of San Salvador did not verify before sending the case [to Rome].[13]

The Congregation for the Doctrine of the Faith is supposed to examine the findings of the preliminary investigation commissioned by the bishop of the diocese and initiate the bishop's request after this examination. In this case, the request was that the priest be dismissed from the clerical state by direct intervention of the Pope. The other serious inconsistency is that the complainant claimed to have been an altar server at the time the alleged events took place, but both the priest and close witnesses said that the priest did not have boys serving as altar servers. He was assisted in the celebration by adult men who usually attended Mass. These two essential aspects were not examined by those in charge of the investigation on behalf of the diocese. Unfortunately, they were not discovered until after the Pope's decree reducing this priest to the lay state.

As Alvarado reports, there were three cases of priests accused of sexually abusing minors, which the Archbishop of San Salvador made public in 2015 and early 2016:

> The announcement that the three former priests had been found guilty at the Vatican was made on December 18, 2016: The speed with which the proceedings were resolved seemed like pounding the table, a clear sign that the Church was committed to fighting this crime. With Molina, it did not even take a year.[14]

The many irregularities on the part of the diocese were blatant injustices. Thus, the former priest decided to sue all those involved for defamation and slander. This civil proceeding helped show the many missteps in the process and the constant contradictions of Isaí and his mother on the facts. In the end, when mother and son were found with their backs against the wall, there was nothing left but to look for a lie big enough to put further questions to rest. The bishop said,

---

13. Ibid.; translation ours.
14. Ibid.; translation ours.

What happened is that there was a phone call, and she told us that she was his mother; she spoke to my secretary and said that her son [Isaí] had died. So we believed because we believe in the person. If she tells us that her son is dead, we believe that he is dead. *We are not concerned with seeing whether it was true or not.*

And then he said that he "also found it strange that they used this as an excuse not to address the civil case."[15]

The damage done to Antonio Molina and to the whole ecclesial community is difficult to repair. In any case, the justice and veracity of the facts require that action be taken against the bishop and his associates for their continuous negligence in exercising their functions. Those in positions of responsibility in the Church may be judged for their negligence in their actions of governance.

IS IT TRULY POSSIBLE TO DEFEND THE PRESUMPTION OF INNOCENCE AND PUT VICTIMS FIRST?

Frequently, when one begins to highlight the importance of the presumption of innocence, one is misjudged, as if one just wants to favor or protect the *system*. And it sets off the anti-clerical rhetoric—based on some legitimate facts—of continued abuse, cover-ups, and attitudes of suspicion about the veracity or the fitness of the victim who dared to report, etc. The right balance and neutrality between the two interests does not exist "a priori": Justice always proves things after the fact. This problem is magnified in the hyperinformed world we live in and is accentuated by the timely judgment of public opinion, especially on the Internet. Before the start of a judicial proceeding, the court of public opinion has already tried everything and issued a verdict. This mechanism is therefore inevitable, so it is almost useless to complain. But can more be done to bring justice to both parties?

In the first place, as in all the institutions where there is a certain hierarchy, the starting point of the priest or religious is not the same as that of the victim: The former belongs to the

---

15. Ibid.; translation ours.

hierarchical structure of the Church and, a priori, enjoys a good social reputation in the eyes of the community and his superiors. The victim does not start with these "structural advantages." The Church has recently recognized this *initial inequality* and wants to improve the situation with a series of legal and governmental measures, so as to remove victims from their position of inferiority: Those who have news of abuse are obligated to report, and each diocese and equivalent are required to have a reporting system; a protocol of reception and active listening; and to help victims with material, medical, and spiritual means from the beginning.

Alongside these mandatory structural measures (established by canon law),[16] authors like Katie van Schaijik suggest adding a theoretical principle to help balance the initial disequilibrium between the presumption of innocence of the priest or religious and the presumption of credibility of the victim. To this end, Van Shaijik suggests the principle of the presumption of *veracity of the victim*, intended to ensure that the initial attitude toward the victim is not one of skepticism but starts with the presumption that the person speaking is sincere. That is, it involves listening to someone who one assumes is speaking in good faith (empathy vs. skepticism). As the author points out, in this context such comments as, "Had you been drinking?" "How were you dressed?" or, "Do you not think you might be exaggerating a bit?"[17] would be inappropriate. That is because they implicitly put the victim in a position of suspicion and inferiority.

Van Shaijik's *presumption of veracity* requires a prior value judgment on the plausibility of the facts, which rests with the one who receives the *notitia criminis*. This was one of the points where there was evolution in recent canonical norms:

> Whenever an ordinary has knowledge, which at least seems true, of a delict, he is carefully to inquire personally or through

---

16. Cf. Pope FRANCIS, *Vos Estis Lux Mundi*, 10.

17. Cf. K. VAN SCHAIJIK, "We Need a New Principle to Balance 'Presumption of Innocence,'" in *The Personal Project* (September 11, 2018), *www.thepersonalistproject.org/home/comments/power-differentials-and-innocent-till-proven-guilty*.

another suitable person about the facts, circumstances, and imputability.[18]

That is to say, the canon speaks of a *probability* that requires discernment: *"notitia saltem verisimilis."*

Claudio Papale points out that there was an evolution of the interpretation of this "judgment of plausibility" in norms of the Church, which can be seen in the "Guidelines of the Bishops' Conferences" that the Vatican ordered them to develop starting in 2011.[19] Taking as an example the first Guidelines of the Italian Bishops' Conference of 2014, which reads, "If the accusation is considered *credible*, then it requires that the case be remanded to the CDF."[20] While in the 2019 Guidelines of the Vicariate of Vatican City, it says, "Whenever the report is *not manifestly unfounded*."[21] As is clear, there is a shift from a more passive perspective (that it is credible), to a more active one (that it is not manifestly unfounded). This reveals a growing awareness on the part of the authority of the Church. Since these delicts of abuse rarely take place in the presence of witnesses, prior investigation should be discarded if the delict is *manifestly impossible*.

The Congregation for the Doctrine of the Faith's *Vademecum* on procedural matters in handling cases of clergy sexual abuse gives some examples of *manifest lack of veracity*:

> If it turns out that at the time of the delict of which he is accused, the person was not yet a cleric; if it comes to light that the presumed victim was not a minor; if it is a well-known fact that the person accused could not have been present at the place of the delict when the alleged actions took place.[22]

---

18. CIC, can. 1717.

19. C. Papale, "L'indagine previa," in *Dispensa Online Pontificia Università Lateranense*, 43–73, *www.pul.it/cattedra/upload_files/19419/Sussidio%20Processo%20penale.pdf*.

20. Italian Bishops' Conference, *Linee guida per i casi di abuso sessuale nei confronti di minori da parte di chierici* (January 2014), 17, *www.chiesacattolica.it/wp-content/uploads/sites/31/2017/08/11/Linee-Guida-abusi-sessuali-2014.pdf*; translation ours.

21. Pope Francis, *Guidelines for the Protection of Children and Vulnerable Persons* (March 26, 2019), no. F.6, *www.vatican.va/resources/resources_protezioneminori-lineeguida_20190326_en.html*.

22. Congregation for the Doctrine of the Faith, *Vademecum* (version 1.0) (July 16, 2020), no. 13, *www.vatican.va/roman_curia/congregations/cfaith/documents/rc_con_cfaith_doc_20200716_vademecum-casi-abuso_en.html*.

Van Schaijik's statement on the presumption of *veracity* may otherwise be described as *presumption of good faith* on the part of the victim, but, in our view, it would be disproportionate to create a new principle, as she argues.[23] As has been demonstrated, the evolution of the regulations has led to adjustments in the process to avoid potential disequilibriums that could harm the victim. In December 2021 there were updates to the norms on delicts reserved for the Congregation for the Doctrine of the Faith, and one of the measures was the improvement of penal action regarding penal proceedings.[24]

THE PRESUMPTION OF INNOCENCE AND CANON LAW

That a person is presumed innocent until proven guilty is a principle with very deep roots in English jurisprudence — but the source is not Anglo-Saxon. As Pennington points out, it is the result of a synthesis between Roman law, canon law, and the jurisprudence of the medieval *Ius comune*. The maxim...

> arose in the late thirteenth century; was conserved by the universal jurisprudence of the *Ius comune*; was used in the defense of marginalized defendants, Jews, heretics, and witches in the early modern age; and, finally, was employed as a powerful argument against torture in the sixteenth, seventeenth, and eighteenth centuries. It was by the latter route that it entered [Anglo-Saxon] common law jurisprudence.[25]

As Pennington explained, the French canon lawyer Johannes Monachus was the first to develop the principle "innocent until proven guilty." He explained the rights of the accused in a

---

23. K. VAN SCHAIJIK, *We Need a New Principle to Balance "Presumption of Innocence"*: "The presumption of innocence is a necessary corrective to the power differential between the State and the individual. The presumption of veracity is a much-needed corrective to the power differential between abuser and his (or her) victims. It should be conscientiously woven into our response to injustice on both a personal and a societal level. It should be codified in ecclesiastical and secular law."

24. Pope FRANCIS, *Rescriptum ex Audientia Ss.mi Which Modifies the Motu Proprio Sacramentorum Sanctitatis Tutela (2001, updated 2010) and Approves the "Norme sui delitti riservati della Congregazione per la Dottrina della Fede"* (December 7, 2021), *press.vatican.va/content/salastampa/it/bollettino/pubblico/2021/12/07/0825/01732.html*.

25. K. PENNINGTON, "*Innocente fino a prova contraria: le origini di una massima giuridica,*" in *Processo penale e tutela dei diritti nell'ordinamento canonico*, ed. D. CITO (Milan: Giuffrè, 2005), 60; translation ours.

commentary on a Decree of Pope Boniface VIII, emphasizing a set of inalienable rights of the accused: to have a summons, to be present in court, for his case to be studied by a public tribunal, the right to have a public judgment; the right not to incriminate himself, to present evidence to defend himself, and to have a lawyer. For Monachus, these rights depended on natural law; not even the Pope, according to him, was above them.[26] Explaining these rights related to due process, he formulated the phrase: "A person is presumed innocent until proven guilty (*item quilibet presumitur innocens nisi probetur nocens*)."[27]

As we have seen with the Magisterium when it comes to communication, the *tradition* of the Church already contains invaluable principles, including from the juridical standpoint, regarding the themes of the presumption of innocence and the burden of proof. Classical general principles such as *onus probandi incumbit ei qui affirmat, non ei qui negat* ("the burden of proof falls on the one who affirms, not who denies"); *actore non probante reus absolvitur* ("if the plaintiff does not prove his argument, the accused is absolved"); and *reus in excipiendo fit autor* ("in disputing, the defendant becomes a plaintiff"). In the *ordo iudiciarius* of the time, there is great respect for individual rights. The difficulty concerning these general principles is their application to particular cases.

The Church has a *unique tradition*, linked to her being the People of God, which naturally shapes these principles.

> From apostolic times, she has developed a distinctive penal discipline, attuned to her original structure and to her spiritual ends, until she has reached a wholly unique "penal system."[28]

For example, in the Church there is no true and proper coercive system — there is no police or prison system, but justice is administered, and offenses are punished with penalties in an effort to repair the damage and correct the perpetrator.

---

26. Cf. Ibid., 61; translation ours.

27. Cited in Ibid., 47; translation ours.

28. G. Cardinale, "Interview with Msgr. B.G. Pighin," in *Avvenire* (December 9, 2021), *www.avvenire.it/chiesa/pagine/i-reati-della-chiesa-giro-di-vite*; translation ours.

In the last few decades, penal prosecutions have in some respects proven inadequate for responding promptly to the wave of crimes of abuse. Misapplication of these procedures as well as negligence have contributed to the damage done. As Pighin says: "Unpreparedness and negligence have been complicit in the negative — even disastrous — effects in this area. Hence the need to enact a new and valid Church penal system."[29]

The reforms that were recently approved by the Church are in this same vein.

In 2020, the Congregation for the Doctrine of the Faith published a *Vademecum* with the goal of offering a resource for faithfully conducting procedures in cases of sexual abuse of minors. There were, among other things, considerations on the protection of privacy, the secrecy of office that everyone is required to respect (although no bond of silence can be imposed on either the accuser or the witnesses), and the presumption of innocence:

> In any event, especially in cases where public statements must be made, great caution should be exercised in providing information about the facts. Statements should be brief and concise, avoiding clamorous announcements, refraining completely from any premature judgment about the guilt or innocence of the person accused (since this is to be established only by an eventual penal process aimed at verifying the basis of the accusation), and respecting any desire for privacy expressed by the alleged victims.[30]

In turn, as Papale explains, it is necessary to inform the accused (and yet also the victims and witnesses):

> Should a judicial seizure or an order to hand over the acts of investigation by the civil authorities intervene, it will no longer be possible for the Church to guarantee the confidentiality of the depositions and the documentation acquired in the canonical setting.[31]

Book VI of penal canon law, which went into effect on December 8, 2021, made this principle explicit.[32] The principle

---

29. Ibid; translation ours.

30. CONGREGATION FOR THE DOCTRINE OF THE FAITH, *Vademecum*, no. 45.

31. C. PAPALE, *L'indagine previa*; translation ours.

32. CIC, can. 1321.

was already present in the canonical system, which does not allow the application of canonical penalties until after there has been a definitive judgment or decree, and in fact, unlike many State systems (such as that of Australia) the appeal or challenge of a nonfinal penal decision always has suspensive effect.[33] Of course, from a practical standpoint it can create confusion (as we shall see later) because it is the first juridical text that makes it explicit. But it can also have a psychological function, thus avoiding a subject being considered guilty after only the news of the delict (which is affirmed, moreover, by the rest of canon 1717) and thus prevent directly "punitive" measures, not, however, measures placed to protect the regular course of the canonical proceeding.

In the last five years, the Church has adopted a mosaic of norms on sexual abuse that speak to how relevant, grave, and urgent this problem is. At the level of juridical technique, there is shortage of criticism for the "normative stratification," neither doubts nor uncertainties about its application by the practitioners of the Law. All this points to the need for a more homogenous order.[34] Many see the new Book VI of penal canon law as a step in this direction.

---

33. CIC, can. 1353.
34. Cf. M. Visioli, *Considerazioni a margine del Rescriptum ex Audientia*, 739–740.

CHAPTER 7

WE BELIEVE IN ONE, HOLY, CATHOLIC, AND... TRANSPARENT CHURCH?

A wound may be bandaged,
and there is reconciliation after abuse,
but whoever has betrayed secrets is without hope.
—*Sirach 27:21*

The positive value of transparency is insufficient because it is considered an absolute principle. Transparency has some limits imposed by the dignity of the human person and the common good for the same reasons that make certain types of censorship and healthy confidentiality necessary.

These general principles "materialize" in concrete values present in daily life (mystery, silence, respect, faith, modesty), which are threatened by the feverish imposition of absolute transparency. These values are essential for life and Church communication. That is why we should take some time to reflect on them and on why unlimited transparency is undesirable.

MYSTERY AND TRANSPARENCY WITHOUT LIMITS

Mystery is continually present in reality: It gives reality meaning and at the same time surpasses it. It is not irrational, absurd, or contradictory. It cannot be overcome by intellectual effort, but it is also not accessible to our search.[1]

Mystery is always beyond the reach of man because it is qualitatively distinct from all other objects of human science. But at

---

1. H. DE LUBAC, *Paradoja y Misterio de la Iglesia* (Salamanca: Sígueme, 2002), 37–39; translation ours.

the same time, it has a relationship with man: It belongs to us and functions in us.[2]

It is comparable to excessive light, which neither our pupils nor the most powerful telescopes will ever be able to reveal. Mystery challenges but welcomes: It produces an inexplicable vertigo that at the same time makes us feel at home, at peace. We are mystery, God is Mystery.

As Byul-Chun Han argues, transparency does not admit mysteries; it is empirical and immanent. It tends to flatten everything, to simplify, and to standardize all asymmetry. Mystery, rather, is inhabited by transcendence; it fascinates; its complexity and density challenge; it generates inner appetite, burning, desire, and therefore love. Transparency does not admit mystery: It renounces the search for any reality that is not apparent and, therefore, does not yearn for deepening and does not, in this sense, admit any appetite. It aims to have everything solved at a glance, manipulated and manipulable, marketable and easy.[3]

> The saint is not transparent. Rather, he or she portrays a myste-rious blur. *The coming reign of peace* will not be called a society of transparency. That is not a state of peace.[4]

Unlimited transparency makes the experience of mystery (mysticism and liturgy) — and certainly its communication (pastoral and theological) — impossible.

SILENCE AND TRANSPARENCY WITHOUT LIMITS

Silence is the privileged environment for the acceptance of mystery.[5] Unlimited transparency is the profusion of words, information, and images. As Søren Kierkegaard said:

> In observing the present state of the world and life in general, [... if] someone asked me 'What do you think should be done?' I would answer, ... the very first thing that must be done is: create silence.

---

2. Ibid., 38–39; translation ours.

3. Cf. B-C. HAN, *La sociedad de la transparencia*, 38–43.

4. Ibid., 38; translation ours

5. Cf. Pope FRANCIS, *Morning Meditation in the Chapel of the* Domus Sanctæ Marthæ (December 20, 2013), *www.vatican.va/content/francesco/en/cotidie/2013/documents/ papa-francesco-cotidie_20131220_mystery.html*.

Most of the flow of information is noisy, empty, banal...

designed merely to jolt the senses or to stir up the masses, the crowd, the public, noise! [...] indeed soon brought to its lowest point with regard to meaning, and simultaneously the means of communication are indeed brought to their highest with regard to speedy and overall circulation; for what is publicized with such hot haste and, on the other hand, what has greater circulation than rubbish! Oh, create silence![6]

This noise is intolerance of silence.

When word and silence become mutually exclusive, communication breaks down, either because it gives rise to confusion or because, on the contrary, it creates an atmosphere of coldness; when they complement one another, however, communication acquires value and meaning.[7]

Silence does not invalidate communication. On the contrary:

From silence springs a communication that is even more challenging, invoking sensitivity and ability to listen, which often reveals the measure and nature of relationships.[8]

Unlimited transparency creates an avalanche of information that is often disconnected and decontextualized and "that on its own does not clarify the world."[9] "The more information we put out, the more entangled the world becomes."[10] We need silence "to discern what is important from what is useless and superficial."[11]

It is necessary to limit transparency (if possible) and the noise it creates in such a way that there can be a human

6. S. KIERKEGAARD, "For Self-Examination," in *Kierkegaard's Writings*, vol. 21, ed. H.V. HONG, E.H. HONG (Princeton: Princeton University Press, 1990), 47–48.

7. Pope BENEDICT XVI, *Message for the 46th World Communications Day, "Silence and Word: Path of Evangelization"* (May 20, 2012), *www.vatican.va/content/benedict-xvi/en/messages/communications/documents/hf_ben-xvi_mes_20120124_46th-world-communications-day.html.*

8. B-C. HAN, *La sociedad de la transparencia*, 79; translation ours.

9. Ibid.

10. Ibid., 80; translation ours.

11. Pope BENEDICT XVI, *Message for the 46th World Communications Day, "Silence and Word: Path of Evangelization."*

communication, which allows us to experience communion:[12] communication made of silence and words organically related to each other.[13]

RESPECT AND TRANSPARENCY

Unlimited transparency, by making mystery and silence impossible, eliminates otherness. We have said it before: It flattens everything; it is overwhelming and disrespectful. That is why offenses are not unusual in the hyperconnected society where everything must be said with absolute transparency. When truth is not taken into account, there is no respect or love:

> The tragedy of disinformation is that it discredits others, presenting them as enemies, to the point of demonizing them and fomenting conflict. Fake news is a sign of intolerant and hypersensitive attitudes, and leads only to the spread of arrogance and hatred. That is the end result of untruth.[14]

In the society of transparency, the other is stripped of his or her mystery and thus becomes vulnerable to judgment: The distance from the other imposed by his or her inner life, conscience, secrets, silence, and soul, is not considered...; since the person has not been fully shown, he or she can be insulted and condemned. This is because that person has been reduced to the mere perception that "the transparent executioner" has of him or her. Unlimited transparency absolutizes subjective perception and disregards the mystery and surprising originality of the other.

The communication of the Church is not compatible with lack of respect or with aggression toward people, both of which derive from the lack of respect from the truth that is typical of unlimited transparency.

---

12. Cf. Pope FRANCIS, *Message for World Communications Day*, "The Truth Will Set You Free" (Jn 8:32): Fake News and Journalism for Peace (January 24, 2018), *www. vatican.va/content/francesco/en/messages/communications/documents/papa-francesco_20180124_messaggio-comunicazioni-sociali.html.*

13. Pope BENEDICT XVI, *Message for the 46th World Communications Day*, "Silence and Word: Path of Evangelization."

14. Cf. Pope FRANCIS, *Message for World Communications Day*, "The Truth Will Set You Free" (Jn 8:32).

TRUST, SUSPICION, AND TRANSPARENCY

The search for unlimited transparency, with a disregard for natural ambiguity, cannot presume innocence. At the same time, it triggers suspicion — it is a society of persecution, of witch hunting. As we have seen extensively in Chapters 1 and 4 with the Calmeyn-Aupetit case and the Rhodes case, the culture of *suspicion* is connected to *prejudice*.

On the contrary:

> Trust means, while not knowing in relation to the other, building a positive relationship with him or her. [...] Where transparency dominates, there is no space for trust.[15]

In a society that relies on trust, demands for transparency should not be extreme.[16]

The society of transparency leaves no room for faith. It is not possible for me to say to my interlocutor, "I believe you," or "because you are the one saying it."[17] Newman's definition of faith, according to Martin Descalzo, as "the courage to bear doubts,"[18] expresses how a society of transparency does not allow for doubt, nor does it take the risk of trusting; it chooses to cling to the false security of suspicion, to the abuse of control. In the realm of unbounded transparency, those closest to you—"yours" (your friends, colleagues, relatives) — who bear witness to your existential ambiguity and who possess so many perceptions about you, according to the logic of civic reporting and in the name of transparency, can not only become a threat but your informants and executioners. Nothing could be further from the Church Christ founded than this.

In the end, affirms Schudson, "Everyday uses of nontransparency lubricate all the small encounters of life that make society function."[19] Our everyday lives are full of friendships and familial

---

15. B-C. HAN, *La sociedad de la trasparencia*, 91; translation ours.

16. Ibid.

17. Cf. Lk 5:5.

18. M. DESCALZO, *La Iglesia nuestra hija* (Salamanca: Sígueme, 1972), 60.

19. M. SCHUDSON, *The Rise of the Right to Know: Politics and the Culture of Transparency*, 276.

relationships that are based on esteem, respect, admiration… and they function when anchored in trust.

IS IT POSSIBLE TO LIMIT TRANSPARENCY?

The concept of transparency is a retrieval because it refers to openness, freedom of expression, the influence of information, and accountability. All these practices have great potential and enormous positive consequences. However, in light of the approach we have called "unlimited transparency," "absolute transparency," or "abuse of transparency," we can see that such transparency is incompatible with respect for human dignity and the common good, and it is therefore irreconcilable with the purposes and communication of the Church.

The problem is that the metaphor of transparency does not admit limits. Reality is either totally transparent or it is not transparent. The quality of transparency does not accept nuance. Minimally tarnished glass or slightly murky water have ceased to be transparent. Used as a metaphor to describe practices of *governance* or communicative processes, transparency always requires contrasting adjectives.

In public opinion, transparency is identified with all that is good, so abuses of this practice are not usually perceived as such because transparency has been secularly *canonized*. The paradox is that while it is presented as a solution to many political, economic, and communication problems, it can give rise to countless injustices, as seen in China and other authoritarian countries. As Peters says:

> Transparency — freedom of information — can be a wonderful tool for exposing lies and cover-ups, but it is not a guarantee of justice. Shows of transparency can often be ways of hiding information in plain sight.[20]

It therefore seems that making mistakes under the mantle of transparency can even be beneficial, while striking under the banner of secrecy can discredit you at the speed of a click.

---

20. J. PUJOL, "Colloquy with John Durham Peters at Yale University on Freedom of Speech," in *Church, Communication & Culture* 4, no. 1 (2019), 105.

The situation created is more serious than it seems because both a decision in favor of secrecy and proper management of transparency are acts of communicating one's identity. They tell who we are with as much force as an official document. That is why Church communicators are reminded of their duty to "to announce without fail or pause the full truth by the means of social communication, so as to give a true picture of the Church and her life."[21]

What will determine for the Church the time to speak and the time to be silent will not be primarily consensus or public opinion. These aspects should be considered a real good but not a fundamental good.[22] Nor should we give in to all demands for transparency out of fear of being branded as "opaque." This is a price that we must sometimes pay to avoid being manipulated or bending to fads. Later on, we shall propose the concept of *translucent communication*.

We should not forget that the Church also bears the sins of her members. Carroggio explains the following regarding the Church in her spiritual dimension:

> As the mystical body of Christ, Christians have (with Saint Paul) affirmed over the centuries that the Church is "holy and without blemish."[23] However, in her most visible, human, and institutional dimension, she shares *perfectibility* and *fallibility* with every other organization involved in social action: the *Catechism of the Catholic Church* recalls that "all members of the Church, including her ministers, must acknowledge that they are sinners."[24] The very Founder of the Church was denied three times by the one who would be His future vicar and sold to death by another one of His twelve immediate collaborators.[25]

Not only does he bring it, but he seems to take it for granted: "Let him who is without sin among you be the first to throw a

21. PCCS, *Communio et Progressio*, 123.

22. Cf. J.M. La Porte, *Introduzione alla comunicazione istituzionale della Chiesa* (Madrid: Palabra, 2012), 257.

23. Eph 5:27.

24. CCC 827.

25. M. Carroggio, "Church Communication in the Face of Vulnerability: A Theoretical Framework and Practical Application for Information Management in Cases of the Abuse of Minors," in *Church, Communication & Culture* 6,1 (2021), 62.

stone."[26] Pope Francis himself clearly and publicly alerted members of the Curia in his 2014 Christmas Message, on a list of "curial diseases," because the Church, "like any body, like any human body, it is also exposed to diseases, malfunctioning, infirmity."[27]

> It is therefore a difficult path between transparency and vulnerability. This is the road we are called to travel. It is not about being transparent in a holy Church, but about how to be transparent in a vulnerable Church.[28]

We must take into account personal weaknesses and institutional vulnerabilities in the way we communicate. In the same way, Professor Magalhães expressed in a Conference on trust and the vulnerability of institutions,

> Trust in the Church, and in institutions in general, will depend largely on the good *they do*: on their capacity for mercy. And it is very common that our goodness is born stained by the shadow of our original sin. Goodness contaminated from within by evil.[29]

In the first place, the Church "speaks" or "remains silent" because she is faithful to herself, to her truth, and to her mission. What is not admissible in any way is for her to be carried away by the temptation to gain consensus at the cost of losing her own identity. A nonnegotiable value in any act of institutional communication is what La Porte calls communicative coherence,[30] which also applies in relation to transparency and secrecy.

By looking at the essence of the Church, a model of original communication can be created that is as original as the Church herself, which, while being open and dialoguing in the midst of the world, does not belong to the world. In fact, in

---

26. Jn 8:7.

27. Pope FRANCIS, *Presentation of the Christmas Greetings to the Roman Curia* (Sala Clementina, Vatican City, December 22, 2014), *www.vatican.va/content/francesco/en/speeches/2014/december/documents/papa-francesco_20141222_curia-romana.html*.

28. D. STURLA, "*Fiducia in una Chiesa vulnerabile?*" in *Inspiring Trust: Church Communications and Organizational Vulnerability*, ed. J. PUJOL, J. NARBONA, J.M. DÍAZ (Rome: EDUSC, 2021), 127; translation ours.

29. G. MAGALHÃES, "*Alcune chiavi per praticare la misericordia cristiana nella società contemporanea*," in *Inspiring Trust: Church Communications and Organizational Vulnerability*, ed. J. PUJOL, J. NARBONA, J.M. DÍAZ (Rome: EDUSC, 2021), 167; translation ours.

30. Cf. J.M. LA PORTE, *Introduzione alla comunicazione*, 257.

the communication of the Church there are spaces for mystery, secrecy, censorship, respect, silence, and modesty—but also for openness, accountability, freedom of expression, and for a way of reporting that is proactive, not defensive.[31]

> Criteria for proper communication will also have to be refined in a time like ours in which the demands of transparency must be reconciled with those of confidentiality: in fact, an unjustified reservation, just like an unchecked disclosure, runs the risk of generating poor communication and not serving the truth.[32]

COMMUNICATION IN THE CHURCH: AN ORGANIC MODEL

To be faithful to her identity, the communication of the Church must harmonize all these values and good practices. Organic logic is what holds all the different dimensions together and not in mutual opposition—to avoid forced exclusions of the "or" variety, "or" to better see "one dimension or reality in the other, or with the other." In this way, the different components will complement each other dynamically. Organic logic is profoundly realistic.[33]

The opposite of organic logic is mechanistic logic or thinking that is hidden behind many deceptive discourses. The mechanistic way of reasoning separates the elements of a whole that are actually united. One is thus unable to see the part in the whole or the whole in its dimensions. The risk is that of distinguishing parts or aspects of reality, separating them or viewing them in contrast with each other, when in reality, they are originally destined to complement each other: In this way we move away from concrete reality. This results in "abstract" thinking that is extraneous to life.[34]

Conceiving secrecy and openness as a polarized antagonism would be an error for the Church that would distance her from an

---

31. Cf. V. ALAZRAKI, *Comunicazione: per tutte le persone,* Presentation in the *Meeting "The Protection of Minors in the Church,"* in *Vatican.va* (February 23, 2019), *www.vatican.va/resources/resources_alazraki-protezioneminori_20190223_it.html*; translation ours.

32. L. GHISONI, *Communio: Agire insieme,* no. 3.6.

33. Cf. R. FERNÁNDEZ DE A., *El 31 de mayo, una misión para nuestro tiempo* (Chile: Nueva Patris, 1997).

34. Ibid.

organic communication that is faithful to her identity. Presenting secrecy and openness as irreconcilable would lead to the imposition of absolutized and distorted visions; it would lead to an abusive mindset that defeats the other, who no longer has a place because he or she has been anathemized.

It is important to always distinguish between the meaning and the context of the term transparency because the Church, which walks through history fulfilling the mystery of redemption, must first of all combat paternalism in governance (in which the superior believes he or she has to answer only to God and has the grace of state to decide what he or she wants) and to develop a transparency among coresponsible subjects, that is, to achieve a true participation from all in the Church's mission by getting people involved. This seems to be one of the biggest issues. It is not knowing everything or communicating everything that allows one to express him- or herself to the world in a "transparent" way; rather, it is necessary to make people feel truly "involved" in the processes that lead to decisions about carrying out the Church's mission. *Synodality* is little understood by those who are accustomed to command by responding only to the "bosses" (usually to make a good impression) and by those who think everything will always stay the same because only a few "chosen ones," in the end, will make the decisions by pretending that everyone has been heard without really taking into account what others have said.

CHAPTER 8

DO NOT TELL ME
YOU ARE ACCOUNTABLE;
SHOW ME!

These things you have done and I have been silent;
you thought that I was one like yourself.
But now I rebuke you, and lay the charge before you.
—Psalm 50:21

Talking about secrecy and transparency in ecclesial communication requires a further reflection on accountability in the Church. The term "accountability" is used in the secular legal system and "has entered the ecclesial juridical context."[1] We are talking about an accountability that is not just economic but concerns in general the capacity to respond and give an account of the procedures and choices made in decision-making and governmental processes. We shall now present a recent case, which helps us understand its necessity in Church governance.[2]

On January 16, 2011, the Congregation for the Doctrine of the Faith concluded its investigation of the priest Fernando Karadima Fariña, who was found guilty of sexual abuse of minors.[3]

> Karadima was a respected figure in the hierarchy of the Church. [...] Almost fifty religious were formed around him, including five bishops. He was a man who attracted many to his parish and had, moreover, great social and even political influence in Chile.[4]

---

1. J. Miñambres, "*Rilevanza canonica dell'accountability degli amministratori di beni ecclesiastici,*" in *Ius Ecclesiæ* 31, no. 1 (2019), 136.

2. Cf. W.M. Daniel, "Accountability and the Juridical Responsibility of the Public Ecclesiastical Administration," in *Ius Ecclesiæ* 30, no. 1 (2018), 35–56.

3. Cf. Redazione Aci Prensa, "*Vaticano: P. Karadima es culpable de abusos sexuales,*" in *ACI Prensa* (February 18, 2011), *www.aciprensa.com/noticias/vaticano-p-karadima-es-culpable-de-abusos-sexuales.*

4. C. Farfán, M.J. López, "*La influencia de Karadima,*" in *Qué pasa* (April 30, 2010), *www.quepasa.cl/articulo/actualidad/2010/04/1-3265-9-la-influencia-de-karadima.shtml/*; translation ours.

One of Karadima's victims identified Monsignor Barros as a person not only close to Karadima but as part of the process of abuse and cover-up. "Juan Barros was there watching when he abused me. They did not tell me about it, it happened directly to me," were the statements of Juan Carlos Cruz, one of the accusers in the Karadima case. According to the accusers, Barros received the first complaints against Karadima when he was secretary to Cardinal Juan Francisco Fresno and, according to Cruz, he "simply tore them up."[5]

After more than twenty years as bishop, Pope Francis nominated Barros as Bishop of Osorno.[6] The protests immediately grew, even during his inauguration.[7] Meanwhile, news had arrived in the Vatican about the accusations against Barros: the story of his complicity with Karadima,[8] entirely credible to bishops, priests, and lay faithful,[9] who expressed their disagreement with the appointment.[10] From the cardinal primate of Chile came this statement:

> Personally I do not know who, how many, or how they informed the Holy Father; I can only say that we have reported to the Holy Father, both personally and as the bishops' con-

5. RECACCIÓN BBC," *Juan Barros, el controvertido obispo cuya presencia encendió la ira de las víctimas de abuso sexual durante la visita del Papa Francisco a Chile,*" in *BBC Mundo* (January 17, 2018), *www.bbc.com/mundo/noticias-america-latina-42719414.*

6. Cf. CONGREGATIO PRO EPISCOPUS (January 10, 2015), in *AAS* 107, no. 2 (2015), 225; cf. REDACCIÓN ACI PRENSA, "*Papa Francisco nombra Obispo de Osorno en Chile,*" in *ACI Prensa* (January 10, 2015), *www.aciprensa.com/noticias/el-papa-francisco-nombra-obispo-de-osorno-en-chile-83850.*

7. Cf. REDACCIÓN ACI PRENSA, "*VIDEO: Episcopado rechaza protesta contra Obispo chileno durante Te Deum,*" in *ACI Prensa* (September 20, 2017), *www.aciprensa.com/noticias/video-episcopado-rechaza-protesta-contra-obispo-chileno-durante-te-deum-63753.*

8. Cf."*Caso Barros: Comisión vaticana entregó en 2015 una carta de Juan Carlos Cruz al papa,*" in *Cooperativa.cl* (February 5, 2018), *www.cooperativa.cl/noticias/pais/iglesia-catolica/caso-barros-comision-vaticana-entrego-en-2015-una-carta-de-juan-carlos/2018-02-05/090107.html.*

9. Cf. REDACCIÓN PURA NOTICIA, "*Parlamentarios envían carta al Papa Francisco en protesta por designación de Juan Barros como obispo de Osorno,*" in *Pura Noticia* (February 16, 2015), *www.puranoticia.cl/noticias/regiones/parlamentarios-envian-carta-al-papa-francisco-en-protesta-por-designacion-de-juan-barros-como-obispo-de-osorno/2015-02-16/135255.html.*

10. Cf. REDACCIÓN SOY OSORNO, "*Destacado sacerdote envía carta al Papa por caso Barros: 'Su figura contrasta con la de nuestro primer obispo,'*" in *Soy Osorno.cl* (March 18, 2015), *www.soychile.cl/Osorno/Sociedad/2015/03/18/311020/Destacado-sacerdote-envia-carta-al-Papa-por-caso-Barros-Su-figura-contrasta-con-la-de-nuestro-primer-obispo.aspx.*

ference, and I can assure you that we have not deceived the Holy Father.[11]

However, Pope Francis heard other sources and on several occasions publicly defended Barros:

> There is not a single piece of evidence against him. [...] It is all slander. [...] Indeed, the only accusation against the bishop was discredited by the judicial tribunal. [...] Osorno suffers? Yes... for being foolish![12]

Juan Carlos Cruz responded on Twitter on January 18, 2018:

> As if it was possible to take a selfie or a photo while Karadima abused me or others with Juan Barros standing next to him, watching everything. These people from above are crazy, and @Pontifex_es talks with victims about redress. We go on just the same, and his apology remains empty.[13]

The Pope insisted, "The day they bring me the evidence against them, I will see. The rest is slander,"[14] and he repeatedly asked the faithful in the Diocese of Osorno to welcome Bishop Barros.

Two days after his apostolic visit to Chile, Pope Francis heard Cardinal O'Malley's criticism of the Pope's call for evidence against Barros. O'Malley introduced an argument that the Church would soon make herself:

> The words, "If you cannot prove your accusations, then you will not be believed," make those who have suffered reprehensible

---

11. Redacción Aci Prensa, "*Cardenal Ezzati: Es grave que hayan engañado al Papa Francisco en caso Barros*," in *ACI Prensa* (April 19, 2018), *www.aciprensa.com/noticias/cardenal-ezzati-es-grave-que-hayan-enganado-al-papa-francisco-en-caso-barros-89984*; translation ours.

12. Cf. Platico cl, "*Papa Francisco se ha desenmascarado: Defensa de obispo Juan Barros*," in *YouTube* (October 3, 2015), *www.youtube.com/watch?v=HTTe06B_UMI*; translation ours. The original words in Spanish: "*No hay una sola prueba contra él [...] todo es una calumnia. [...] De hecho, la única acusación contra el obispo fue desacreditada por la Corte judicial [...] ¿Osorno sufre? Sí... ¡por tonta!*"

13. J.C. Cruz Chellew, personal Twitter account (January 18, 2018), *twitter.com/jccruzchellew/status/953992484140519424?ref_src=twsrc%5Etfw%7Ctwcamp%5Etwe etembed%7Ctwterm%5E953992484140519424%7Ctwgr%5E%7Ctwcon%5Es1_&ref_url=https%3A%2F%2Fwww.bbc.com%2Fmundo%2Fnoticias-42733493*; translation ours.

14. Cf. Redacción BBC: "*'Son todas calumnias': la polémica defensa del papa Francisco al obispo Juan Barros, acusado de encubrir abuso sexual de menores en Chile*," in *BBC Mundo* (January 18, 2018), *www.bbc.com/mundo/noticias-42733493*.

violations of their human dignity feel abandoned and relegate survivors to discredited exile.[15]

The Pope recognized his error of claiming evidence in that way and apologized to the victims. Twelve days later he sent Charles J. Scicluna—Archbishop of Malta and President of the College for the examination of appeals (in matters of *delicta graviora*) in the Ordinary Session of the Congregation for the Doctrine of the Faith—to Chile with the mission of "hearing those who (had) expressed a willingness to furnish basic information in their possession." The visit concluded with a report of sixty-four testimonies totaling more than 2300 pages [16] not only on the Barros case but evidently including it.

After reading the report, Pope Francis recognized his error:

> With regard to myself, I recognize, and I would like you to convey this faithfully, that I have made serious errors in the assessment and perception of the situation, in particular through the lack of reliable and balanced information. I now beg the forgiveness of all those whom I have offended.[17]

In the letter, the Pontiff requested to visit the Episcopal Conference of Chile to discern and reflect with them in order to remedy the difficult situation of the Church in the Andean nation.

THE BISHOPS' ACCOUNTABILITY

Evidently, in the process that led to the nomination of Barros as Bishop of Osorno either there were elements that were missing, or the opinion prevailed of those who persisted in denying their complicity with Fernando Karadima. For three years, the latter version of events found a privileged channel to reach Pope Francis, and this contributed, against the Pope's own will, to the worsening of the crisis that most affected the Church in Chile.

15. REDACCIÓN EFE, "*El cardenal O'Malley critica los comentarios del papa sobre el obispo chileno Barros,*" in *Agencia EFE* (January 21, 2018), *www.efe.com/efe/america/ sociedad/el-cardenal-o-malley-critica-los-comentarios-del-papa-sobre-obispo-chileno-barros/20000013-3498841*; translation ours.

16. S. RODRÍGUEZ, M.J. NAVARRETE, "*Scicluna asegura que su informe no será entregado a la fiscalía,*" in *La Tercera* (May 30, 2022), *www.latercera.com/nacional/noticia/scicluna-asegura-informe-no-sera-entregado-la-fiscalia/601429/*.

17. Pope FRANCIS, "Letter to the Bishops of Chile Following the Report of Archbishop Charles J. Scicluna," in *Vatican.va* (April 8, 2018), *www.vatican.va/content/francesco/ en/letters/2018/documents/papa-francesco_20180408_lettera-vescovi-cile.html*.

I saw it with my own eyes during Pope Francis's visit to Chile in 2008. There was no indifference there: There was indignation and anger at the systemic cover-up, at the silence, and at the deception of the faithful for the pain of the victims who for decades were neither heard nor believed.[18]

Despite the many communications of men and women of good will—lay faithful, priests, deacons, bishops, and the bishops' conference—the Pope thought he was acting according to justice, taking advice from people who were actually taking advantage of their closeness to him in order to manipulate him.

The mainly *upward* accountability in the Church (except in the financial sphere) is intended to protect the independent decision-making process of those in positions of authority, but at the same time it isolates them in their judgments and decisions and blocks the participation of the faithful in decision-making processes that concern everyone. On the other hand, while decisions made in secret are protected from the influence of public observation, they also "protect" leaders from accountability.[19] In fact, in the case we are looking at, the faithful's recurrent appeal to Church leaders has been that "they have done absolutely nothing in these three years to listen to God's people, much less the victims."[20]

As one can deduce from this case, any responsibility toward the people ("downward" accountability) would not have limited the authority of the Pope or the bishops but would have enriched it, helping them make decisions that would have effectively taken measures to remedy the problem of abuse and of cover-ups by superiors and bishops.

"Downward" accountability in the Church would foster a climate of trust that would have opened the way for those who hold power as a service to access information that, although potentially uncomfortable, would help them govern better. As

---

18. V. ALAZRAKI, "*Comunicazione: per tutte le persone*," Presentation in the *Meeting "The Protection of Minors in the Church"* (February 23, 2019), *www.vatican.va/resources/resources_alazraki-protezioneminori_20190223_it.html*; translation ours.

19. Cf. R. SHAW, *Nothing to Hide*, 69.

20. REDACCIÓN, "*Los laicos de Osorno escriben una dura carta a los obispos chilenos*," in *Alfa e Omega* (April 19, 2018), *www.alfayomega.es/149005/los-laicos-de-osorno-escriben-una-dura-carta-a-los-obispos-chilenos*; translation ours.

Monsignor Scicluna highlighted when he was speaking of the responsibility of the bishops: "A good steward will empower his community through information and formation."[21]

> Transparency, trust, and speaking truth to power are complexly interrelated ethical and organizational concepts. To create cultures that manifest those characteristics, leaders must do several practical things: provide equal access to information to all, refrain from punishing those who constructively demonstrate imperial nakedness, refrain from rewarding spurious loyalty, and empower and reward principled contrarians. But that is easier said than done, as recent experiences at the highest levels of government illustrate.[22]

Of course, it is not a matter of *unlimited accountability*, which would compromise the necessary independence of the decision-making process that ultimately falls within the competence of the one who has been placed as the shepherd of God's people. But we should indeed favor a system that is not exclusively *vertically ascending*.

> A view of accountability that limits it to the model of upward accountability only [...] takes for granted an ecclesiology according to which authority flows only downward... a "pyramidal view" of the Church.... At the base the faithful people play a passive role and seem to have a lower position in the Church.... Inasmuch as the Church is hierarchical and institutional, this view is at least partly correct; but to take it as the only and the *comprehensive* legitimate way of thinking of the Church is a mistake that breeds more mistakes.[23]

A system that is not only vertical ascending allows for greater participation, enriches those decisions, and purifies them of the toxic influences that exploit the secretive, one-way system for their own interests. It would also be a model of accountability that would better reflect the Church's identity (which is communion and hierarchy) in terms of service.

> If the case for openness and accountability in human affairs generally is a strong one, the case for living by these values in

---

21. C.J. Scicluna, "*Taking Responsibility for Processing Cases of Sexual Abuse Crisis and for Prevention of Abuse,*" Presentation in the Meeting "*The Protection of Minors in the Church*" (February 21, 2019), *www.vatican.va/resources/resources_mons-scicluna-protezioneminori_20190221_en.html.*

22. W. Bennis, D.P. Goleman, et al., *Transparency*, ch. 2.

23. R. Shaw, *Nothing to Hide*, 140–141.

the Catholic Church is even stronger. It lies in the fact that the Church is a *communio* — a unique divine-human community whose human members also are bonded to one another in and through their "membership" in Jesus Christ and the action of the Holy Spirit. In this *communio* all should be, and should act as mature, contributing members. All should know what they need to know for that to come about.[24]

Pope Francis himself, in asking forgiveness and acknowledging that he had committed "grave errors" due to a lack of "truthful and balanced information," was in a certain sense taking responsibility before God's people for why his actions were incorrect. This fact, while noteworthy as an act of humility, is also a demand for accountability on the part of those who, called to edify all, have committed an error. In any case, the error itself was inevitable, but the structure did not help.

This includes the dispositions of the Motu Proprio *Vos Estis Lux Mundi* on the need to open channels for listening and reporting. It is not an appeal for anonymous accusations but to break with the "enclosure of information," desired by those who think that "dirty laundry should be washed at home" (or in the *Curia*, as we would say in the case of the Church) and with a lack of downward accountability.

A recent case of accountability highlighted the following. The "Munich Report" on abuse cases in the diocese of Munich-Freising (1945–2019) accused Pope Benedict XVI of negligence during his tenure as Archbishop of Munich-Freising forty years ago. The main accusation of "covering up" the case of Peter Hullermann had been clarified with documents back in 2010. What brought attention back to the Pope Emeritus was an error in the eighty-two-page memo written by the law firm assisting the Pope Emeritus in defending himself against accusations revealed in the report. This memo denies Ratzinger's presence in the meeting about the acceptance of Hullermann. And Pope Benedict XVI publicly apologized for this oversight.[25] It was an

---

24. Ibid., 119.

25. Cf. R. Regoli, "Pope Benedict, Sex Abuse and the Catholic Church's Future," in *Wall Street Journal* (February 17, 2022), *www.wsj.com/articles/pope-benedict-xvi-sex-abuse-catholic-church-meeting-ratzinger-archbishop-munich-german-synodal-path-sauve-commission-hullerman-11645132639*.

error, not a lie. This mistake triggered a new media storm against Ratzinger, from which we only want to highlight two important elements regarding the accountability of the Church authorities: the assumption of downward responsibility (Pope Benedict XVI's public apology) and, on the other hand, the fact of the Pope Emeritus's legal defense through a law firm. As the historian Regoli pointed out in an interview, the latter aspect means that when faced with *accountability* one must respond not only with press conferences or speeches but also with teams of lawyers. A path of *accountability* is being set into motion that does not allow for backtracking.[26]

As in the economic sphere, and even more in other sectors of governance and administration, the lack of accountability toward the faithful, as in the Barros case, serves as a refuge for those who manipulate the authorities with errors, conceal their crimes, or simply act irresponsibly in their mission of governance. In fact, bishops who have covered up crimes of pederasty, even though by their episcopal dignity they were responsible only to the Roman Pontiff, were urged by him to be accountable to the justice system as well.[27]

Among the measures that would contribute to guaranteeing a greater "culture of care" in relation to minors, Bergoglio indicated the responsibility of those who have abused or have covered up abuse, independently of their ecclesiastical dignity:

> I am conscious of the effort and work being carried out in various parts of the world to come up with the necessary means to ensure the safety and protection of the integrity of children and of vulnerable adults, as well as implementing zero tolerance and ways of making all those who perpetrate or cover up these crimes accountable. We have delayed in applying these actions and sanctions that are so necessary, yet I am confident

26. Cf. J.M. Brocal, "¿*Cómo afectará al legado de Benedicto XVI su respuesta al informe de Munich?*," in *Rome Reports* (February 10, 2022), *www.romereports.com/2022/02/10/como-afectara-al-legado-de-benedicto-xvi-su-respuesta-al-informe-de-munich/*.

27. Cf. Redacción Aci Prensa, "*El Papa Francisco quiere que rindan cuentas todos los culpables de abusos, incluso obispos*," in *ACI Prensa* (August 20, 2018), *www.aciprensa.com/noticias/el-papa-francisco-quiere-que-rindan-cuentas-todos-los-culpables-de-abusos-incluso-obispos-47098*.

that they will help to guarantee a greater culture of care in the present and future.[28]

THE QUESTION OF THE LEGAL RESPONSIBILITY OF ORGANIZATIONS

The Church—like all bodies and individuals—assesses the most suitable way to assume responsibility for unjustly caused harm. Her credibility hangs in the balance. Baura points to *juridical responsibility* as the (free) capacity and the duty (the due act) to respond to a damaging situation that must be repaired because there was an underlying obligation.[29] This general principle was recognized by canon law:

> Whoever illegitimately inflicts damage upon someone by a juridic act or by any other act placed with malice or negligence is obliged to repair the damage inflicted.[30]

In the study of canon law, there is a rich discussion on the specificity of the cited canon, which we shall leave aside in order to focus on the element that has to do with our topic: accountability on the part of those governing the Church.

Zuanazzi argues that this materializes in the *personal accountability* of those who perform a function of governance in the Church, regarding the content and modalities, and within the scope of their own competence.[31] That is, the leading authorities will be different depending on whether they have *direct power* (their own or vicarious) or *delegated power*. However, beyond the principle of personal accountability according to one's competence, there is also *accountability of the juridical person* (or

---

28. Pope FRANCIS, *Letter to the People of God.*

29. Cf. E. BAURA, "*Il principio della colpa e la responsabilità oggetiva,*" in *La responsabilità giuridica degli enti ecclesiastici,* ed. E. BAURA and F. PUIG (Milan: Guiffrè, 2020), 79–80. There is a great deal of literature on this topic: F. D'OSTILIO, *La responsabilità per atto illecito della Pubblica Amministrazione nel diritto canonico* (Rome: Pontifical Lateran University, 1966); I. GORDON, "*La responsabilità dell'amministrazione pubblica ecclesiastica,*" in *Monitor Ecclesiastico* 98 (1973), 384–419; H. PREE, *La responsabilità giuridica dell'Amministrazione Ecclesiastica in La giustizia nell'attività amministrativa della Chiesa. Il contenzioso amministrativo,* ed. E. BAURA, J. CANOSA (Milan: Giuffrè, 2006).

30. CIC, can. 128.

31. Cf. I. ZUANAZZI, "*La responsabilità dell'Amministrazione Ecclesiastica,*" in *La responsabilità giuridica degli enti ecclesiastici,* ed. E. BAURA and F. PUIG (Milan: Guiffrè, 2020), 296.

entity), for what the entity actually does, and juridical situations pertaining to the patrimony of the entity.[32]

When we speak of accountability, we are thinking about compensation, which is why we always look to the top. As Otaduy explains, the relationship of subordination between the cleric and the bishop is not comparable to *professional* relationships in the secular realm. Canonical subordination has a twofold heading: the Sacrament of Holy Orders on one hand and, on the other, incardination to serve in a specific local Church.[33] His consecration demands a lifestyle consistent with the obligations of the clerical state (not of his private life). The second sphere that is most prominent in juridical responsibility is that of the exercise of his canonical office. This position is not a "job" but a *munus* (a received canonical office) in which he is directly responsible for his actions. "The bishop could be juridically responsible for the action of the priest by virtue of his *obligation to supervise*"[34] when this supervision is legally established.

In canon law, the bishop can never be culpable for acts done by the priest in the exercise of his office. It is not enough to inculpate the bishop that the person was "a priest" and "incardinated" in his diocese.[35] This is true in canon law, but it does not work in State systems (for example, in France), where the legal figure of the Church has no specific legal status and is equated with normal civil and religious organizations. In civil law, it will be undeniable to say that there is a *relationship of dependence* between the priest and the bishop. The same *simplification* happens in the sphere of communications: It is assumed that the superior has responsibilities with respect to the actions of the priest without considering the *atypical nature* of the priest's performance and of the relationship between bishop and priest.

One of the aspects of the aforementioned Sauvé Report is the request that the Church assume civil responsibility for sexual

---

32. Ibid., 303–304.

33. J. OTADUY, *Responsabilità civile degli enti dell'organizzazione ecclesiastica*, 405.

34. Ibid; translation ours.

35. Ibid., 405–406.

abuses committed by clerics in the period from 1950 to 2022. Recommendation No. 23 reads:

> Recognize, for the entire period analyzed by the Commission, the civil and social responsibility of the Church, irrespective of individual fault and the criminal and civil liability of the perpetrators of sexual violence and, as the case may be, Church officials.[36]

In other words, the Commission recommends that the Catholic Church in France assume juridical responsibility (including in terms of compensation) derived from penal offenses for a period of more than seventy years. This demand poses several problems.

First, it does not take into account the principle of *individual accountability* already mentioned in these pages. It should be added that penal responsibility is always personal and never institutional. Only individuals commit crimes. Second, the call to assume civil responsibility for crimes committed for over seventy years raises the issue of the *statute of limitations*. The "statute of limitations" refers to a time within which a crime can be prosecuted by law, beyond which society's interest in seeing it penalized lapses not least because it becomes difficult to reconstruct the truth of the facts. The principle of the statute of limitations is not a "legalized washing of hands"; rather, it is about a sign of civility present in all legal systems. Third, the Church is being called upon to assume institutional responsibility when it is well known that in France the Catholic Church has no legal personhood. Since the French Revolution, according to French law, the Church does not enjoy legal status as such (i.e., it does not legally exist). For these reasons, Recommendation No. 23 is inadequate and legally inconsistent.

In summary, regarding the juridical responsibility of the organizations, at the canonical level the cleric is autonomous when it comes to his private acts (he and he alone is personally liable). For conduct in the exercise of his office, the bishop or diocese can only be vicariously liable for fault (negligence) *in eligendo*

---

36. CIASE, *Final Report "Sexual Violence in the Catholic Church France 1950–2020,"* 39, *www.ciase.fr/medias/Ciase-Summary-of-the-Final-Report-5-october-2021.pdf.*

or *in vigilando* (e.g., for a crime of abuse).[37] As Otaduy says, the problems arise with the intermediate situations such as when the cleric commits an offense *on the occasion of ministry* or *taking advantage* of his priestly status, although the acts are not done at times, places, or instances of Church activity. In such cases the subsidiary responsibility of the hierarchical superior could be admitted if fault in selection or supervision were demonstrated.[38]

The *Code of Canon Law* provides for the removal of the bishop from office, with a sanction that tends to be perpetual. This removal is due to "grave causes"[39] such as the *negligence* of the bishop. In issues of governance as serious as those concerning the abuse of minors by clerics, canon law speaks of gross misconduct or negligence. A law promulgated by Pope Francis in 2016 aimed to establish the conditions for the removal from office of those whose actions have proven to be grossly negligent. In article 1 § 2, it describes the case in which the subject has "objectively lacking in a very grave manner the diligence that his pastoral office demands of him, even without serious moral fault on his part."[40] In this case, "objectively lacking" ought to mean that a negligent action attributable to the ecclesiastical authority in the performance of the pastoral office has been ascertained, from which certain damage has resulted. What is new is that from this lack of due diligence (negligence), the new law promulgated by Pope Francis includes the subsequent loss of the office, also initiating a proceeding.[41]

---

37. Cf. J. Ferrer Ortiz, "*La responsabilità civile della diocesi per gli atti dei suoi chierici,*" in *Ius Canonicum* 45 (2005), 576–577.

38. Cf. J. Otaduy, *Responsabilità civile degli enti dell'organizzazione ecclesiastica*, 407.

39. CIC, can. 193.

40. Cf. Pope Francis, Motu Proprio *As a Loving Mother*, in *AAS* 108 (2016), 715–717, *www.vatican.va/content/francesco/en/motu_proprio/documents/papa-francesco-motu-proprio_20160604_come-una-madre-amorevole.html.*

41. For an even deeper analysis, consult, F. Puig, "*I doveri di vigilanza dell'autorità ecclesiastica,*" in *La responsabilità giuridica degli enti ecclesiastici*, ed. E. Baura, F. Puig (Milan: Giuffrè, 2020), 345–352; F. Puig, "*La responsabilità giuridica dell'autorità ecclesiastica per negligenza in un deciso orientamento normativo,*" in *Ius Ecclesiæ* 28 (2016), 716–734.

THE OBLIGATION TO COMPENSATE AND TO REDRESS DAMAGE: BENEVOLENCE AND JUSTICE

As Otaduy and others argue, the canonical regime of account-ability and compensation for damages is practically nonexistent beyond the enunciation of the general principle[42] and some dispositions of the *Code* that concern particular situations. With this normative lacuna it is difficult to establish a dialogue with State systems.[43] One option to fill this silence and normative void may be to refer to civil law (in this matter).[44] Church law provides for the possibility of making the provisions of civil law its own.[45] However, as Otaduy warns, this option must be interpreted with caution, because...

> the civil regulations in force in most countries are difficult to reconcile with the reality of the Church and its law. [...] The na-ture of the *relations of dependence* in the secular sphere, public or private, and the criteria for transferring responsibility are far removed from the provisions of canon law on the *relationships of subordination* to the hierarchical superior.[46]

In this civil framework, the pastoral activity of the priests would be judged (erroneously) in the manner of professional relationships, that is, priests would appear to be "employees" of the Church.[47]

Finally, because of the cases of sexual abuse in the United States, the question has been raised as to whether the Vatican

---

42. Cf. CIC, can. 128.

43. J. Oταδυγ, *Responsabilità civile degli enti dell'organizzazione ecclesiastica*, 409; translation ours: "Nothing is expressly said in the canonical order, for example, on the various forms of accountability, either directly (for one's own acts) or indirectly (for the acts of others); whether the principle of fault without exception applies or whether cases of objective responsibility are admitted; whether under certain circumstances there might be a reversal of the burden of proof. [...] There are no explicit rules for imputing an act to the hierarchical superior, nor is the nature of the legal relationship of dependence between function holders specified, nor the types of damage that could generate legal liability, nor the means of redress."

44. In countries with an Anglo-Saxon tradition, civil responsibility is also used with a preventative and dissuasive function. In this respect, there are punitive damages for wanton and willful disregard and misconduct that are particularly intolerable. Cf. L.F. REGLERO CAMPOS, J.M. BUSTO LAGO (eds.), *Trattato sulla responsabilità civile* (Cizur Menor, Navarra: Thomson Reuters Aranzadi, 2014).

45. Cf. CIC, can. 1290.

46. J. Oταδυγ, *Responsabilità civile degli enti dell'organizzazione ecclesiastica*, 411; translation ours.

47. Cf. Ibid.

should answer to national courts for crimes committed in the countries of origin of the bishops, priests, and religious.

> It is argued that the Church is a hierarchical and centralized organization, which is why the superior of the bishops, priests, and religious would be the Pope, upon whom vicarious responsibility would be projected as the result of such crimes. As is easy to guess, the goal would be to reach the most conspicuous wealth—the deep pocket—in order to meet demands for multi-million-dollar figures.[48]

THE OBLIGATION OF SUPERVISION IN THE GOVERNANCE OF ECCLESIASTICAL AUTHORITY

Professor Puig expresses a question that is often repeated in cases of damages caused by ministers of the Church: "Where were the ecclesiastical authorities who were supposed to ensure that this did not happen?"[49] The request for explanation and redress is not only addressed to those who caused the harm but also to the institutional reality to which he belongs: his representatives and leaders.

The explicit mention of the term "vigilance" in canon law mainly concerns the general sphere of the vigilance of those who govern—especially the bishop and the ordinaries—over aspects of ecclesiastical discipline.[50] In this sense, the *function of vigilance* could be understood as something "inherent in the function of governance, which has as its general purpose the regulation of the social structure of the Church, as well as the condition and activity of the faithful in relation to the purpose of the Church."[51]

Returning to the general obligation of accountability, *negligence*[52] in *due supervision* is attributed to fault or malice as the main criteria of the attribution of accountability. In the normal order of things, the cause of failure in duties of vigilance is

---

48. Ibid., 414; translation ours.

49. F. Puig, *I doveri di vigilanza dell'autorità ecclesiastica*, 315; translation ours.

50. Cf. CIC, can. 392.

51. F. Fabene, "*Vigilanza (diritto e dovere di),*" in *Dizionario generale di Diritto canonico* VII, l, ed. A. Viana, J. Otaduy, J. Sedano (Pamplona: Istituto Balestruccio di Azpilcueta, 2012), 902; translation ours.

52. Cf. CIC, can. 1389 § 2: "A person who through culpable negligence illegitimately places or omits an act of ecclesiastical power, ministry, or function with harm to another is to be punished with a just penalty."

culpable negligence (not malice) understood as the lack of *due diligence*. Being negligent in the duty to be vigilant for harm caused by another cannot be done with malice, because in that case it would necessarily be *aiding in the crime*, not simple negligence. That is, the failure to be vigilant may be the failure to pay *attention* or the failure to *foresee* the event (where any diligent person could have foreseen it). When faced with a nonpositive event that "foreseeably will happen," the authority is required to activate specific means to prevent it.

> [Regarding the] available means of ecclesiastical authority to make vigilance effective, the simplest and most traditional answer might be the [pastoral and canonical] visitation and the *various forms of reporting*.[53]

It is advisable to add to the traditional forms of hierarchical vigilance, vertical and circumscribed in time and space, others that are more horizontal and collaborative such as identifying *potentially risky situations*.[54] As Puig explains, the hierarchical paradigm of responsibility points to the position of superiority in the functions of governance (e.g., the function of a metropolitan who is obliged to supervise the suffragan dioceses), while the horizontal one points to the control and verification of results, from positions of professional neutrality, or taking inspiration from parameters that tend to be objective or technical. "The horizon of canonical oversight could benefit from these trends, which are often linked to the need for accountability and transparency."[55]

Giraldina Boni argues that the faithful of the Church have a right to be *well governed*, hence the "instruments for reacting to the installation in ecclesiastical offices of persons who are unsuitable, lack the necessary qualities, or are inept."[56] The author does not stop at theoretical considerations; she goes into specifics:

> Because the right to good government is not relegated to mere enunciation of magnanimous intentions [...] it is therefore nec-

---

53. F. PUIG, *I doveri di vigilanza dell'autorità ecclesiastica*, 354; translation and emphasis ours.

54. Cf. Ibid.

55. Ibid., 355; translation ours.

56. G. BONI, *Il buon governo nella Chiesa: inidoneità agli uffici e denuncia dei fedeli* (Modena: Mucchi Editore, 2019), 17; translation ours.

essary to sound out the canonical order in detail in search of props to build with the chrism of juridicism and to configure in its identifying features a "popular legitimation," so to speak, to externalize the pathological situation of unsuitable people invested in ecclesiastical offices so that provision is made.[57]

She explores the normative paths to lay the foundation of this right and the possibility of juridical institutions with which to compare or assimilate.

AN ORGANIZATIONAL AND GOVERNANCE CULTURE OF SELF-ACCOUNTABILITY

In this area, it is clear that the Church's confrontation with secular rights is of primary importance. As Puig would suggest, following the structure of the harm prevention and compensation system, adapting the supervisory duties of Church bodies to meet civil standards of *victim protection* and *harm prevention*, would be a way of self-accountability.[58]

It is common for the system of vigilance in regard to harm prevention to be habitually delegated to the market than to the civil authority. Puig gives two examples: the *vigilance of the security of real estate* or, in certain cases, the *security of persons*.

> Where the insurance system for material damage is in force and reasonably accessible, the ecclesial agent must certainly have it; the authority's vigilance, in principle, should not go beyond the verification that this relative insurance relating to material damages exists.[59]

With regard to the *safety and integrity of persons*, Church authorities will rely on the action of law enforcement and will cooperate with civil judicial authorities.

The *culture of prevention* increasingly leads to requirements that institutions — legally — comply with organizational and management models that include measures of vigilance and checks to prevent crimes and reduce risks. This compliance with the law is not designed to prevent everything. This is about *preventing* objectively unlawful conduct and proactively calculating

---

57. Ibid., 112; translation ours.

58. Cf. F. Puig, *I doveri di vigilanza dell'autorità ecclesiastica*, 356.

59. Ibid., 357; translation ours.

risks in order to reduce eventualities (e.g., attacks on information systems for financial crimes, crimes against intellectual property, personal data, etc.). The institution is called to have an up-to-date map of risks and to take security and monitoring measures.

To this end, institutions adhere to the codes of conduct and best practices of sectors that provide parameters of diligence. This introduces the institution into an orbit of self-accountability and self-regulation, establishing its own levels of requirement, which are verified by certification entities through periodic audits. Good intentions in governance are not enough; we are asked to work better and with a purpose connected to the mission. The Pope wrote in this regard:

> The renewal of structures demanded by pastoral conversion can only be understood in this light: as part of an effort to make them more mission-oriented.[60]

---

60. Pope Francis, Apostolic Exhortation *Evangelii Gaudium*, no. 27.

CHAPTER 9

A CULTURAL TRANSFORMATION FOR THE CHURCH

The Church is a mystery in a theological sense,
but not a mystery in a secular sense—
at least it shouldn't be.
— Martin H. Work

Pope Saint Paul VI, citing the theologian Congar, stated that "we can make the program of an ongoing Church reform our own: *Ecclesia sempre reformanda.*" The Church is always in need of purification and conversion. And this is a process that must include the entire People of God, both pastors and lay faithful, and must encompass all the dimensions of ecclesial being, including law and communication.

It is not the search for something that is missing or extraneous but rather a purification with which the Church continuously conquers her own original image, expressed in her identity. In the field of communication, this "ongoing reform" is driven by events that have weakened the Church's credibility and that require cultural change.

This is not a matter of facing a vacuum of doctrine or legislation but rather of rereading the Magisterium and listening attentively to what recent history itself tells us. It has indicated paths and styles that, while quite coherent with the identity of the Church, continue to be blocked by the inertia of, "It has always been done this way." People find security in repetition, even if that *security* is often false because it is evident that certain ways of doing things no longer work.

As we have seen the previous examples, the abuse of secrecy, excessive transparency, and a sense of accountability that is exclusively "vertical and ascending" produce opposite effects of those we want to obtain. That is, those who abuse secrecy do so to hide a reality that they do not want known, but in this way they only manage to generate rumors, which then turn out to be gigantic and make people see amplified situations, with much more devastating effects. Those who abuse transparency, on the contrary, seek to make the whole of reality known as it is and, without meaning to, foster a simplified and deceptive communication — based on slogans — that actually distorts reality. Finally, when accountability is only exercised vertically, one seeks to protect the decision-making process and preserve the authority of those who govern but in fact exposes them to misinformation; manipulation to gain advantage; and, consequently, to committing governing errors that damage the authority when the intent was to protect it.

We intend to deal with this cultural transformation by first addressing the arguments from the juridical standpoint and then from the perspective of institutional communication.

At the Juridical System: New Concepts That Shake up the Canonical System

Concepts such as accountability, transparency, vulnerability, zero tolerance, risk prevention, and civil liability, which do not properly belong to the canon law *system*, have appeared in these pages. Some of these concepts are not juridical (including transparency, responsibility, or vulnerability) and come from different disciplines. Others, however, are: such as civil accountability, oversight, and risk prevention.

On one hand, the canonical system considers these principles to be elements extraneous to the system: not out of closure but because a system is a universe of meanings unto itself. A biological ecosystem (tropical, desert, etc.) has its own predetermined equilibrium that functions and makes sense in itself. In a certain way, canon law forms a determined and defined (juridical)[1] eco-

---

1. Prof. Joaquín Llobell liked to speak of the procedural ecosystem as a "harmonious and healthy consideration of the protection apparatus"; quoted in M. Del Pozzo, "*Il giusto processo e l'ecosistema processuale nel pensiero di Joaquín Llobell,*" in *Ius Ecclesiæ* 33, no. 1 (2022), 453; translation ours.

system. As Del Pozzo points out: "The ecosystem alludes precisely to care for the natural and organic habitat of cultivation."[2] Altering an ecosystem with extraneous elements is not always beneficial and positive. This is evident in nature: We have many negative examples, perhaps the most widespread and universal being that of climate change. The alteration of climate conditions is causing disequilibrium in many ecosystems.

On the other hand, juridical systems are already finished creations and have an important component of universality, in the sense of permanence and inalterability. At the same time, they are open because they can be completed, enriched, and updated. We will see this in a moment, when we speak of the juridical process, which is not an invention of the Church. It has taken various cues from other traditions, which have contributed to its uniqueness.

Accidental or transitory elements (like the principles mentioned above) can be stabilized over time and perpetuated. As Álvaro D'Ors said,

> The living are limited by the ancestors who respected those limits of a community's coexistence; that is why we say that *customs* are second *nature*. Since these customs that come from our ancestors are determined by different accidental factors, they can vary between different communities.[3]

Transparency, responsibility, and other terms generate the juridical debate—from the outside, we might say—as elements that are beyond the juridical ecosystem but highlight deficiencies and demands that are worth listening to and developing. In any case, it is a slow process, unlike the rhythm imposed by contemporary society.

Pope Francis has approved legal reforms in reference to economic issues, the fight against corruption in Church government, and the abuse of minors or vulnerable persons, which include terms and demands outside of the canonical legal tradition. On one hand, this poses problems of coherence and consistency, as shown by legal practitioners and experts, including Visioli. On the

---

2. Ibid., 454; translation ours.
3. Á. D'Ors, *Derecho y sentido común. Siete lecciones de derecho natural como límite del derecho positivo* (Madrid: Civitas, March 2001), 31–32; translation ours.

other hand, the assumption of these notions and standards in the Church's juridical texts generates certain expectations: In the civil sphere, in fact, when we read "transparency" or "accountability" in a canon law text, we associate them with the requirements of civil law (continental or common law), which is, moreover, the context from which these concepts come.

The collaboration and dialogue between canon law and secular orders is *also essential*, especially in certain areas. The cooperation in the fight against the abuse of minors and vulnerable persons is undoubtedly one of the best joint efforts that can be made (between legal systems). As we have already mentioned when dealing with the partial abolition of the pontifical secret (for certain cases), the main purpose of this measure was "to demolish the impediment of information" for certain types of conduct and in certain procedural instances. The main beneficiaries have been the victims, to whom the sentence can now be made known "without the institutional obstacle,"[4] as Scicluna has said. And, on the other hand, they favor cooperation and the fluidity of requests and exchanges of documentation (through international letters rogatory) with the authorities of other legal systems.

As Giuseppe della Torre explained, this measure approved by the Pope helps the Church move from a defensive attitude, almost one of distrust toward State systems, to one of trust and favoring a healthy collaboration:

> When the law of the State includes an obligation for those with the facts to report, the disappearance of the pontifical secret and the specification of its limits of secret of office quietly allow the implementation of what is prescribed by the law, thus fostering full collaboration with the civil authorities and avoiding illegitimate incursions by the civil authority into the canonical sphere.[5]

---

4. D. Verdú (interview by), "'La revoca del segreto pontificio non risolverà tutti i problemi, ma non ci sarà più l'ostacolo istituzionale,' Interview with Charles J. Scicluna," in El País (December 18, 2019); translation ours.

5. G. Della Torre, "Contributo sulla pubblicazione del Rescritto del Santo Padre Francesco sull'Istruzione Sulla riservatezza delle cause," in Vatican News (December 17, 2019); translation ours.

This sincere (not tactical) collaboration with the victims and secular systems will, in the long run, help to regain lost credibility.

Growth in respect and collaboration can continue to move toward a greater mutual listening. The canonical order, which has been the source of the secular order in many respects, has invaluable elements to contribute to important debates: elements such as privacy and the protection of personal information or the legal status of artificial intelligence. For her part, the Church can be open and take into consideration these requirements and standards (transparency, responsibility, risks, etc.). In weighing the legal consequences, she may choose not only to assimilate secular regulations but also to develop her own criteria and regulations.

However, cultural changes are not uniform or linear and cannot be completely controlled. We are currently in the midst of a process of cultural change driven by a technological revolution, which also concerns the Church. In this context, such terms are knocking on the door of canon law and, in some cases, have been allowed to enter or are even there now. Some think that this is creating unsustainable contradictions. The more pessimistic think that this may irreparably break the canon law ecosystem. Others, with a more skeptical view, think that these changes will not last and that the system itself will reject them in years to come. Finally, there are the more pragmatic ones: those who think that the Church must listen and incorporate these requirements (of transparency, responsibility, etc.) and integrate them into her system, even with its foundations. This requires stopping and understanding both the legal tradition and the foundations of the canonical system.

THE INQUISITORIAL AND ADVERSARIAL JURIDICAL TRADITIONS

Penal canon law, especially from the thirteenth century, has developed three models of proceedings: The *adversary system* began with a written complaint in which the plaintiff had the burden of proof. The prosecutor also had the burden of proof and, if he or she did not prove the accusations, the plaintiff was sentenced to the same punishment as the accused. The accused was the beneficiary of many safeguards.[6] The second model was the *inquisitorial system*, which left a great deal of *initiative* to judges to initiate cases and gather evidence. The accused maintained the same rights of defense as in the adversary system. As Arroba Conde explains, the proliferation of heresy and the need to act more quickly against lack of orthodoxy led to these due process guarantees being seen as an impediment to the administration of justice.[7] This led to the development of a variation of the inquisitorial model in which some of these rights to defense disappeared. Indeed, torture has become a legal means for discovering the truth. Even with this inversion of due process, *citatio* and *defensio* remained as procedural safeguards "under penalty of nullity of decisions."[8]

The inquisitory procedure confers many attributes and powers to the judge, who not only presides over the proceeding but plays a direct role promoting and taking initiatives: for example, investigating or collecting evidence—on his or her own initiative—to find out the truth.[9] In the adversary procedure, on the other hand, each side is responsible for conducting its own investigation. Each party determines the object of the dispute, presents materials for the knowledge of the facts, and cross-examines witnesses.[10] Each also has the power to prevent the judge from exceeding the limits placed on the dispute by the will of the two parties themselves.

These two principles, which distinguish between the role of the judge and that of the parties in the proceeding, are present in all legal traditions, both canonical and secular (whether continental or common law). They are two shared roots that become evident in different ways in different parts of the proceeding.

As has been said, the inquisitorial principle and the adversary principle meet in the canonical proceeding. Arroba distinguishes

---

6. Cf. M.J. Arroba Conde, *Giusto processo e peculiarità del processo canonico* (Canterano, Rome: Aracne, 2016), 17; translation ours.

7. Cf. Ibid., 18.

8. Ibid.; translation ours.

9. Cf. Encyclopedia Britannica, "Inquisitorial procedure," *www.britannica.com/topic/inquisitorial-procedure*.

10. Cf. Encyclopedia Britannica, "adversary procedure," *www.britannica.com/topic/adversary-procedure*.

between *initiative* and the *procedural impulse* and argues that, in the Church, the procedural push is inspired by the adversary model. Where a public good of the Church is at stake (as in penal cases), the law confers to the judge the inquisitorial power to promote the process and act *ex officio*.[11]

In turn, not all cases are equal, but a hierarchy of gravity is conferred (right, serious, or very serious); these differences "allow the judge to deviate from a certain solemnity provided by law in relation to the performance of each procedural act."[12] In the most serious cases, the judge may modify the form provided by the exercise of the rights of defense—for example, the judge may delay making the content of the complaint known to the accused. Although, in very serious cases, some of these guarantees of the defense are excluded; for example, the imposition of secrecy (nonpublication) of a procedural act.[13]

To understand the aforementioned, it may help to look at a specific example of the stage of the prior investigation. At this stage, explains Papale, the *accused* is in the dark about his position; and he will learn of the investigation into him if he is given precautionary or disciplinary measures by the Ordinary. For example, he could be removed from his office or residence; he could be ordered not to wear clerical garments; and he could, among other things, be barred from participating publicly in the Eucharist.

Thus, as the *Vademecum* points out,

During the investigative process, a particularly sensitive task ⸱ling to the Ordinary of Hierarch is to decide *if* and *when* to ⸱erson being accused.[14]

here is no uniform norm or criterion for decid-
⸱cretion—the prudence—of the official to
⸱v: the reputation of the parties, the risk
⸱ion, and the scandal to the faithful.
⸱re not punishments, even though

⸱uliarità del processo canonico, 152.

⸱ act that is *essential* for defending oneself.
⸱ THE FAITH, *Vademecum*, no. 52.

public opinion (as well as the subjective opinion of the accused) may perceive them as such. In these respects, the *manner* of proceeding is crucial. Along with prudent discernment by the Ordinary, the accuracy and formality of the law and care in communication are essential since law is cold and formal, and the relationships of communion in the Church call not only for justice but also for charity. Priests are summoned to meet in the chancery; sometimes, however, these restrictions are communicated directly by a telephone call.

As Montini pointed out, it is very difficult to reconcile the need to impose these *precautionary measures* with the *accused* person's right to a good reputation.[15] In addition to the likely damage to a priest's personal reputation, these restrictions—if they go on for a long time—can lead to great difficulties for his economic situation and livelihood.

Church law seeks justice and the truth of the facts, and as we have seen when speaking of the presumption of innocence, the Church protects the rights of the person, regardless of race, religion, or circumstances. However, she does not exactly follow the tradition of secular law, which is based on the mere protection of individual rights. The inquisitorial tradition is not "absolute" as regards individual rights. Within the unique juridical tradition of the Church, not only is the incriminated person or the victim protected, but the preservation of ecclesial communion is also considered, preventing scandal and protecting the *salus animarum* of the Mystical Body that is the Church.

At the Level of Communication: Secrecy Cannot Be a Common Practice

The *Boston Globe* case clarifies that secrecy contradicts fre expression, denies the faithful their right to know the tr seriously undermines the exercise of justice, inverts auth and weakens relationships in the Church, contradict essential principle of communion and distorting the

---

15. G.P. Montini, "*Provvedimenti cautelari urgenti nel caso di accus di ministri sacri. Nota sui canoni 1044 e 1722,*" in *Quaderni d* (1999), 191–204.

of its hierarchical organization. The abuse of secrecy in the Church was also revealed as a weapon of clerical manipulation, which prevents shared responsibility in the Church as well as accountability.

Excessive secrecy harms the Church's image in the eyes of the media and, through it, in the eyes of public opinion.[16] A Church that conceals and does not inform offers reasons and motivations to those who already have prejudices, and this fosters speculation and slander. We live in a world in which...

> someone hiding something is not necessarily corrupt, but all corrupt people are hiding something. Not everyone who keeps secrets is abusing power, but all abuses of power are typically hidden.[17]

And, unfortunately, the Church has been no exception.

Abuses of secrecy (as well as abuses of transparency) in the Church unfortunately diminish her prophetic capacity on key issues inherent to human dignity. This is true not only when it comes to issues related to bioethics and social justice but also for issues facing the journalistic and communication world itself. In a media environment often contaminated by fake news and by a press that frequently censors, decontextualizes, exaggerates, or silences the truth — and is mostly run by influential people from the political, economic, or ideological lobbies — the prophetic voice of the Magisterium of the Church becomes more necessary than ever. But what we are and do sometimes screeches so loudly in people's ears that it prevents what we say from being heard.[18]

On the other hand, the abuse of secrecy compromises information about the Church. When Church authorities refuse to give information to the media, the latter look for alternative sources

---

16. Cf. R. SHAW, *Nothing to Hide*, 94.

17. V. ALAZRAKI, "*Comunicazione: per tutte le persone,*" Report in the *Meeting "The Protection of Minors in the Church"* (February 23, 2019), *www.vatican.va/resources/resources_alazraki-protezioneminori_20190223_it.html*; translation ours.

18. "What you are screams so loudly in my years that I cannot hear what you are saying": This is a paraphrase of a phrase written by COVEY; quoted in Y. DE LA CIERVA, *La Chiesa casa di vetro,* 72.

that often do not reveal the truth of the facts with the accuracy of the original source — in this case, the Church.[19]

As often takes place with injustices, the abuse of secrecy generates "alienation, anger, rebellion, and a rejection of authority that go far beyond reasonable crticism."[20] A closely related consequence of this practice is the proliferation of rumors and half-truths, with their attendant half-lies, which in the long run damage trust and bonds between members and with institutions.[21]

Secrecy and confidentiality should protect only established juridical goods (for example, sacramental secrecy, secrecy in trial instruction, professional secrecy, as well as confidentiality that requires the organizational autonomy of the Church: archives, the conclave, the election of bishops, etc.), and therefore they have their place in the life and governance of the Church. However, the norm of common practice should not be secrecy[22] but openness, participation, and accountability, always in the manner proper to the Church. It must foster the flow of information in every sense,[23] showing with facts a Church communication that everyone is part of — through Baptism — and therefore participate coresponsibly, each with his or her specific mission.[24]

A TRANSFORMATION FROM WITHIN

When Cardinal Pell returned to Rome months after his release from prison, the *Program of Church Management* at the Pontifical University of Santa Croce in Rome invited him to give a presentation on the culture of transparency as part of its webinar series *Building a Transparent & Accountable Church*. Pell spoke

---

19. Both canon law and secular law contemplate the option for a judge to decree the secrecy of a proceeding. Transparency is important and necessary, but discretion is essential for the penal investigation to be such.

20. Cf. R. SHAW, *Nothing to Hide*, 32.

21. B. CLARIOND, *Comunicar y participar*, 189.

22. Cf. Pope St. JOHN PAUL II, *The Rapid Development*, no. 72.

23. Cf. PCCS, *Communio et Progressio*, 120.

24. Cf. B. CLARIOND, *Comunicar y participar*, 191.

about the need for a "cultural change for Church organizations,"[25] emphasizing that transparency is important but that it is found at the end of a list of values that precede it, such as honesty, professional competence (effectiveness), service, and a sense of community. For Pell, transparency is an important concept because it allows light to enter and satisfies the legitimate need to "know," but it is not the cornerstone. According to Cardinal Pell, this *cultural change* — as an organization — requires competent people in key positions who enforce clear policies because "grace does not exempt us from bad practices."[26]

González Alorda, an expert in organizational transformation procedures, came to the following conclusion after more than fifteen years of work in the field: "Transformation of a company is merely superficial unless a wave of personal transformations of the people in the organization is set in motion."[27] The qualities Pell talked about have a lot to do with *personal development*: the creation of habits and skills that directly relate to the tasks of a leader, such as thinking about and deciding on strategy, relationships with team members, and day-to-day managerial activities.[28]

This "wave of personal transformation" does not depend on enthusiasm or motivation: "Transformation requires a methodology"; it is not improvised. Alorda associates this personal development with a process of character growth, with the acquisition of new habits and skills, through the direction of a mentor who guides and gives feedback. This type of personal transformation *is painful* because it means accepting a challenge. The mentor corrects and suggests discipline and a concrete desire to excel in skills that one does not have. This growth is associated with personal talent, but it requires motivation.

In the area of motivations and goals, Professor Guillén shows how important the role of the Church is in proposing horizons

---

25. Cf. G. Pell, Presentation in PCM Program of Church Management, Webinar "Creating a Transparent Culture in the Catholic Church" (January 14, 2021), *www.youtube.com/watch?v=xEGEE4Po1Cs*.

26. Ibid.

27. Á. Gonzalez Alorda, "Transforming Organizations from Within," in *Inspiring Trust: Church Communications and Organizational Vulnerability*, ed. J. Pujol, J. Narbona, J.M. Díaz (Rome: EDUSC, 2021), 201.

28. Ibid., 203.

of personal fulfillment and happiness through the development of the highest desires (love of God and others). Along with other colleagues at Harvard, he developed a proposal that revolves around meaningful work, focusing on the highest human and spiritual ideals.[29] The set of personal virtues Pell mentioned, which precede transparency and accountability, cannot be taken for granted in the Church.

INCORPORATING THE PRACTICE OF ACCOUNTABILITY IN THE CHURCH AS AN EXPRESSION OF HER COMMUNION

In light of the *cultural change* Pell suggests and of what has been said about the Barros case, we see the necessity of incorporating responsibility in the internal culture of the Church: that is, openness to sharing information, evaluating, accepting criticism, and being accountable for the options chosen and the goals identified by the authority.[30] This change would open the door to shared responsibility, which would greatly enrich the governance decisions and would reinforce authority.

The underlying idea of *enriching* the "decision-making process" is the result of the experience of living a well-established collaborative spirit at work ("Together we go further," or, "Nobody is more intelligent than all of us together"). However, if we dig a little deeper, an undeniable advantage of accountability is that authority, in accounting for its decisions, is exposed to healthy confrontation. The bishop, though chosen by the mercy of God, is placed at the head of the people as shepherd — he acts as Christ-Head and has full power over the local Church entrusted to him. We add to that the fact that we are still influenced by a clerical culture in which the faithful and pastors have lived for a long time. Here it should not surprise us that the associates of the bishops often fall prey to a reverential fear, which ceases to be a

---

29. M. GUILLEN, "Regaining Trust: Three Key Players," in *Inspiring Trust: Church Communications and Organizational Vulnerability*, ed. J. PUJOL, J. NARBONA, J.M. DÍAZ (Rome: EDUSC, 2021), 217–231; *Motivation in Organizations: Searching for a Meaningful Work-Life Balance* (London–New York: Routledge, 2021).

30. L. GHISONI, *Communio: Agire insieme*, no. 3.6.

virtue when it leads them to withhold *uncomfortable* information from the bishop.

> A universal problem is that when staff speak to their leader, the very nature of the message tends to change. The message is likely to be spun, softened, and colored... if only to make the message more palatable and to make the messenger appear more valuable.[31]

When the leader gives an account of what he or she is doing and the information he or she is managing, it opens the door to new sources that can help that person tread more solid ground in order to take safer measures.

Accountability also allows the head of the organization to hear everyone and discover who are the *controllers* of information. This is a necessary measure because...

> whoever controls information does not have to convince but rather has absolute power over the subject matter. Therefore, not being *accountable* to anyone, he or she can freely cover up his or her own errors and misdeeds as well as those of colleagues [...] and friends, thus forming intolerable chains of favors.[32]

Similarly, accountability is a tool that helps guarantee that information held at intermediate levels of government is not blocked or used as power but flows to those who need it to make firm decisions.[33]

Another advantage of accountability is that it allows one to address errors frankly and to learn from them because accountability is also evaluation. In the face of organizational errors, there is a strong temptation to respond with a purely informational solution. If, rather, one has opted for a system of openness, participation, and accountability, then there will be no doubts about the fact that the first step in crisis management must be to address its causes for the benefit of the organization's public, and matters of information will only come after that.[34] Addressing and evaluating errors allows us to resolve them and learn from them,

---

31. W. Bennis, D.P. Goleman, et al., *Transparency*, ch.1.
32. Y. De la Cierva, *La Chiesa casa di vetro*, 213; translation ours.
33. W. Bennis, D.P. Goleman, et al., *Transparency*, ch.1.
34. Cf.Y. De la Cierva, *La Chiesa casa di vetro*, 100.

making the experience a treasure, which, if there is a healthy flow of information, will be passed on within the institution and can be exported to other dioceses or religious families, in the case of the Church, or even to other organizations to prevent repeat occurrences. What happened in *The Boston Globe* case was the exact opposite, and this had very unfortunate consequences.

A Church in which openness and shared responsibility are the norm, in which there is not a dearth of necessary information, is a Church that does not fear accountability and that knows how to live and make this practice a part of her culture, as an expression of her essence. It is not just a "practice of good governance" in response to the needs of Western societies.

The general attitude of secular nonprofit organizations, which are accountable also to their beneficiaries,[35] is exemplary: The Church, which is born from the mystery of the One and Triune God, has reasons to do much more.

The view of the Church as communion, as image of the Trinity, offers the key to understanding the various charisms and mysteries of the Church and gives dynamism and organicity to the participation of all the People of God:

> Lay people and those in consecrated life are not called to be mere executors of what the clergy commands since we are all servants of the one vineyard, in which each does his or her part with his or her own contribution, engaging him- or herself in the discernment that the Spirit imparts to the Church.[36]

A deeper experience of the communal character of the Church implies this shared responsibility, for which two-way information channels are necessary: going to the lay faithful and to the pastors, fostering greater mutual knowledge and thus fruitful dialogue.[37] This shared responsibility, which aims at the Christian

---

35. Downward accountability is exemplary in this. It refers to an organization's engagement with its beneficiaries as well, with how it builds relationships and accounts for how it conducts its business. Cf. M. Rey-Garcia, K. Liket, L.I. Álvarez-González, K. Maas, "Back to Basics: Revisiting the Relevance of Beneficiaries for Evaluation and Accountability in Nonprofits," in *Nonprofit Management and Leadership* 27, no. 4 (2017), 497.

36. L. Ghisoni, *Communio: Agire insieme*; translation ours.

37. Cf. Y. Congar, *Una Chiesa contestata* (Brescia: Queriniana, 1969), 98–99.

transformation of the world (even within the Church) makes the common good, that is, salvation, more visible.[38]

For his part, the charism of governance in the Church is the charism of the pastor; it has a strong missionary character, and the exercise of power is literally service. In this way, accountability cannot be extraneous to it; on the contrary, a pastor of the Church is confirmed by accountability in his mission to remain in the midst of the people as one who serves, as one who gives his life. The accountability of the superiors toward the subordinates, far from compromising the hierarchical structure of the Church, reinforces and purifies it, showing by its deeds its markedly evangelical character, reinforcing relationships of trust within the Church, and reinvigorating the authority of those who are at the head of the community.

Accountability understood from the truth of ecclesial communion prevents against prejudices and divisions within the Christian community whereby one may come to think that "only a bishop can know what is best for another bishop, or a priest for a priest, or a lay person for a lay person."[39] One of the lessons of the tragedy of sexual abuse and cover-ups is that since it is a problem in the Church, it must be addressed by the Church, which is all of us, together.

Being inspired by the mystery of the Church, the image of the Trinity—and taking it as a model of what we are called to live—enriches, strengthens, and guards against any type of division, unjust discrimination, or self-sufficiency, whether done by a group or an individual.

It would be an error to reduce accountability to the mere confession of errors. Even if authority fails and must account for its errors,

> This will not constitute a judgment from which to defend oneself for the purpose of regaining credit, a stain on one's honor, or a barrier to ordinary and immediate power. On the contrary, this will be the testimony of a journey made together, a testimony that only together can we find the discernment of a truth,

---

38. Cf. Ibid., 71.
39. Cf. L. GHISONI, *Communio: Agire insieme*; translation ours.

a justice, a charity. The logic of communion does not support an accusation and a defense but a challenge to the good of all. Accountability is therefore a form — even more necessary today — of this logic of communion.[40]

It is highly desirable that, just as happened with accountability in the economic sphere at the beginning of the Christian era, the accountability of ecclesial communion now become a paradigm that marks present and future history.

---

40. Cf. Ibid.

CHAPTER 10

TRANSLUCENCY: A STYLE OF ORGANIC COMMUNICATION TAILORED TO THE CHURCH

The Church in our time is striving more and more
to become a "glass house," transparent and credible.
And that is to be welcomed.
—Pope Saint John Paul II [1]

The communication of the Church, faithful to her identity, cannot follow the canons of transparency, but, as we said earlier, it must be organic. It must be an open communication, where the following have their rightful place: silence, accountability, secrecy, trust, the correct flow of information, modesty, and freedom of information. The image we propose to ensure this organic relationship is translucency.

Webster's Dictionary defines translucent (and translucence) as the quality of a body "[to permit] the passage of light" and not show objects clearly. Like frosted glass, "transmitting and diffusing light so that objects beyond cannot be seen clearly." [2] That is to say, it lets light through and opens the possibility of seeing, but it does not show everything automatically or by default.

Applied to communication, translucency allows the passage of light; that is, it favors openness and responsibility, but it prevents that "obscene nudity" which does not contemplate mystery. Translucency admits of degrees in the unveiling of truth,

---

1. Pope St. JOHN PAUL II, *Address to the Conference of Austrian Bishops* (June 21, 1998), no. 9.

2. *Webster's Third New International Dictionary of the English Language, Unabridged* (Springfield, MA: Merriam-Webster, 1993); continually updated as *Merriam-Webster Unabridged, unabridged.merriam-webster.com.*

so it does not offer an exact "problem-solving recipe," as does transparency.

Translucency offers no guarantees of success because neither during the decision-making process nor at the level of communication do we give up the effort to contextualize and discern. In any case, it will be necessary to find new and unique boundaries in order to assess the adequacy of information taking into account important elements such as human dignity, the common good, public interest, justice, etc.

Mauro Rivella speaks of a...

> communication *that leaves no room for shaded areas* and is not reticent about what happened, giving the impression of wanting to keep silent or cover up the facts.[3]

For this reason, "we cannot remain silent about our faults, no matter how much this causes suffering and may lend itself to further exploitation."[4] For the Church, the comparison with other social groups with more widespread criminal activity cannot be an excuse for not coming to terms with herself.

As Shaw argues, "More openness is not the total solution, but it is part of it."[5] Translucent communication implies a mindset of openness; it requires informing and accounting for one's actions, and it requires sharing responsibilities: This allows all members of the organization to be "participants." The Church must continue to discover the critical role of the baptized as active members. In the words of Vatican II, the laypeople are not only *collaborators* but also *coresponsible* members. Indeed, it is good to see how lay women and men share more responsibility in more areas. Pope Francis appealed to this in his letter following the publication of the Pennsylvania sex abuse investigation:

> It is impossible to think of a conversion of our activity as a Church that does not include the active participation of all the members of God's People.[6]

---

3. M. Rivella, "*Trasparenza nella Curia Romana,*" in *Trasparenza. Una sfida per la Chiesa,* ed. M. Merlini (Rome: Studium, 2020), 74; translation and emphasis ours.

4. Ibid., 75; translation ours.

5. R. Shaw, *Nothing to Hide,* 35.

6. Pope Francis, *Letter to the People of God.*

At the same time, translucency reminds us of those limits imposed by justice and prudence which must be respected. In his novel *The Circle*, Eggers promotes transparency in the absolute sense, where the guiding rule for individuals, communities, and organizations is that of living in full *transparency* in order to achieve perfect societies and governments. However, utopia is recognized by its results: It promises too much but offers too little. A world without privacy would be inhumane.

Translucency is an attitude that preserved the human ecosystem, which requires a certain level of secrecy and mystery in order to be healthy. Translucency, and not absolute transparency, preserves the value and beauty of secrecy, which is revealed in the organic dynamics of friendship:

> Of course, this is the proper mark of friendship: that one reveal his secrets to his friend. For, since charity unites affections and makes, as it were, one heart of two, one seems not to have dismissed from his heart that which he reveals to a friend.[7]

The human soul needs space to be alone with itself, without a spotlight or media scrutiny. Moreover, not everyone needs to know *everything all the time*: In addition to being impossible, there are things that concern some people and not others.

First of all, it is worthwhile to distinguish a private life from related concepts, such as intimacy. *Private* has multiple meanings; we can reduce it to mainly two: (a) coinciding with confidential or reserved, that is, something that is done in front of few people, in a familial or domestic way, and (b) the opposite of public, belonging to a singular person, an individual (private property, private correspondence, etc.).[8] Etymologically, *Intimacy — intus, intumus, intimus —* refers to that which is most internal, to psychological intimacy and the intimacy of conscience, to the deepest interiority of the human being.[9] Thus, "Nobody is required to reveal what

---

7. St. Thomas Aquinas, *Summa Contra Gentiles*, Book IV, trans. Charles J. O'Neill, ch. 21, *genius.com/St-thomas-aquinas-summa-contra-gentiles-book-iv-annotated*.

8. Cf. N. González Gaitano, *El deber de respeto a la intimidad* (Pamplona: EUNSA, 1990), 16–42.

9. For a deeper linguistic analysis, cf. Ibid., 17–29.

his or her interlocutor does not have a right to know. A consequence of the right to intimacy is the *ability to have secrets.*"[10]

Intimacy is something sacred, and thus one can communicate something intimate by imposing the obligation of not revealing it to anybody. In the Church, this obligation is of great importance: We see it primarily in sacramental secrecy but also in secrecy relating to spiritual direction.

Countries with an Anglo-Saxon tradition do not distinguish between *private life* and *intimacy*; the term *privacy*[11] captures both aspects. Although the word *intimacy* exists, it is usually used in another sense. Privacy is the normal term to encompass both meanings (confidential and intimate). Only physical persons can have intimacy; legal persons and institutions cannot: They enjoy "private life" figuratively speaking, by extension.[12] Intimacy resides in the core of the human person, in the heart. When we talk about the privacy of party X, we are speaking metaphorically to refer to what is known the least and usually remains hidden from public view.

This respect for the human being, a kind of *holy fear*, is the condition for the presumption of innocence, a right that translucency does not ignore. Translucent communication does not coerce, require, or furnish information that should not be given either because of its nature or because the time is not right to do so. In a communicative environment in which this concept of translucency is applied, authentic human relationships are cultivated because in respect for each person's privacy, one gives and receives without violence: The bonds of trust are strengthened, and this favors a greater and healthy openness. The translucent model of communication ensures that necessary information goes

---

10. E. BAURA, *Accompagnamento e formazione: diritti e doveri dei fedeli*, Lecture delivered at the XLV Study *Accompagnare, Discernere, Integrare: Profili e Prospettive Giuridico-Ecclesiali*, organized by the Associazione Canonistica Italiana: GRUPPO ITALIANO DOCENTI DI DIRITTO CANONICO [Italian Canon Law Society: Canon Law Teachers, Italian Group] (Borca di Cadore, Belluno, Italy, July 3, 2018), *www.youtube.com/watch?v=Va4cBLcCFoY*; translation and emphasis ours.

11. A "right to privacy" is mentioned for the first time in 1890 in the now famous article by the lawyers Warren and Brandeis: Warren was a lawyer who was tired of being pursued by the local press after he married a woman from a wealthy Boston family.

12. Cf. N. GONZÁLEZ GAITANO, *El deber de respeto a la intimidad*, 23–25.

in all directions, albeit according to its natural and appropriate course.

While transparency—with its demand to dominate everything—fosters aggression, translucency fosters respectful listening, which implies welcoming silence. In this way the dialogue is enriched. As Monsignor Ocáriz said in a communications lecture on dialogue and respect:

> Those who respect others, the reality of things, and the essence of the profession become more "respectable" and better interlocutors in public debates. Seeking to understand others, to comprehend their perspectives, one discovers specific aspects that one had not considered, refines one's proposals, and ultimately makes oneself more "understandable." If instead the work of communication ignores the other person's questions or misgivings, then monologue replaces dialogue.[13]

In the "society of translucence," those who fear the light (of truth and justice) are self-excluded and hide in the opacity of the abuse of secrecy or in the hypocrisy of absolute transparency, where everything is on display. As the German philosopher Han says, absolute transparency (which disregards modesty and respect), becomes "pornographic."[14] Translucency, on the other hand, requires a certain "prudential censorship" that, far from limiting, exalts the good, the beautiful, the just, and the true; with appropriate restraint in interpersonal dialogue, "Man can freely search for the truth, express his opinion and publish it."[15]

A society in which everything can be shown leaves no room for modesty. Modesty is the guardian of the person's mystery and intimacy: of that unexplored and captivating world that is hidden behind the pure gaze, the innocent smile, and the dignified dress. Modesty reinforces otherness in the relationship. Its purpose is not to hide but to preserve: It does not allow the immediate exposition of transparency; instead, it predisposes one to the revelation of mystery, which remains a mystery and

---

13. F. Ocáriz, "*Saluto finale di chiusura del XI Seminario Professionale sugli Uffici di Comunicazione della Chiesa: Dialogo, rispetto e libertà di espressione nella sfera pubblica*," ed. J. Pujol, C. Mendoza, in *Catholic Church and the Public Sphere* (Rome: EDUSC, 2018), 148; translation ours.

14. Cf. B-C. Han, *La sociedad de la transparencia*, 51; translation ours.

15. Cf. Vatican Council II, *Gaudium et Spes*, no. 59, ch. II.

is not possessed, much less instrumentalized. Modesty guards self-giving. It conserves, and it grows respect for oneself and for others; modesty serves love.

Unlimited transparency, with its overexposure, seeks to eliminate the person's original mystery; it seeks his or her total unveiling. This leads to the "logic of appropriation."[16] "A view that reveals what is hidden — which evidently goes beyond the mere exposure of body parts and the objectivization that this provokes — and what must remain hidden would undermine the very foundation of existence; it would mean the end of the human being's humanity, of what distinguishes him or her from other living beings."[17]

While boundless transparency, with overexposure, shows people as a desecrated and obscene commodity, reducing their value to "being exposed,"[18] the function of modesty is to "hide the image to protect the self."[19] The communication of the Church in the service of human dignity and the common good must be a strong ally of modesty and, in this sense, will have to find ways to internalize what is good in greater openness and responsibility, which is in line with the supernatural ends of the Church without being confused with what are only fleeting sociocultural trends — in our case study, the society of unlimited transparency.

Translucent communication is positive and may be the best solution because, as we have already said, it opts for the light[20] and moves away from ferocious and bloody media circuses, even if it must for this reason pay the price of not bending to models

---

16. Sexual abuse occurs in the pretense of unlimited transparency. The abuser instrumentalizes the victim and reduces the latter to the object of his or her pleasure, removing the mystery of the victim's otherness, his or her value, and thus violates his or her most basic rights. Cf. A. Cencini, *È cambiato qualcosa nella Chiesa dopo gli scandali sessuali? Analisi e proposte di formazione* (Salamanca: Ediciones Sígueme, 2016), 110–111; translation ours.

17. M. Selz, *Modestia* (Salamanca: Ediciones Sígueme, 2018), 113–114; translation ours.

18. Cf. B-C. Han, *La sociedad de la trasparencia*, 50–51; translation ours.

19. M. Selz, *Modestia*, 114; translation ours.

20. Pope St. John Paul II, *Message for the 18th World Communications Day* (June 3, 1984), *www.vatican.va/content/john-paul-ii/en/messages/communications/documents/hf_jp-ii_mes_24051984_world-communications-day.html*, no. 4: "Do not corrupt society, and in particular youth, by the approving and insistent depiction of evil, of violence, of moral abjection, carrying out a work of ideological manipulation, sowing discord!"

of *transparency*. This was the image that Pope Francis used when Philip Pullella of *Reuters* asked him if he was running into resistance to his reforms in the Curia, and the Pope responded that there was some, as in society:

> There are saints in the Curia. And there are some who are not so saintly, and these are the ones you tend to hear about. You know that one tree falling makes more noise than a whole forest growing."[21]

The organic model of translucency reflects the Church much more than one of exclusive poles of transparency-secrecy. This model promotes the truth of the Church that is mystery, that exists to communicate, and that is communion; it better presents her evangelical understanding of her Magisterium, her hierarchical authority, the richness of her Tradition, her commitment to truth and charity, and the distinctive way she defines effectiveness.

The Church is by her structure and mission a communion of believers and not a *political democracy*, a nongovernmental organization, or a *nonprofit*, so borrowing notions from political science, management, or economics has limitations. This, however, cannot become an excuse for not adopting requisites and practices of good governance that can be critical to church life. In this sense, the Church, as the "People of God" and the "Body of Christ" (Vatican II definitions), is called to be a model in the public sphere.[22]

For the Church to be correctly understood, she must therefore be viewed — internally and externally — as a communion of believers (baptized lay people and ordained members) with spiritual *ends* (the salvation of souls), which is present in the public *sphere* through many activities and institutions, and which is *governed by the professional standards consistent with her structure and mission*. That is why the Church has particular elements that

---

21. Pope Francis, *Press Conference during the Return Flight from Rio de Janeiro on the Occasion of the XXVIII World Youth Day* (July 28, 2013), *www.vatican.va/content/francesco/en/speeches/2013/july/documents/papa-francesco_20130728_gmg-conferenza-stampa.html*.

22. R. Shaw, *Nothing to Hide*, 9.

should guide her in how to internalize the culture of transparency and responsibility, making this synthesis her own:

a) The Church acts in the public sphere, but because of her structure and mission, she is not a political community, but rather a spiritual community.

b) Social projection is inseparably linked to her spiritual character.

c) The Church was organized around specific values received from Divine Revelation.

d) On the practical and prudential level, the Church is not a democratic society but a hierarchy. The leaders assume their position of ministry out of service and should not be motivated by political or economic interests.

e) Her mission is not to profit but to follow the apostolic spiritual mandate.

A final consideration about translucency leads us to reflect on the *prophetic dimension* of communication in the Church. Both the abuse of secrecy and presumed absolute transparency deprive the Church of her prophetic capacity. On the contrary, an organic and translucent communication in the Church is a communication that is always original and dynamic and, by building a dialogue on the mystery of the Church and from the human person, it leaves the way open for prophetic communication.

The Church of Christ should not be an institution that is closed in on itself in an indolent abuse of secrecy; however, it also cannot be an institution that is only concerned with pandering to the ups and downs of history and then, since transparency is now fashionable, irresponsibly becoming transparent.

The Church, the People of God, is always on the move; mystery that she is, she can be renewed only by *being more herself*. Only in this way can she discover herself open to being challenged by the signs of the times and can give the world a prophetic message that saves.[23]

> If the Church wants to renew herself, if she wants to adapt to the demands of our times, then she must first develop a full image of herself; she must know herself thoroughly.[24]

In this open, respectful, and fruitful dialogue, it will be possible to discern and discover a timeless truth: "There is [...] a time to keep silence, and a time to speak."[25]

But in this dialogue, it will be important for the Church to really listen. The commitment to this transformation must be serious...

> Even though the questions they ask are "sometimes embarrassing or disappointing, especially when they in no way correspond to the message we have to get across."[26]

Recalling that "these disconcerting questions are often asked by most of our contemporaries,"[27] Pope Saint John Paul II concluded:

> For the Church to speak credibly to people today, those who speak for her have to give credible, truthful answers to these seemingly awkward questions.[28]

THE WAY OF "CEASELESS COMMUNION"

We have tried in different ways to explain how the communication of the Church requires an organic model that goes beyond transparency. Translucency is the (imperfect) metaphor we have found to convey what we mean: Translucency has in

---

23. R. BLÁZQUEZ, *La Chiesa*, 110–111; translation ours: "The Church, which seeks to carry out her mission, must first deepen her self-awareness to define herself with greater clarity, and second, she must renew herself, returning to the origins of her identity. For only by conforming to her original model will she be able to adequately distinguish herself from the world and, at the same time, dialogue with it in an amicable and proactive way (evangelizing)."

24. K. WOJTYŁA, *Il rinnovamento della Chiesa e del mondo. Riflessioni sul Concilio Vaticano II* (Madrid: LAC, 2016), 286; our tranlation.

25. Eccl 2:7.

26. PCCS, *Ethics in Communications*, no. 26; quoting PONTIFICAL COUNCIL FOR CULTURE, *Towards a Pastoral Approach to Culture* (May 23, 1999), no. 34.

27. PONTIFICAL COUNCIL FOR CULTURE, *Towards a Pastoral Approach to Culture* (May 23, 1999), no. 34, *www.vatican.va/content/dam/wss/roman_curia/pontifical_councils/cultr/documents/rc_pc_pc-cultr_doc_03061999_pastoral_en.html*.

28. PCCS, *Ethics in Communications*, no. 26.

common with transparency the *capacity to transmit light*. It does so in a different, thoughtful way, according to the identity of the Church. Now, the starting point is openness and communication. Translucent communication is very well suited to the concept of ceaseless *communication*, which we presented in Chapter 5.

In a context of widespread disinformation (fake news, deep-fakes, floods of information) "ceaseless communication" carries out the mission of making sources about the Church's teachings available so that texts are readily available to users who want to verify sources.[29]

In our view, the Church can be categorized as a *high-reliability organization* (HRO)[30] that operates in high-risk contexts. Sanders describes the guiding principles of these types of organizations that revolve around *reliability* with an emphasis on how they communicate. See how in these types of organizations characterized by *complexity* in a world of *risk*, trust depends largely on their type of communication.[31] The risk environment and the culture of security are the ecosystem in which these organizations operate.

The experts summarize the characteristics of HROs into five points:[32] (a) preoccupation with failure, (b) reluctance to simplify, (c) sensitivity to operations, (d) commitment to resilience, and (e) deference to experience.

Sanders organizes and incapsulates them in four principles, which can serve as inspiration for the translucent communication

---

29. Cf. M. Mosconi, "*Comunicazione ecclesiale e vigilanza canonica nel contesto degli attuali strumenti di comunicazione sociale,*" in *Quaderni di diritto ecclesiale* 31, no. 1 (2018), 84.

30. The initials HRO can correspond both to "high-reliability organizations" and to "high-risk organizations"; Professor Sanders uses them interchangeably. In the context of "the Catholic Church," it is more appropriate to say "reliability," as is explained in these pages. Cf. K. Sanders, "*Communicating Effectively in High-Risk Organizations: Learning from High Reliability Organizations,*" in *Inspiring Trust, Church Communications and Organizational Vulnerability,* ed. J. Pujol, J. Narbona, J.M. Díaz (Rome: EDUSC, 2021).

31. Cf. Ibid., 57.

32. Cf. K.E. Weick, K.M. Sutcliffe, *Managing the Unexpected: Resilient Performance in an Age of Uncertainty* (San Francisco: Jossey-Bass, February 2007); K.E. Weick, K.M. Sutcliffe, *Managing the Unexpected: Sustained Performance in a Complex World* (Hoboken, NJ: John Wiley & Sons, 2015); C. Lekka, "*High Reliability Organisations: A Review of the Literature,*" in *Health and Safety Executive*, Report Review 899 (2011).

we propose for the Church: (a) mindful leadership, (b) just culture, (c) problem anticipation, and (d) containment of unexpected events.[33]

When Professor Sanders speaks of "mindful leadership," she is referring to a proactive leadership style that listens and is on the ground, fostering cooperation and seeking collaboration. One can say that this management style involves being somewhat *on the lookout* for "bad news" because there is an interest in always knowing what is going on.[34] It is a style that fits perfectly with the policies imposed by Pope Francis, who calls for "active listening" to victims, requires people to "report abuse" (even those working in the Curia), and presses for the "opening of reporting channels" on potential cases of abuse in the dioceses and constituencies of the Church. In turn, this *style of governance* ties into Sanders's second principle: a just culture.

The "just culture," unlike the guilt culture or the shame culture, seeks not only to identify the person responsible but also, primarily, to understand the cause of the problem. It is about deeply understanding why what is happening is happening, making the principles of the HRO our own (sensitivity to failure and to error and rejection of simplification).[35]

The Catholic Church, in various ways, has shown that she is seriously committed to justice and to getting at the truth of cases of abuse. She is not content with diagnoses but seeks to deeply understand the phenomenon in different cultures and parts of the world. There are still cracks in the prevention system, and management errors continue to occur, but that is not synonymous with total failure. For an HRO like the Church, the most important thing is to continue to listen to reality to look for causes and thus to be able to refine the remedies and measures to be taken. In an organization of around 1.5 billion members spread throughout the world, crises will take many forms and will have many different causal factors.

---

33. Cf. K. SANDERS, *Communicating Effectively in High-Risk Organizations*, 58.
34. Cf. Ibid., 59–60.
35. Cf. Ibid., 60.

After his visit to Chile, Pope Francis began spending hours listening to abuse victims and realized that the bishops lacked awareness and understanding of the problem. On this occasion he convened the Meeting on the Protection of Minors in the Church, calling the presidents of the bishops' conferences from around the world to Rome with the aim of increasing their awareness about this issue. In fact, he asked them to listen to the victims themselves before traveling to Rome in February 2019. In an organization that listens, measures are constant and never definitive because reality is not static.

Regarding errors committed by the organization's personnel, HROs make a threefold distinction: (1) examining human error caused by *deficient processes* or lack of *training*; (2) errors resulting from *at-risk* behavior in which things are done that should not be, albeit with the best of *intentions*; and (3) *reckless behavior* that must be punished.[36] This threefold distinction also sheds light on the useful strategy for assessing and addressing prevention and crisis in the Church.

The last two principles Sanders distinguishes (problem anticipation and containment of unexpected events) are understood in the context of the above: They foster an open and translucent organizational culture that lives with error and failure on a daily basis and, in the face of error and mishaps, does not generate *fear* but encourages *improvement*. The Church, carried on by sinners (from the Roman Pontiff to the last Christian to reach the age of reason), should take this fallibility of her members into account without idealizing anyone. As Sanders points out,

> An organizational culture that suggests that everything is wonderful and "world-beating" can be conducive to a complacency inimical to a high reliability culture which seeks to know and be alert to what's going wrong and why it is going wrong.[37]

As has been relentlessly repeated throughout these pages, bidirectional communication, both vertical and horizontal, is fundamental. This is compatible with the hierarchical principle of the Church. Starting from this hierarchical structure, processes

---

36. Cf. Ibid., 61–62.
37. Ibid., 62.

will have to be created to promote channels of communication and to avoid erroneous models of the exercise of authority such as the clericalism or elitism that we have denounced so much.

Indeed, this is a key point in the HRO proposal on which the Church could stand to greatly improve:

> When things are detected, that are not working well, [in the HRO] there is a reluctance to simplify and a commitment to look at the real causes and the real reasons for why events unfolded as they did.[38]

Sometimes one might think of these organizations as...

> very hierarchical, rigidly and centrally run bodies burdened with endless controls, trying to ensure that nothing goes wrong. However, in high reliability organizations there is a combination of central control and great local agility.[39]

This *agility* depends on the sensibility of those who govern. Church leaders are those who *effectively* promote this "organizational culture." Sanders states that this type of leadership "is vital for high reliability organizations because without it, risk increases."[40] And she gives examples of behaviors by leaders that have seriously damaged their organizations: mediocrity, complacency, blame, not listening, etc. In *scrutinizing* candidates for the episcopacy, good preparation and honesty cannot be taken for granted.

We referred to Pope Francis's various words of encouragement and to the motivations of Cardinal Pell in order to embrace this cultural transformation in the Church based on openness and responsibility.

This is therefore our proposal: We need an organic form of communication based on translucence, that is, openness, shared responsibility, ceaseless communication, and the maintenance of due confidentiality, starting from the identity of the Church and from her mission, assuming and sharing commitments, being accountable for decisions and mistakes, creating communion.

---

38. Ibid., 62.
39. Ibid.
40. Ibid., 63.

As illustrated throughout this book, our proposal moves along three coordinate axes: communication, theology, and law. These three disciplines work together to define the boundaries of transparency and secrecy. In these pages we speak a lot about communication and the Magisterium of the Church. Many authors before us have closely analyzed the link between these two realities, but now we will focus on another binomial, which we have already presented in this study but will now make more explicit since it is certainly a new nuance with respect to previous works on the institutional communication of the Church.

Communications and the Law Must Work Together

In view of the current technological context and the problems facing the Church in terms of transparency and responsibility in different areas (sexual abuse, problems linked to finances or mismanagement of the Church government), we believe that the communications department of the Church (of a diocese or an ecclesiastical institution) must develop a certain *juridical mindset* in its work and decision-making procedures in order to be effective. This awareness requires training in conformity with legal requirements, building a bridge between civil law and canon law in these critical areas.

Considering the complexity of the public sphere and the wide dissemination of information due to the Internet, the Church's communication style must *also* take into account legal aspects in order to be successful. This communication implies respect for victims, protection of the personal information of the faithful, and respect for copyright laws. This legal sensitivity feeds the reputation and authority of the Church in the public sphere.

Because law and communications are distinct specializations, they often operate completely disconnected from one another, achieving disconnected solutions. We believe that this lack of collaboration is a great challenge for internal communication at the organizational level. "Communications without a juridical mindset" often leads to a set of cosmetic solutions that may seem successful in the short term but whose superficiality will soon damage the institutional reputation. On the other hand, "legal action without communications" easily forgets the whole, sometimes to the detriment of the institutional identity, for example, prioritizing compensation or litigation over demonstrating sensitivity and neighborliness. Legal action on its own struggles to account for other important aspects such as institutional apologies, willingness to talk, and interest in healing.

In many human spheres, change does not happen automatically or spontaneously, without taking any action. In familial education, people (whether children or parents) do not see the necessity of changing their attitudes until they go through a major setback or disaster. In organizations, sometimes there is no openness to seeing or acknowledging a problem until a concrete problem or crisis occurs. Therefore, crises and hard times can be the catalysts that build momentum for institutional and personal transformation.

The juridical mindset and the magisterial tradition of the Church can foster communications by thinking in the *long term*. That is, they help overcome the temptation of popularity, or of results at any cost, which often prevail in the field of communications. She can resist being dazzled by technological innovations. Toni Segarra, a well-respected advertising professional in Spain and the rest of Europe, in a social context in which spectacle and the most obscene transparency prevail, highlights two qualities of the Church: "thinking long-term," and "preserving the mystery," "the inexplicable,""the elusive,"[41] the sacred.

The "mystery of the sacred" is different from "the mystery of secrecy." In the first case it promotes translucency because it has that characteristic of transmitting light, albeit in a particular, not absolutely transparent, way. This is the characteristic of the mystery of the *Church*, in the deepest and most positive sense of the term.

Toni Segarra himself, in his speech as Doctor "Honoris Causa" of Nebrija University (Madrid, Spain), praised communications and in particular the advertising profession, and among other things recalled the passage of the priest and writer Pablo D'Ors,

---

41. A. Segarra, *Desde el otro lado del escaparate* (Madrid: Espasa, 2009).

when he criticized this drift toward fear and the simplicity of darkness:

> There is no literature on light. We are enamored with evil. It is useful to know the shadows, obviously, but not to be trapped in or latched onto them. It is harder to see the light than it is to see the darkness; seeing the light requires training.[42]

This *formation* comes from the creativity of communication and from a certain connaturality with hope that is the fruit of a lived faith.

Therefore, this organic model that we propose must include the juridical mindset necessary for communications not to become a sham.

THE LAW IS A PRACTICAL SCIENCE, JUST LIKE COMMUNICATIONS

Law and the legal system are not the same thing. For Roman jurists, law was a practical science: the science of justice and injustice, keeping in mind that the origin of "justice" was not legal norms but something preceding them. The classical understanding of justice is that of "giving to each the right that corresponds to him or her." This classical understanding of justice is very practical and realistic, open to all human beings of good will.[43]

The law is a practical science, and *common sense* is the practical philosophy of jurists. As D'Ors says: Common sense is "the simplicity of one's common individual reasoning."[44] *Common sense*, like the natural practical reason that everyone possesses, leads us to see with simplicity what must be done.

Thus, developing a *juridical mindset* does not mean to simply teach mere legality but to learn to think legally beyond the legal sphere, seeking truth and justice (what is due to each person) through this organic mindset. It is also important to learn to see the legal implications behind the designs and photographs

---

42. A. SEGARRA, *Discurso doctor honoris causa por la Universidad de Nebrija* [Madrid] (September 24, 2021), *forbes.es/nombre-del-dia/118069/hombre-del-dia-toni-segarra-doctor-honoris-causa-por-la-universidad-de-nebrija/*; translation ours.

43. Cf. J. HERVADA, *Cos'è il Diritto* (Rome: EDUSC, 2013), 27–29.

44. A. D'ORS, *Derecho y sentido común*, 29; translation ours.

that are used, the messages that one intends to convey, and the communicative relationships that one intends to establish.

This way of reasoning and dealing with reality leads to the design of new strategies (newsletters, social media campaigns, etc.), taking into account respect for personal information and the copyright of the music and photos used. In this way, communications and the law are present—equally—from the beginning. This is a mindset that leads to tackling challenges by seeing communications not as a "trick," and having a legal mindset not to find *legal validations* but to cultivate an organic strategy.

Finally, at the time this book was about to go to press, studies in media consumption in the United States and in various European countries show that in 2022 the Internet is already ahead of television in terms of hours consumed. This fact is not trivial and has implications that should give us food for thought. On one hand, the context of this translucent communication no longer distinguishes between analog and digital; we live and relate to each other with remote or face-to-face messages indistinctly. On the other hand, the models of information creation and consumption as well as the models of free time are changing. Platforms like Instagram, Twitteer, TikTok, YouTube, and Patreon generate huge audiences with high levels of loyalty. Stories no longer have a journalist as narrator.

Successful amateur content creators—or "influencers," depending on how one wants to view them—with a good smartphone and good ideas produce pieces that, due to their emotional and experiential content, reach a massive audience, much greater than that of television. The impact of this change of language has a decisive influence on the Church's ways of communicating and listening. The institutional communications of the Church must continue to devote attention to understanding this evolution[45] in order to effectively structure this ceaseless communication.

---

45. Cf. G. TRIDENTE, B. MASTROIANNI (eds.), *La missione digitale. Comunicazione della Chiesa e social media* (Rome: EDUSC, 2016).

CHAPTER 11

FIFTEEN IDEAS
FOR TRANSLUCENT
COMMUNICATION

APPLICATIONS OF IDEAS
FROM THE MAGISTERIUM

1. Rediscover the Magisterium of the Church
in Terms of Openness, Transparency, and Responsibility.

Study and better highlight the richness of the Magisterium of the Church when it comes to communication, especially in relation to ecclesiology, social doctrine, and anthropology. When the Church does something, speaks, or is silent, she reflects what she is and what she has received: the truth revealed by God himself. The Church is not "late" in her Magisterium on these matters but has often kept her knowledge on paper—in *writing* or *declarations*. The great challenge as communicators is to put it fully into practice.

2. Openness as the Standard for Communication and
Bidirectional Channels of Information:
Criteria for Effectiveness.

Prioritize openness, shared responsibility, and information, both internally and externally. Keep in mind that not everyone should know everything. The general criterion for the circulation of information is the "need to know" according to the responsibility that is exercised.

Openness means that internal communication is fluid and the members of the institution have access to the information that is useful and appropriate for them; it also means that journalists find Church doors to information open. Save for exceptional cases (e.g., when an item of news needs to be given at a certain time / context) the Church should communicate freely, without special impediments.

Since 2001, the Church has invited her leaders and members to...

> use the Internet as a *tool of internal communications*. This requires keeping clearly in view its special character as a direct, immediate, interactive, and participatory medium.[1]

3. Implement Accountability Processes for Church Leaders, Not as a Witch Hunt But as an Expression of the Communion of the Church.

The Church is a Body that we are all members of: she is communion. Downward accountability is an essential aspect of her identity. Far from weakening the Church — for example, by undermining the authority of bishops and superiors — this attitude strengthens her because it protects her from countless dangers such as misinformation by leaders, manipulation of information, and decisions that affect everyone. Moreover, it curbs corruption in general and leaves the door open to contributions that help in the pursuit of the institution's objectives.

Accountability is a good that should not be subject to each person's good will and free interpretation, but when exercised in the manner of the Church, it must be incorporated as an effective tool that confirms her identity and mission.

4. Promote and Protect Some Endangered "Nontransparent" Principles: Confidentiality, Silence, Modesty, Respect, and Mystery.

There are values, anchored in the Gospel, that the society of *transparency* rejects but that are nevertheless important and worth conserving: confidentiality, silence, modesty, respect, and mystery. It is necessary to present them as values that, if put into practice, make life more humane and the world more habitable. It is important to reintroduce them because they manifest the

---

1. PCCS, *The Church and Internet*, no. 6 (February 22, 2002), *www.vatican.va/roman_ curia/pontifical_councils/pccs/documents/rc_pc_pccs_doc_20020228_church-internet_ en.html*; emphasis ours.

truth of the human person and are therefore part of the Church's evangelical preaching and institutional communication.

These elements should not be presented as "antagonistic" to openness, informing, freedom of expression, and *accountability* but rather as complementary: highlighting the importance of all these aspects in a positive communication that reflects and promotes human dignity and the common good.

5. Overcome a Defensive Attitude Toward the Media.

We need to overcome a defensive attitude in the face of just criticisms from the press and cultivate a positive and amicable rapport with communicators and journalists. A deeper understanding of the Magisterium of the Church will help bishops and superiors *conquer their fear* of the media and achieve a pastoral closeness that, from the standpoint of evangelization, is also strategic.

> It requires that Church leaders and pastoral workers respond willingly and prudently to media when requested, while seeking to establish relationships of mutual confidence and respect, based on fundamental common values, with those who are not of our faith.[2]

APPLICATIONS OF IDEAS FROM LAW

6. The Right to Information in the Church (Transparency and Accountability).

The right to information *about* the Church on the part of the faithful and the general public has not yet been formalized in the Church. This *juridical* vacuum is, in fact, partially filled by communication, which establishes *criteria* for the release of information: who and what should be known or not known. However, the general principles should be juridical and magisterial.

Unlike public entities, a private organization should be accountable primarily to its members. It is required to report to the public only in cases of legitimate public interest. The Catholic Church is a private institution with about 1.5 billion members;

---

2. PCCS, *Ætatis Novæ*, no. 8.

therefore, even if she is not formally a *public* entity, she can be considered one. That is why the attitude should be one of openness.

7. In the Fight Against Abuse, the Victims Are the Starting Point, and Bishops and Superiors Must Be Well Aware of the Current Legal Framework.

Abuse can be sexual; there may also be abuse of power or abuse of conscience. In all cases, the victims are the starting point and the Church's main concern.

It is necessary to open channels of active listening, which allow for the reporting of abuse in conformity with canonical legislation and the recommendations of the bishops' conference itself. A team consisting of men and women who are specialists (in law, psychology, and communication) should be created in order to guarantee empathy and to safeguard the parties' privacy and presumption of innocence.

The bishops and superiors must be aware and must apply the Church's current juridical framework regarding sexual abuse. However, in addition to prosecuting them criminally and having an effective organization for handling and following up on such complaints, there is a need to collectively take responsibility. This does not mean repeatedly declaring in the public eye that we are "sinners" but having an organic prevention strategy. This involves creating safe spaces in multiple dimensions: legal, psychological and medical, communicative, educational, and formative. One must also think about a spiritual itinerary of conversion.[3]

---

3. J. Bertomeu, "*Hacia una espiritualidad de la prevención,*" in *Ecclesia* 4036 (June 13, 2020), 7; translation ours: "Instead of actions and strategies, only a *prevention itinerary* that recovers the project of the Kingdom Proposed by Jesus and conversion toward Him will make it possible to repair what has been broken and to guarantee to the victims that their suffering will not be in vain. This itinerary passes through individual and synodical discernment of the inconsistencies themselves and of the persevering presence of a God who is not silent in the face of abuses, whatever they may be. It passes through the focusing of our gaze on the mystery of evil and the mystery of God. It also passes through the prophetic critique of those dynamics and those processes that promote a culture of abuse, uncritically assuming power relationships that are too asymmetrical, that do not seek the good of the other but rather a selfish self-interest."

8. The Administration of Justice Is Not a Matter of Harshness or Magnanimity: Attention to Unlimited Transparency and Zero Tolerance as Slogans.

In the Church's style of governance there is no opposition between *caritas pastoralis* and *rigor iuris*. Correcting those who make mistakes and avoiding harm to the community is an essential part of the office of governance in the Church.

The bishop and the hierarchical superior must know and apply the laws of the Church as a guarantee to avoid arbitrariness. In turn, the law of the Church has a threefold purpose of seeking redress for the scandal, the reestablishment of justice, and the repentance of the offender.

9. A Juridical Mindset Is Essential for Cultural Change: Communications and Law Must Work Together.

Developing a juridical mindset does not mean teaching mere legality but learning to think legally beyond the legal world, seeking truth and justice (what *is due* to each person) through this responsible and organic mindset.

In the field of communications, this way of thinking and approaching reality leads to designing strategies (newsletters, social media campaigns, etc.) taking into account respect for personal information, copyright of the photos and music used, etc. Thus, communications and law are present—equally—from the beginning.

10. Vigilance, Diligence, and Risk Prevention: Virtues of Good Governance.

Legal responsibility can be personal (of the one exercising the function), or of the legal person (in some cases). The attribution of liability is determined by malice or fault, and it signals a lack of due diligence, that is, punishable negligence.

The function of vigilance is part of the office of governance. There are some areas where the bishop has an obligation of vigilance. *To be vigilant* means to pay attention (check), to anticipate (monitor), and to prevent risks.

In the Church there is no general obligation of accountability (only in some specific areas, like economics). Now, Pope Francis, after discovering the case of the cover-up in Chile, pointed to *downward* accountability as a measure of good governance and also prevention. As Scicluna says, "A good steward will empower his community through information and formation."[4]

Applications of Ideas from Communication

11. Implement Ceaseless and Organic Communication.

The path of ceaseless communication suggests taking the informational initiative, starting from the presupposition that the Church is one of the high-reliability organizations. There are many eyes on her, and the contexts in which she lives are high risk.

We need to overcome the mechanism that views as opposing realities what should actually be held together organically. When it comes to communication, silence and communication are not in opposition but refer to each other. Communication without silence is noise: It is false and harmful. Silence is a dimension of truth that must be communicated. The flood of data and information, in fact, does not imply that we will be better informed; on the contrary, it often causes us to lose perspective and sensibility.

Silence, on the other hand, is not healthy when it excludes communication.

12. Start from Within: Internal Channels of Communication.

Define the internal channels of communication (official and informal) and relevant information that each one must know and to which everyone is called to participate. Keeping these channels and streams running is an ongoing task. This internal culture generates cohesion and prevents crises.

---

4. C.J. Scicluna, *Taking Responsibility for Processing Cases of Sexual Abuse Crisis and for Prevention of Abuse.*

Communion and *synodality* will be empty talk or eternally pending tasks if communication in the various ecclesial organizations is not renewed *from within*.

13. Relationship with the Media: From Enemies to Allies.

Maintaining quality relationships with journalists is necessary because:

a) They and their audiences are people with dignity, whom we can serve and from whom we have much to learn.

b) In the Church, stories of common people are constantly arising that deserve to be told because what these stories show is something our world needs to know.

c) Journalists deserve to find a welcoming Church that is interested in the truth. A Church that respects them and facilitates them in their work and makes relevant content available... and assists them spiritually when they ask.

d) We need not wait for a crisis to create good relationships with the media, if for no other reason than "using" journalists, even for the "good of the Church," is immoral and therefore not very evangelical.

14. Good Communications Requires Formation and Resources: A Requirement for Current and Future Leaders (in Seminaries and Novitiates).

If the Church exists to communicate, she must form good *communicators* who carry out their task in a clear, simple, and deep way, showing as relevant — for today's men and women — the truth of the Gospel. This is an art that cannot be improvised.

"Organic communication" means *cultural change*, in which it is normal to exchange ideas, to foster channels of information, to be accountable for one's actions, and to respect the realm of silence, confidentiality, and reservation.

This transformation requires a significant investment of time, talent, and treasure (see Appendix II).

15. Designing a Program of Positive and Professional Communications: Concrete Measures.

Positive, proactive, and professional communications is fully coherent with the identity of the Catholic Church. It is *positive* because it does not compete to be impactful but to build. In this sense it is proactive because in that enthusiasm, it seeks, discovers stories, and communicates them. It is not a "defensive" communication: It takes the initiative to inform, aware that it is serving the truth and responding to the public's legitimate right to know. It respects journalists but is not afraid of them.

Now, if the ideal of positive and professional communications does not land on a series of concrete measures, it runs the risk of remaining an abstract desire. We must begin by developing a *communications plan* (see Appendix I) in a professional way, that is, by *allocating* human and material resources (see Appendix II). These concrete measures will not work as foolproof recipes, but they will be the result of dynamic and constant work.

APPENDIX I

COMMUNICATION PLANNING: A BASIC SKETCH [1]

A.

Above all, it is essential to begin with an understanding and in-depth study of the institution itself: its identity, who its specific target audience is, what its needs and interests are, and the best channels or means to access these audiences.

A key aspect for Church communicators is to create and maintain open channels of feedback with the target audiences. They should not be satisfied with just knowing them but should aim to be very much in a personal relationship with them. This relationship and the knowledge that comes with it are vital to communication.

To be professional in communication, the first thing to do is not to buy devices but to know the institution itself very well, in our case the Church and the Gospel, and to know our audience well: that is, to know what we need to communicate and to ask ourselves how and why.

B.

Secondly, we must think that the work of communication should be planned. One cannot do everything at once, even though there is the temptation to succumb to impulsivity or personal preferences.

The plan must be concrete and realizable in order to have a specific date of execution and to be assessable. We must establish general and specific objectives for the short, medium, and long

---

1. Cf. J.M. La Porte, *Introduzione alla Comunicazione Istituzionale della Chiesa.*

term and then establish performance benchmarks. Planning is very useful and nonrigid schedules can be a good tool.

C.

There comes the time to do what was planned, and it is the moment to be methodical and consistent with the defined plan. At the same time, this phase requires the *"flexibility of* landing," that is, the capacity to adapt to the specific terrain. It is a critical moment but extremely valuable for getting to know the public and our previous work better, based on the impact that it can have.

In the implementation phase, it is important not to get discouraged in the face of obstacles because, through setbacks and failures, we can learn and grow a lot individually and as a group. Trying again is the only thing that will make us experts.

D.

Evaluation is extremely important: Evaluate "without mincing words," seeking as much objectivity as possible. Avoid oversatisfaction and even hyper-criticism to ensure that what emerges from the evaluation can be translated into concrete action, into correction... in short, into growth. SWOT (strength, weakness, opportunity, and threat) analyses can be particularly useful for this phase.

The four points just listed do not occur in a succession of stages, where when one ends you begin with the next; they occur simultaneously. They are dimensions of a single, planned, and professional communication process. If one of these dimensions were missing, the entire communication would suffer: It would lose impact; it would cease to be professional; it would be "less communication." Of course, planning is not enough to be professional, but it is nevertheless fundamental to the communication process. These four dimensions apply to a communication plan in general but also to in-house communication planning, or to communication planning focused on specific channels such as digital communication plans, etc.

APPENDIX II

PROFESSIONAL COMMUNICATION REQUIRES AN INVESTMENT OF RESOURCES

A.

First of all, quality time is needed because communication cannot be improvised. It is not enough for one person (busy with many other things), to devote — like an amateur or hobbyist — snatches of time to update a Web page, send newsletters, respond to messages, and manage social media accounts.

B.

To communicate well, one needs a team, as we have already said: No one is smarter than an "us working together," and if the Church is a nucleus and a synod, then this — along with many other things — means that "we are very much a team."

A communications team that wants to work will have a thousand tasks with no set schedule because neither stories, nor events, and even less crises simply arise during work hours. This profession's relationship with time is always distressing. On the one hand, communication, like "death," is very unpredictable, and on the other, it has a great deal of work that must be done while "fighting the clock."

Teamwork requires specialization and complementarity. Budgetary shortages lead the communicator to be as well-rounded a figure as possible: He or she must have technological knowledge, audiovisual editing skills, the ability to write, the gift of synthesis, etc. It is good that there are technicians in some areas, but budget limitations will always exist; it does no good to complain about this.

C.

Communication requires training and talent. Communication is a practical science, but innate talent requires study, it requires science — to be capable and serious, to be reliable, to be hard-working, and to challenge people. It is not enough to be motivated and to have "good will"; one needs to hone one's skills and prepare.

Not everything is helpful. "Yes-men" can do particular damage in the field of communication. Discovering and valuing people with talent for communication and entrusting them with the communication of the Church, giving them a seat in meetings where decisions are made, and listening to their opinion will all have very positive effects on the mission of the Church. There is nothing more frustrating and sterile than a leader (bishop or superior) who thinks he knows communication, when in fact he does not, or one who is not open to being advised (because he already knows everything).

D.

Resources: Good communication costs money. This is a principle that not everyone understands. It is worth investing in it so that the world may know the truth and the beauty of the Gospel. Also, because in that field — as in others — the game is played with "the children of darkness," who are not normally known for mediocrity nor an inability to arouse interest.

The Church has always invested resources and talent in communication: Think of the painters, sculptors, architects, poets, and musicians of all eras... think of the Constantinian basilicas, the Byzantine Hagia Sophia, or the Sagrada Familia in Barcelona... think of the genius of the great sculptors and painters, such as Da Vinci, Michelangelo, Caravaggio, Chagall... or think of the illustrious *maestri* of music: Händel, Bach, Beethoven, Verdi. There was no lack of greats in literature and poetry, from St. Augustine and Dante to C. S. Lewis and Tolkien... or in film, theatre, or photography. The list would be endless!

"In order to communicate the message entrusted to her by Christ, the Church needs art."[1] What was the Baroque style if not a great communication operation, following the Protestant Reformation, that flooded culture in every sense with a great visual and musical catechesis? Investing in lawyers and insurance but not in communication reveals a short-sighted view.

The Church still needs the art and creativity of the written and spoken word, of the technologies of communication, to arouse amazement at the mystery of man and God and at the wonders of nature.[2] From this amazement comes the communication of enthusiasm and hope, which is why Dostoevsky claimed that "beauty would save the world."[3]

Lack of communication damages and empties the Churches: People leave tired of a Church that seems to have nothing relevant to say.

In the information society, not communicating is like not existing.

---

1. Pope St. JOHN PAUL II, *Letter to Artists*, no. 12 (April 4, 1999), *www.vatican.va/content/ john-paul-ii/en/letters/1999/documents/hf_jp-ii_let_23041999_artists.html*.

2. Cf. R. VAN BÜHREN, "Caravaggio's 'Seven Works of Mercy' in Naples: The Relevance of Art History to Cultural Journalism," in *Church, Communication & Culture* 2, no. 1 (2017), 64; explored extensively in a special issue: R. VAN BÜHREN, S. DE ASCANIIS, L. CANTONI, "Special Issue on Tourism, Religious Identity and Cultural Heritage," in *Church, Communication & Culture* 3:3 (2018), 195–418.

3. F. DOSTOEVSKY, *The Idiot*, trans. Eva MARTIN, (June 21, 2021), ch. 5, *www.gutenberg.org/ files/2638/2638-h/2638-h.htm*.

AFTERWORD

RESEARCH AND COMMUNICATION OF THE TRUTH ARE AT THE FOUNDATIONS OF JUSTICE

by Charles J. Scicluna

The timeliness and immediacy of digital communication pushes the Church to move toward a more proactive way of communicating, aware that she must accompany, dialogue with, and be close to the faithful. The right to information has shifted gears with the digital age. Concepts such as transparency, accountability, access to information, and a two-way relationship between the faithful and Church authorities are cultural milestones on which there is no going back.

As Pujol and Montes de Oca show, these changes introduce new demands; they call for greater accountability in terms of transparency and accountability, and they challenge legal aspects of the canonical system, especially in the area of child sexual abuse by Church ministers. However, this is not merely a media issue; it is not merely a matter of coming to terms with public opinion: We are faced with a new call—that of confronting truth and justice in a deeper sense.

The search for truth, not only from the formal standpoint but also, above all, from the material standpoint, is the first task of every juridical order, which translates the aim of making truth radiate (*veritatis splendor*) both in legislating (*splendor legis*) and in carrying out justice (*splendor iustitiæ*). The recent reforms of the canonical penal system—which aim to address the tragedy of sexual abuse committed by priests and negligence on the part of the authorities—are part of this desire for truth and justice within the Church. The Church, in her prophetic mission, is aware that "respect for the truth engenders confidence in the role of the law, while disrespect for the truth engenders distrust and suspicion."[1]

1. A Proactive Attitude of "Seeking the Truth"

The reform of Book VI of the *Code of Canon Law*, proposed by Pope Francis following a long period of discernment at different ecclesial levels and made public with the Apostolic Constitution *Pascite Gregem Dei* of May 23, 2021, is an expression of the Church's determined will as a community to discern in reasonableness and goodness. It is a sign that she intends to provide herself with an effective norm to punish the most serious behaviors against communion, in particular, those that we know are *delicta graviora contra mores* or *contra sextum præceptum Decalogi cum minore*. Norm, community, discernment, and consent would be the four elements necessary for any true *receptio legis*.[2]

The effective and affective reception of this ecclesial penal law, *ordinario rationis* (rule of reason) endowed with *rationabilitas* (reasonableness) and obedience to the ethos of the Gospel, is also expressed in a set of other norms and, above all, in ecclesial consensus. For this reason, the aforementioned reform would not be understood in its proper scope without knowing the previous legislative reforms and without taking note of the benevolent reception by the People of God.

In particular, the Apostolic Letter in the form of Motu Proprio *Vos Estis Lux Mundi* (VELM), dated May 7, 2019, stands out. It imposed a set of obligations for a rigorous, serious, and speedy investigation that would allow for an eventual penal trial. The entire ecclesial community understood that it is impossible to bring justice to victims without promptly reporting any abuse or neglect to ecclesiastical authorities.

---

1. C.J. Scicluna, "*La ricerca della verità nei casi di abuso sessuale: un dovere morale e legale*," in *Verso la Guarigione e il Rinnovamento*, ed. C.J. Scicluna, H. Zollner, D.J. Ayotte (Bologna: EDB, 2012), 89; translation ours.

2. Cf. M.C. Ruscazio, "*Considerazioni sulla receptio legis alla luce del Motu Proprio Mitis iudex Dominus Iesus*," in *Stato e Chiese* 9 (2018), *www.statoechiese.it/images/uploads/articoli_pdf/Ruscazio.M_Considerazioni.pdf?pdf=considerazioni-sulla-receptio-legis-alla-luce-del-m.p.-mitis-iudex-dominus*.

The good *receptio legis* of the new aforementioned criminal legislation noted in the previous months also shows Pope Francis's ability of discernment in interpreting, in the light of God and of a true synodal experience, the needs of our Church already immersed in the twenty-first century: a Church that until recently has been too corporativist and even self-referential, afraid of the scandal that such cases could have aroused, and full of shame and denial. Today we are witnessing the birth of an ecclesial community that is more aware of the need to listen with dignity and respect to all, but especially to the victims, and to share their suffering.

On the other hand, we see a Church that is committed to guaranteeing fair trials on the most elementary principles of defense, impartiality and legality, with an attitude of awakening and greater timeliness both in initiating the investigation and in completing it (*iustitia delata, iustitia negata*).

In my opinion, it would be necessary to establish *præter legem* an agent for victims under article 5 of VELM, maintaining pastoral contact with them and, crucially, informing the complainants of what is happening throughout the process.[3] In this way, we follow the line established by the Holy Father, who on December 6, 2019, promulgated a *Rescriptum ex Audientia SS.mi* on the confidentiality of cases to abolish the pontifical secret in three procedural instances (accusation, trials, and decision) for cases of sexual abuse, following *Vos Estis Lux Mundi* and article 6 of the *Normæ de Gravioribus Delictis* reserved to the Congregation for the Doctrine of the Faith. Communication with those concerned about the progress of the canonical criminal process, without precluding the principle of the presumption of innocence of the accused, especially when the complainant is the presumed victim, should no longer be a difficulty due to the rather formalist interpretation of an acerbic juridical-canonical system.

---

3. Cf. C.J. Scicluna, "The Rights of Victims in Canonical Penal Processes," in *Periodica* 109 (2020), 500.

2. Positive Attitude: Being "Collaborators with the Truth"

The obligation to inform the ordinary or the religious superior does not eliminate the possible obligation to report to the civil authorities if that is established by one's civil order. In this regard, article 19 of VELM establishes for the first time the Church's obligation to submit and collaborate with the competent civil authorities, transforming into a legal obligation what until now was only a moral obligation.[4]

The Church has thus imposed on herself a high standard of respect and collaboration with State authorities and laws, accepting many of the recommendations of the Royal Commission of Australia, the John Jay Rapport, etc., because she is aware that she wants to move in the same direction as society regarding the safeguarding and protection of minors and vulnerable persons.

Not only do these measures solidify the idea that there is an obligation to collaborate with the various institutions of society and therefore with the media as cultural mediators, but the Church also expresses the will to combine the right of citizens and of the faithful to truthful information with the right to privacy and the protection of good reputations. Considering the latter as a nonabsolute right will allow for better protection of privacy in the Church as well as an easier procedure, distinguishing true accusations from calumnies, insinuations, rumors, and defamations.

As I have reiterated on other occasions, the Church does not like it when "justice becomes a spectacle." The legislation on sexual abuse was never intended as a prohibition against reporting to civil authorities but as a foundation for a rigorous and secure management of the rights of all persons involved in such procedures.

3. Renewing a "Culture of Truth" in Ecclesial Leadership

The reforms undertaken in the Church in recent years have made it possible to launch new norms for canonical processes.

---

4. Cf. VELM, art. 3.

But that is not all: Such legislation also calls for real "organizational and governance changes."

The Church as the mystical and living Body of Christ on earth is always *reformanda*, in a constant process of updating and renewal. As Pope Francis often reminds us, this renewal today passes through "initiating processes" rather than "occupying spaces,"[5] preserving tradition not as an archaeological fact but as the constant development of the Lord's presence in his Church. Without listening to those who are our companions on this pilgrimage, the treasure that the Lord has entrusted to us for our growth as children of God cannot come to light, and neither a true synodal journey nor pastoral governance is possible.

On a personal level, in terms of my work in my Maltese diocese, I have learned that effective management of the abuse crisis in the Church is not possible without the spirit of affective and effective collegial communion and, above all, without the indispensable collaboration and help of lay experts. Pastors and faithful, together, can build a "culture of truth" that can oppose the current "culture of abuse" denounced by Pope Francis during the abuse crisis in Chile in 2018.

As I said in my meeting at the Vatican with the presidents of the world's bishops' conferences in February of 2019, "Discernment on the part of ecclesial authority cannot but be collegial."[6] Furthermore, I am constantly asking the laity for medical, legal, and communicative advice because I cannot and should not rely on my judgment alone in decision making. From my experience of service to both the diocesan and universal Church in the Roman Curia, Church leaders, when making decisions, would do well to count on a group of experienced lay persons whom they can entrust responsibilities, ask for advice on the direction to be taken, and discern with them each situation for a true and righteous judgment.

---

5. Pope FRANCIS, *Visita pastorale del Santo Padre Francesco a Milano: Incontro con i sacerdoti e i consacrati* (March 25, 2017), *www.vatican.va/content/francesco/it/speeches/2017/march/documents/papa-francesco_20170325_milano-sacerdoti.html*.

6. C.J. SCICLUNA, *Taking Responsibility for Processing Cases of Sexual Abuse Crisis and for Prevention of Abuse.*

The Lord is opening before us a road that is difficult to travel but also very exciting. He asks of us that conversion of heart sufficient to allow for a *receptio legis* that is not only an obedient assent to the dispositions of the Supreme Lawgiver but also an experience that is both psychological-spiritual and one of faith.

ACKNOWLEDGMENTS

At the end of this work, we would like to first of all thank the *Centro per la Difesa Sociale del Minore* (otherwise known as the *Istituti Riuniti di San Girolamo della Carità*) of Rome, which along with Fr. Peter V. Armenio, Edmundo Martinez, and Stephen J. Chojnicki of Midwest Theological Forum, made this project possible and effective.

Our special thanks go to our fellow communications and legal experts: José Mª La Porte, Giovanni Tridente, Davide Cito, Marc Teixidor, Fernando Puig, Jordi Bertomeu, and Fr. Mark Gurtner for their valuable suggestions and observations. We also thank Kira Howes for her patient and important linguistic work in translating this book.

Finally, we would like to thank many people who are close to us and who have encouraged our work: Roberto Regoli, Francisco Insa, and many students of Communication Law who with their questions and accounts of many cases have enriched this book.

BIBLIOGRAPHY

AGUILAR, M.A. *The Communicative Values of Transparency in the New Financial System of the Diocese of Calbayog.* Licentiate thesis, Pontifical University of Santa Croce (PUSC), 2018.

ALAZRAKI, V. *Comunicazione: per tutte le persone*, Presentation in the *Meeting: "The Protection of Minors in the Church,"* February 23, 2019. *www.vatican.va/resources/resources_alazraki-protezioneminori_20190223_it.html.*

ALVARADO, M. *"Antonio Molina: el exsacerdote salvadoreño al que el papa Francisco destituyó por un caso no probado de violación y amenazas." Séptimo Sentido*, February 18, 2018. *7s.laprensagrafica.com/antonio-molina-exsacerdote-salvadoreno-al-papa-francisco-destituyo-caso-no-probado-violacion-amenazas/.*

ANTON, M. *The Stakes: America at the Point of No Return.* Washington, DC: Regnery Publishing, 2020.

AQUINAS, Thomas. *Summa Contra Gentiles*, Book IV. Translated by Charles J. O'Neill. *genius.com/St-thomas-aquinas-summa-contra-gentiles-book-iv-annotated.*

ARRIETA, J.I. "A Presentation of the New Penal System of Canon Law." *The Jurist* 77 (2021).

———. *"Dimensione di governo: Prendere le decisioni, spiegare le proprie ragioni." Teoria e pratica del giornalismo religioso. Come informare sulla Chiesa Cattolica: Fonti, logiche, storie, personaggi*, edited by G. TRIDENTE. Rome: EDUSC, 2014.

ARROBA CONDE, M.J. *Giusto processo e peculiarità del processo canonico.* Canterano, Rome: Aracne, 2016.

ASTIGUETA, D.G. *"Trasparenza e segreto. Aspetti della prassi penalistica." Periodica de Re Canonica* 107, no.3 (2018).

———. *"Lettura di Vos estis lux mundi." Periodica de Re Canonica* 108, no.3 (2019).

BACHIOCHI, E. *The Rights of Women: Reclaiming a Lost Vision.* Notre Dame, IN: Notre Dame University Press, 2021.

BALL, C. "What Is Transparency?" *Public Integrity* 11, no.4 (2009).

BARAGLI, E. *"Segreto ed informazione nella Chiesa." La Civiltà Cattolica* 124, no. 2 (1973).

BARTOLONI, B. *Le orecchie del Vaticano*. Florence: Mauro Pagliai Editore, 2012.

BAURA, E. *"L'attività sanzionatoria della Chiesa: note sull'operatività della finalità della pena." Ephemerides Iuris Canonici* 2 (2019).

———. *Il principio della colpa e la responsabilità oggetiva, in La responsabilità giuridica degli enti ecclesiastici*, edited by E. BAURA, F. PUIG. Milan: Guiffrè, 2020.

———. *Accompagnamento e formazione: diritti e doveri dei fedeli*. Lecture delivered at the XLV Study *Accompagnare, Discernere, Integrare: Profili e Prospettive Giuridico-Ecclesiali*, organized by the Associazione Canonistica Italiana: GRUPPO ITALIANO DOCENTI DI DIRITTO CANONICO [Italian Canon Law Society: Canon Law Teachers, Italian Group]. Borca di Cadore, Belluno, Italy, July 3, 2018, *www.youtube.com/watch?v=Va4cBLcCFoY*.

BENEDICT XVI. Encyclical Letter on Integral Human Development in Charity and Truth *Caritas in Veritate*. June 29, 2009.

———. *Pastoral Letter to the Catholics of Ireland*. October 19, 2010. *www.vatican.va/content/benedict-xvi/en/letters/2010/documents/hf_ben-xvi_let_20100319_church-ireland.html*.

———. *Message for the 46th World Communications Day*, "Silence and Word: Path of Evangelization." May 20, 2012. *www.vatican.va/content/benedict-xvi/en/messages/communications/documents/hf_ben-xvi_mes_20120124_46th-world-communications-day.html*.

———. *"La Chiesa e lo scandalo degli abusi sessuali." Klerusblatt*, April 11, 2019. *www.catholicnewsagency.com/news/41013/full-text-of-benedict-xvi-essay-the-church-and-the-scandal-of-sexual-abuse*.

BENEDICT, R. *The Chrysanthemum and the Sword*. Boston: Houghton Mifflin, 1946.

BENNIS, W., D.P. GOLEMAN, J. O'TOOLE. *Transparency: How Leaders Create a Culture of Candor*. New York: John Wiley & Sons, Inc., 2008.

BERTOMEU, J. *"La respuesta de la Iglesia a la cultura del abuso." Vida Nueva* 3248 (November / December 2021).

———. *"Hacia una espiritualidad de la prevención." Ecclesia* 4036 (June 13, 2020).

BIRKINSHAW, J., D. CABLE. "The Dark Side of Transarency." *The McKinsey Quarterly*, February 1, 2017. *www.mckinsey.com/ business-functions/people-and-organizational-performance/ our-insights/the-dark-side-of-transparency.*

BLACKTONE, W. *Commentaries on the Laws of England*, Book IV. Oxford: Clarendon Press, 1769.

BLÁZQUEZ, R. *La Chiesa. Mistero, Comunione, Missione.* Salamanca: Seguimi, 2017.

———. *"Ministerio y poder en la Iglesia." Communio* 6, no. 3 (1984).

———. *La Iglesia del Concilio Vaticano II.* Salamanca: Seguimi, 1988.

BOK, S. *On the Ethics of Concealment and Revelation.* New York: Vintage Books, 1989.

BONI, G. *Il buon governo nella Chiesa: inidoneità agli uffici e denuncia dei fedeli.* Modena: Mucchi Editore, 2019.

BRENNER, M. "American Nightmare: The Ballad of Richard Jewell." *Vanity Fair*, February 1997. *archive.vanityfair.com/article/ share/1fd2d7ae-10d8-474b-9bf1-d1558af697be.*

CALABRESE, G., et al. *"Magisterio." Dizionario di Ecclesiologia.* Madrid: LAC, 2016.

CARDINALE, G, "Interview with Msgr. B.G. Pighin." *Avvenire*, December 9, 2021. *www.avvenire.it/chiesa/pagine/i-reati-della-chiesa-giro-di-vite.*

———. *Interview of Msgr. Charles Scicluna on the Strictness of the Church in Cases of Pedophilia.* March 13, 2010. *www.vatican. va/resources/resources_mons-scicluna-2010_it.html.*

CARROGGIO, M. "Church Communication in the Face of Vulnerability: A Theoretical Framework and Practical Application for Information Management in Cases of the Abuse of Minors." *Church, Communication & Culture* 6, no. 1 (2021).

"Caso Barros: Comisión vaticana entregó en 2015 una carta de Juan Carlos Cruz al papa." Cooperativa.cl. February 5, 2018. *www.cooperativa.cl/noticias/pais/iglesia-catolica/caso-barros-comision-vaticana-entrego-en-2015-una-carta-de-juan-carlos/2018-02-05/090107.html.*

Catechism of the Catholic Church. Vatican City: LEV, 2002.

Cencini, A. *È cambiato qualcosa nella Chiesa dopo gli scandali sessuali? Analisi e proposte di formazione.* Salamanca: Ediciones Sígueme, 2016.

Cencini, A., S. Lassi, eds. *La formazione iniziale in tempo di abusi, Servizio Nazionale per la tutela dei minori.* CEI, February 2021.

Cernuzio, S. *Il velo del silenzio. Abusi, violenze, frustrazioni nella vita religiosa femminile.* Milan: Edizioni San Paolo, 2021.

Chardo, F. *Bishop Kevin Rhoades Cleared of Any Wrongdoing Following Referral by Diocese.* Dauphin County District Attorney's Office. September 13, 2013. *dauphin. crimewatchpa.com/da/310/post/bishop-kevin-rhoades-cleared-any-wrongdoing-following-referral-diocese.*

Ciocca, C. *Webinar: Transparency and Governance in the Church.* May 5, 2020. *www.pusc.it/article/webinar-transparency-and-governance-church.*

Cito, D. *"Brevi annotazioni canonistiche sul concetto di abuso di potere e di coscienza." Tredimensioni.* 2020.

Clariond, B. *Comunicar y Participar: La comunicación institucional en la Iglesia y su relación con la tutela y promoción del bien común.* Rome: Ateneo Pontificio Regina Apostolorum, 2018.

Clemenzia, A. *Sul luogo dell'ecclesiologia. Questioni epistemologiche,* Rome: Città Nuova, 2018.

Code of Canon Law (CIC). January 25, 1983, in *AAS* LXXV.

Cohn, R. *The PR Crisis Bible.* New York: St. Martin's Press, 2000.

Congar, Y. *Una Chiesa contestata.* Brescia: Queriniana, 1969.

Congregation for the Doctrine of the Faith. *Vademecum,* version 1.0. July 16 2020. *www.vatican.va/roman_curia/ congregations/cfaith/documents/rc_con_cfaith_doc_20200716_ vademecum-casi-abuso_en.html.*

CONGREGATION FOR CATHOLIC EDUCATION. *Guidelines for the Use of Psychology in the Admission and Formation of Candidates for the Priesthood*. June 29, 2008.

CONGREGATION FOR THE CLERGY. *The Gift of the Priestly Vocation*. Ratio Fundamentalis Institutionis Sacerdotalis. December 8, 2016. *www.clerus.va/content/clerus/en/notizie/new11.html*.

CONGREGATIO PRO EPISCOPUS. January 10, 2015.

CRUZ CHELLEW, J.C. personal Twitter account. January 18, 2018. *twitter.com/jccruzchellew/status/953992484140519424?ref_src =twsrc%5Etfw%7Ctwcamp%5Etweetembed%7Ctwterm%5 E953992484140519424%7Ctwgr%5E%7Ctwcon%5Es1_& ref_url=https%3A%2F%2Fwww.bbc.com%2Fmundo%2Fnotic ias-42733493*.

DANIEL, W.M. "Accountability and the Juridical Responsibility of the Public Ecclesiastical Administration." *Ius Ecclesiæ* 30, no. 1. (2018).

DANS, E. "Why Textbooks and Education Are to Blame for Fake News." *Forbes*, March 9, 2018.

DE LA CIERVA, Y. *La Chiesa casa di vetro*. Rome: EDUSC, 2014.

———. *"Comunicación Institucional en situación de crisis." Introducción a la Comunicación Institucional de la Iglesia*, edited by J.M. LA PORTE. Madrid: Palabra, 2012.

DE LUBAC, H. *Paradoja y Misterio de la Iglesia*. Salamanca: Sígueme, 2002.

DEL POZZO, M. *Lo statuto giuridico fondamentale del fedele*. Rome: EDUSC, 2018.

———. *"Il giusto processo e l'ecosistema processuale nel pensiero di Joaquín Llobell." Ius Ecclesiæ* 33, no. 1 (2022).

DELLA TORRE, G. *"Contributo sulla pubblicazione del Rescritto del Santo Padre Francesco sull'Istruzione Sulla riservatezza delle cause." Vatican News*, December 17, 2019.

DESCALZO, M. *La Iglesia nuestra hija*. Salamanca: Sígueme, 1972.

DOMINGUEZ-LOPEZ, J.I. "The Presumption of Innocence." *The Tablet*, February 5, 2020, *thetablet.org/the-presumption-of-innocence/*.

DONATI, P., A. MALO, G. MASPERO, eds. *Social Science, Philosophy and Theology in Dialogue: A Relational Perspective*. London: Routledge, 2019.

D'ORS, Á. *Derecho y sentido común. Siete lecciones de derecho natural como límite del derecho positivo*. Madrid: Civitas, March 2001.

D'OSTILIO, F. *La responsabilità per atto illecito della Pubblica Amministrazione nel diritto canonico*. Rome: Pontificia Università Lateranense, 1966.

DOSTOYEVSKY, F. *The Idiot*, trans. Eva Martin. June 21, 2021, *www. gutenberg.org/files/2638/2638-h/2638-h.htm*.

FABENE, F. *"Vigilanza (diritto e dovere di)." Dizionario generale di Diritto canonico* VII, 1, edited by A. VIANA, J. OTADUY, J. SEDANO. Pamplona: Istituto Balestruccio di Azpilcueta, 2012.

FARFÁN, C., M.J. LÓPEZ. *"La influencia de Karadima." Qué pasa*, April 30, 2010. *www.quepasa.cl/articolo/presente/2010/04/1-3265-9-la-influencia-de-karadima.shtml/*.

FERRER ORTIZ, J. *"La responsabilità civile della diocesi per gli atti dei suoi chierici." Ius Canonicum* 45 (2005).

FLORIDI, L., ed. *The Onlife Manifesto. Being Human in a Hyperconnected Era*. New York-London: SpringerOpen, 2015.

FRANCIS. Apostolic Exhortation on the Proclamation of the Gospel in Today's World *Evangelii Gaudium*. November 24, 2013, *www.vatican.va/content/francesco/en/apost_exhortations/documents/papa-francesco_esortazione-ap_20131124_evangelii-gaudium.html*.

———. Post-synodal Apostolic Exhortation to Young People and to the Entire People of God *Christus Vivit*. March 25, 2019, *www.vatican.va/content/francesco/en/apost_exhortations/documents/papa-francesco_esortazione-ap_20190325_christus-vivit.html*.

———. Motu Proprio *As a Loving Mother*. 2016, *www.vatican.va/content/francesco/en/motu_proprio/documents/papa-francesco-motu-proprio_20160604_come-una-madre-amorevole.html*.

———. Motu Proprio *Vos Estis Lux Mundi*. May 10, 2019, *www.vatican.va/content/francesco/en/motu_proprio/documents/papa-francesco-motu-proprio-20190507_vos-estis-lux-mundi.html*.

———. *Rescripta ex Audientia SS.mi*. December 3 and 6, 2019. *L'Osservatore Romano* 288, no. 4 (December 18, 2019).

———. *Rescriptum ex Audientia Ss.mi Which Modifies the Motu Proprio Sacramentorum Sanctitatis Tutela (2001, updated 2010) and Approves the "Norme sui delitti riservati della Congregazione per la Dottrina della Fede."* December 7, 2021, *press.vatican.va/content/salastampa/it/bollettino/pubblico/2021/12/07/0825/01732.html*.

———. *Guidelines for the Protection of Children and Vulnerable Persons*. March 26, 2019, *www.vatican.va/resources/resources_protezioneminori-lineeguida_20190326_en.html*.

———. *Letter to the People of God*. August 20, 2018, *w2.vatican.va/content/francesco/en/letters/2018/documents/papa-francesco_20180820_lettera-popolo-didio.html*.

———. *Letter to the People of God in Chile*. May 31, 2018, *www.catholicnewsagency.com/news/38567/full-text-of-pope-francis-letter-to-the-church-in-chile*.

———. *Letter to the Bishops of Chile Following the Report of Archbishop Charles J. Scicluna*. April 11, 2018, *www.vatican.va/content/francesco/en/letters/2018/documents/papa-francesco_20180408_lettera-vescovi-cile.html*.

———. *Letter to Priests on the 160th Anniversary of the Death of the Holy Curé of Ars*. August 4, 2019, *www.vatican.va/content/francesco/en/letters/2019/documents/papa-francesco_20190804_lettera-presbiteri.html*.

———. *Pope Francis' In-flight Press Conference from Greece*. December 6, 2021, *www.catholicnewsagency.com/news/249798/full-text-pope-francis-in-flight-press-conference-from-greece*.

————. Appeal at the *Conference "Promoting Child Safeguarding in the Time of COVID-19 and Beyond,"* organized by the Pope John XXIII Community with Azione Cattolica Italiana and the Centro Sportivo Italiano, in collaboration with the Centro per la Vittimologia e la Sicurezza [Center for Victimology and Security] of the University of Bologna, held in the Sala San Pio X in Rome. November 4, 2021.

————. *Press Conference on the Return Flight from Rabat to Rome.* March 31, 2019, *www.vatican.va/content/francesco/en/ speeches/2019/march/documents/papa-francesco_20190331_ marocco-voloritorno.html.*

————. *Press Conference on the Return Flight from Dublin to Rome.* August 26, 2018, *www.vatican.va/content/francesco/en/ speeches/2018/august/documents/papa-francesco_20180826_ irlanda-voloritorno.html.*

————. *Presentation of the Christmas Greetings to the Roman Curia.* Sala Clementina, Vatican City, December 22, 2014, *www.vatican.va/content/francesco/en/speeches/2014/december/ documents/papa-francesco_20141222_curia-romana.html.*

————. *Morning Meditation in the Chapel of the* Domus Sanctæ Marthæ. December 20, 2013, *www.vatican.va/content/ francesco/en/cotidie/2013/documents/papa-francesco- cotidie_20131220_mystery.html.*

————. *Homily in the Chapel of the* Domus Sanctæ Marthæ *with a Group of Clergy Sex Abuse Victims.* July 7, 2014, *www. vatican.va/content/francesco/en/cotidie/2014/documents/papa- francesco-cotidie_20140707_vittime-abusi.html.*

————. *Address to Participants in the Plenary Assembly of the Congregation for Institutes of Consecrated Life and Societies of Apostolic Life.* Sala Clementina, Vatican City, December 11, 2021, *www.vatican.va/content/francesco/en/speeches/2021/ december/documents/20211211-plenaria-civcsva.html.*

————. *Message for World Communications Day, "The Truth Will Set You Free" (Jn 8:32): Fake News and Journalism for Peace.* January 24, 2018, *www.vatican.va/content/ francesco/en/messages/communications/documents/papa- francesco_20180124_messaggio-comunicazioni-sociali.html.*

―――. *Press Conference during the Return Flight from Rio de Janeiro on the Occasion of the XXVIII World Youth Day*. July 28, 2013, *www.vatican.va/content/francesco/en/speeches/2013/july/documents/papa-francesco_20130728_gmg-conferenza-stampa.html*.

―――. Introduction to the *Meeting "The Protection of Minors in the Church."* February 21, 2019, *www.vatican.va/content/francesco/en/speeches/2019/february/documents/papa-francesco_20190221_incontro-protezioneminori-apertura.html*.

FERNÁNDEZ DE A., R. *El 31 de mayo, una misión para nuestro tiempo.* Chile: Nueva Patris, 1997.

GALDÓN, G. *Informazione e Disinformazione.* Rome: Armando Editore, 1999.

GANDOLFI, M.E. *"Quante sono le donne nella Chiesa? Conoscere i dati per riconoscere una presenza."* Orientamenti Pastorali 10 (2020). *www.centroorientamentopastorale.it/organismo/wp-content/uploads/2021/02/Gandolfi_102020.pdf*.

GENNARI, C. *"Sul segreto del S. Ufficio."* Il Monitore ecclesiastico 19 (1897).

GHISONI, L. *Communio: Agire insieme,* Presentation in the *Meeting "The Protection of Minors in the Church."* February 22, 2019, *www.vatican.va/resources/resources_lindaghisoni-protezioneminori_20190222_it.html*.

JOHN XXIII. Encyclical Letter on Establishing Universal Peace in Truth, Justice, Charity, and Liberty *Pacem in Terris*. April 11, 1963, *www.vatican.va/content/john-xxiii/en/encyclicals/documents/hf_j-xxiii_enc_11041963_pacem.html*.

JOHN PAUL II. Post-synodal Apostolic Exhortation on Reconciliation and Penance in the Mission of the Church Today *Reconciliatio e Pænitentia*. December 2, 1984, *www.vatican.va/content/john-paul-ii/en/apost_exhortations/documents/hf_jp-ii_exh_02121984_reconciliatio-et-paenitentia.html*.

―――. *Address to the Cardinals of the United States*. April 23, 2002, *www.vatican.va/content/john-paul-ii/en/speeches/2002/april/documents/hf_jp-ii_spe_20020423_usa-cardinals.html*.

———. *Discorso ai partecipanti al Congresso Nazionale del Movimento di "Impegno Culturale."* January 16, 1982, *www. vatican.va/content/john-paul-ii/it/speeches/1982/january/ documents/hf_jp-ii_spe_19820116_impegno-culturale.html.*

———. *Discorso ai giornalisti riuniti in vaticano per celebrare il Giubileo della Redenzione.* January 27, 1984, *www.vatican. va/content/john-paul-ii/it/speeches/1984/january/documents/ hf_jp-ii_spe_19840127_giornalisti.html.*

———. *Letter to Artists.* April 4, 1999, *www.vatican.va/content/ john-paul-ii/en/letters/1999/documents/hf_jp-ii_let_23041999_ artists.html.*

———. *Message for the 18th World Communications Day.* June 3, 1984, *www.vatican.va/content/john-paul-ii/en/messages/ communications/documents/hf_jp-ii_mes_24051984_world-communications-day.html.*

GONZALEZ ALORDA, Á. "Transforming Organizations from Within." *Inspiring Trust: Church Communications and Organizational Vulnerability,* edited by J. PUJOL, J. NARBONA, J.M. DÍAZ. Rome: EDUSC, 2021.

GONZÁLEZ GAITANO, N. "More Than a Media System Failure? Reason, Faith, and Mercy as Comprehensive Paradigms for Communication." *Church, Communication & Culture* 2, no. 1 (2017).

———. *El deber de respeto a la intimidad.* Pamplona: EUNSA, 1990.

GORDON, I. *"La responsabilità dell'amministrazione pubblica ecclesiastica." Monitor Ecclesiastico* 98 (1973).

GOULDING, G. "Towards a Theological and Synodal Response to the Abuse Crisis." *New Blackfriars* 102, no. 1097 (2020).

———. "Truth and Silence: Learning from Abuse." *The Way* 42, no. 4 (2003).

GOYRET, P. *El Obispo, Pastor de la Iglesia. Estudio teológico del munus regendi en Lumen Gentium* 27. Pamplona: EUNSA, 1998.

GRISEZ, G. *Living a Christian Life.* Quincy: Franciscan Press, 1993.

GUILLEN, M. "Regaining Trust: Three Key Players." *Inspiring Trust: Church Communications and Organizational Vulnerability*, edited by J. PUJOL, J. NARBONA, J.M. DÍAZ. Rome: EDUSC, 2021.

———. *Motivation in Organizations. Searching for a Meaningful Work-Life Balance.* London–New York: Routledge, 2021.

HAN, B-C. *La sociedad de la trasparencia.* Barcelona: Herder, 2018.

HAWTHORNE, J. "The Scarlet Letter by Nathaniel Hawthorne Reviewed." *The Atlantic*, April 1886.

HAWTHORNE, N. *The Scarlet Letter.* New York: Barnes &Noble Classics, 2003.

HEALD, D. "Transparency as an Instrumental Value," *Transparency: The Key to Better Governance?* edited by C. HOOD and D. HEALD. New York: Oxford University Press, 2006.

HENRIQUES, A. *Corporate Truth: The Limits to Transparency.* London: Earthscan, 2007.

HERVADA, J. *Cos'è il Diritto.* Rome: EDUSC, 2013.

HOLY SEE, *Letter N. 484.110.* February 26, 2020, *www.catholic. org.au/images/Observations_of_the_Holy_See_to_the_ Recommendations_of_the_Royal_Commission.pdf.*

HOYEAU, C. (interview by), "*Laetitia Calmeyn : 'Si j'avais été un homme, la question de l'amitié avec Mgr Aupetit ne se serait pas posée.'*" *La Croix*, December 12, 2021. *international. la-croix.com/news/religion/if-i-had-been-a-man-the-question- would-not-have-come-up/15355.*

INDEPENDENT COMMISSION ON SEXUAL ABUSE IN THE CATHOLIC CHURCH. *Final Report "Sexual Violence in the Catholic Church France 1950-2020," www.ciase.fr/medias/Ciase-Summary-of-the- Final-Report-5-october-2021.pdf.*

INDYSTAR. "Fort Wayne Bishop Cleared of wrongdoing in Pennsylvania Investigation." *IndyStar*, September 13, 2018. *eu.indystar.com/story/news/crime/2018/09/13/catholic- church-bishop-fort-wayne-cleared-wrongdoing-after- probe/1288974002/.*

ITALIAN BISHOPS CONFERENCE. *Linee guida per i casi di abuso sessuale nei confronti di minori da parte di chierici.* January 2014, *www.chiesacattolica.it/wp-content/uploads/sites/31/2017/08/11/Linee-Guida-abusi-sessuali-2014.pdf.*

KENT, A., K. SALWEN. *Il caso Richard Jewell. La storia di un uomo in cerca di giustizia.* Milan: Mondadori, 2020.

KIERKEGAARD, S. "For Self-Examination." *Kierkegaard's Writings,* vol. 21, edited by H. V. HONG and E.H. HONG. Princeton: Princeton University Press, 1990.

KIMES, John Paul. "Reclaiming 'Pastoral': *Pascite Gregem Dei* and Its Vision of Penal Law." *The Jurist* 77, (2021).

KOUVEGLO, É. "*I fedeli laici e l'esercizio della potestà nella Chiesa. Status quæstionis e ricerca di una chiave funzionale di lettura.*" *Apollinaris* 90, no. 1 (2017).

LA PORTE, J.M. *Introduzione alla comunicazione istituzionale della Chiesa.* Madrid: Palabra, 2012.

LAUCIRICA, J.M. *Secreto pontificio, in Diccionario general de derecho canónico,* vol. VII, edited by J. OTADUY, A. VIANA, J. SEDANO. Madrid: Thomson Reuters Aranzadi, 2013.

LEKKA, C. "High Reliability Organisations: A Review of the Literature." *Health and Safety Executive,* Report Review 899 (2011).

LEONARDI, M. *Wojtyła, Wanda Poltawska e il "mistero" di una Meditazione scomoda.* April 26, 2014, *www.ilsussidiario.net/news/cronaca/2014/4/26/il-caso-wojtyla-wanda-poltawska-e-il-mistero-di-una-meditazione-scomoda/494515/.*

LÓPEZ MARINA, D. "*Develan falso caso de abusos sexuales que acabó con un sacerdote muerto en prisión.*" *ACI Prensa,* February 2, 2016. *www.aciprensa.com/noticias/develan-falso-caso-de-abusos-sexuales-que-acabo-con-un-sacerdote-muerto-en-prision-35151.*

"*Los laicos de Osorno escriben una dura carta a los obispos chilenos.*" *Alfa e Omega,* April 19, 2018. *www.alfayomega.es/149005/los-laicos-de-osorno-escriben-una-dura-carta-a-los-obispos-chilenos.*

LUCAS, B. "The Seal of the Confessional and a Conflict of Duty." *Church, Communication & Culture* 6, no. 1. 2021.

MAGALHÃES, G. "*Algunas claves para practicar la misericordia cristiana en la sociedad contemporánea.*" *Inspiring Trust: Church Communications and Organizational Vulnerability,* edited by J. PUJOL, J. NARBONA, J.M. DIAZ. Rome: EDUSC, 2021.

MENDOZA, C. "*Trasparenza (principio di).*" *Glossary.* CASE Stewardship. *casestewardship.org/glossario/trasparenza/.*

———. "What Kind of Transparency for the Church? Proposing Operational Transparency for Processes, Solutions, and Decisions in the Catholic Church." *Church, Communication & Culture* 5, no. 2 (2020).

MERAYO, A. *Técnicas de comunicación oral.* Madrid: Editorial Tecnos, 2012.

MERING, N. *Awake, Not Woke: A Christian Response to the Cult of Progressive Ideology.* Gastonia, NC: TAN Books, 2021.

MIÑAMBRES, J. "*Rilevanza canonica dell'accountability degli amministratori di beni ecclesiastici.*" *Ius Ecclesiæ* 31, no. 1 (2019).

———. "*Corresponsabilità [Stewardship].*" *Glossary.* CASE Stewardship, *www.casestewardship.org/320.html.*

MONTINI, G.P. "*Provvedimenti cautelari urgenti nel caso di accuse odiose nei confronti di ministri sacri. Nota sui canoni 1044 e 1722.*" *Quaderni di diritto ecclesiale* 12 (1999).

MORRIS-MARR, L. "Priest Who Confessed to Abuse 1500 Times 'Proves Need for Change.'" *The New Daily,* June 14, 2018. *thenewdaily.com.au/news/national/2018/06/14/confession-child-abuse-royal-commission/.*

MOSCONI, M. "*Comunicazione ecclesiale e vigilanza canonica nel contesto degli attuali strumenti di comunicazione sociale.*" *Quaderni di diritto ecclesiale* 31, no. 1 (2018).

NACINOVICH, M. "Priest's Defamation Suits Are the Latest Wrinkle in Sex-Abuse Fallout." *National Catholic Reporter,* November 25, 2020. *www.ncronline.org/news/accountability/priests-defamation-suits-are-latest-wrinkle-sex-abuse-fallout.*

NATIONAL REVIEW BOARD. "A Report on the Crisis in the Catholic Church in the United States." *Origins,* March 11, 2004.

Ocáriz, F. "*Saluto finale di chiusura del XI Seminario Professionale sugli Uffici di Comunicazione della Chiesa: Dialogo, rispetto e libertà di espressione nella sfera pubblica,*" Catholic Church and the Public Sphere, edited by J. Pujol, C. Mendoza. Rome: EDUSC, 2018.

Papale, C. "*L'indagine previa.*" *Dispensa Online Pontificia Università Lateranense. www.pul.it/cattedra/upload_files/19419/ Sussidio%20Processo%20penale.pdf.*

Pell, G. Presentation in PCM Program of Church Management, Webinar "Creating a Transparent Culture in the Catholic Church." January 14, 2021, *www.youtube.com/ watch?v=xEGEE4Po1Cs.*

Pennington, K. "*Innocente fino a prova contraria: le origini di una massima giuridica.*" In *Processo penale e tutela dei diritti nell'ordinamento canonico,* edited by D. Cito. Milan: Giuffrè, 2005.

Perlasca, A. "*Il segreto pontificio.*" *Quaderni di diritto ecclesiale* 26 (2013).

Piacenza, M. *Presentazione della nota sull'importanza del foro interno e l'inviolabilità del sigillo sacramentale.* June 29, 2019, *www.vatican.va/roman_curia/tribunals/apost_penit/ documents/rc_trib_appen_pro_20190629_forointerno- cardpiacenza_it.html.*

Pius XII, *Discorso di Papa Pio XII ai giornalisti cattolici riuniti a Roma per il loro IV Congresso Internazionale.* February 17, 1950, *www.vatican.va/content/pius-xii/it/speeches/1950/ documents/hf_p-xii_spe_19500217_la-presse.html.*

Platico cl. "*Papa Francisco se ha desenmascarado: Defensa de obispo Juan Barros.*" *YouTube,* October 3, 2015. *www.youtube. com/watch?v=HTTe06B_UMI.*

Półtawska, W. *Diario di un'amicizia. La famiglia Poltawski e Karol Wojtyła.* Milan: Edizioni San Paolo, 2010.

Pontifical Council for Social Communications. Pastoral Instruction *Communio et Progressio.* May 23, 1971, *www. vatican.va/roman_curia/pontifical_councils/pccs/documents/ rc_pc_pccs_doc_23051971_communio_en.html.*

———. *Ethics in Communications.* June 4, 2000, *www.vatican.va/ roman_curia/pontifical_councils/pccs/documents/rc_pc_pccs_ doc_20000530_ethics-communications_en.html.*

———. Pastoral Instruction *Ætatis Novæ.* February 22, 1992, *www. vatican.va/roman_curia/pontifical_councils/pccs/documents/ rc_pc_pccs_doc_22021992_aetatis_en.html.*

Puig, F. *"I doveri di vigilanza dell'autorità ecclesiastica." La responsabilità giuridica degli enti ecclesiastici,* edited by E. Baura, F. Puig. Milan: Giuffrè, 2020.

———. *"La responsabilità giuridica dell'autorità ecclesiastica per negligenza in un deciso orientamento normativo." Ius Ecclesiæ* 28 (2016).

Pujol, J. *"El contexto eclesiológico y los principios que guiaron la revisión del Libro VI del CIC." Ius Canonicum* 61, no. 122 (2021).

———. "Transparency Is Not a Utopia But a Non-stop Process." *Church, Communication & Culture* 2, no. 1 (2017).

———. "Colloquy with John Durham Peters at Yale University on Freedom of Speech." *Church, Communication & Culture* 4, no. 1 (2019).

———. *"Chi dobbiamo incolpare per la crisi delle* Fake News? *Tre fattori in gioco sulla verità online." Medic* 26, no. 1 (2018).

Pree, H. *"La responsabilità giuridica dell'Amministrazione Ecclesiastica." La giustizia nell'attività amministrativa della Chiesa. Il contenzioso amministrativo,* edited by E. Baura, J. Canosa. Milan: Giuffrè, 2006.

Rédaction Paris Match. December 8, 2021, on the cover of the print version, *www.parismatch.com/Actu/Societe/Exclusif-Monseigneur-Aupetit-perdu-par-amour-1775067.*

Redacción ACI Prensa. *"Al grito de 'Por todos los niños' atacan a sacerdote que no es culpable de abusos." ACI Prensa,* August 21, 2018. *www.aciprensa.com/noticias/al-grito-de-por-todos-los-ninos-atacan-a-sacerdote-que-no-es-culpable-de-abusos-20805.*

———, *"Cardinale Ezzati: es grave que hayan engañado al Papa en el caso Barros."* ACI Prensa, April 19, 2018. *www.aciprensa. com/noticias/cardenal-ezzati-es-grave-que-hayan-enganado-al-papa-francisco-en-caso-barros-89984.*

———. *"Declaran inocente a sacerdote acusado falsamente de abusos en Irlanda."* ACI Prensa, March 13, 2014. *www.aciprensa.com/ noticias/declaran-inocente-a-sacerdote-acusado-falsamente-de-abusos-en-irlanda-36857.*

———. *"El Papa Francisco quiere que rindan cuentas todos los culpables de abusos, incluso obispos."* ACI Prensa, August 20, 2018. *www.aciprensa.com/noticias/el-papa-francisco-quiere-que-rindan-cuentas-todos-los-culpables-de-abusos-incluso-obispos-47098.*

———. *"Luego de tres años de prisión liberan a sacerdote falsamente acusado de abusos en Colombia."* ACI Prensa, October 15, 2015. *www.aciprensa.com/noticias/luego-de-tres-anos-de-prision-liberan-a-sacerdote-falsamente-acusado-de-abusos-en-colombia-48776.*

———. *"Papa Francisco nombra Obispo de Osorno en Chile."* ACI Prensa, January 10, 2015. *www.aciprensa.com/noticias/ el-papa-francesco-nomina-vescovo-di-osorno-in-cile-83850.*

———. *"Vaticano: P. Karadima es culpable de abusos sexuales."* ACI Prensa, February 18, 2011. *www.aciprensa.com/noticias/ vatican-p-karadima-è-colpevole-di-abuso sessuale.*

———. *"VIDEO: Episcopado rechaza protesta contra Obispo chileno durante Te Deum."* ACI Prensa, September 20, 2017. *www. aciprensa.com/noticias/video-episcopado-rechaza-protesta-contra-obispo-chileno-durante-te-deum-63753.*

REDACCIÓN BBC. *"Juan Barros, el controvertido obispo cuya presencia encendió la ira de las víctimas de abuso sexual durante la visita del Papa Francisco a Chile."* BBC Mundo, January 17, 2018. *www.bbc.com/mundo/noticias-america-latina-42719414.*

———. *"'Son todas calumnias': la polémica defensa del papa Francisco al obispo Juan Barros, acusado de encubrir abuso sexual de menores en Chile."* BBC Mundo, January 18, 2018. *www.bbc.com/mundo/noticias-42733493.*

REDACCIÓN PURA NOTICIA. *"Parlamentarios envían carta al Papa Francisco en protesta por designación de Juan Barros como obispo de Osorno." Pura Noticia*, February 16, 2015. *www.puranoticia.cl/noticias/regiones/parlamentarios-envian-carta-al-papa-francisco-en-protesta-por-designacion-de-juan-barros-como-obispo-de-osorno/2015-02-16/135255.html.*

REDACCIÓN SOY OSORNO. *"Inédito: 30 curas y diáconos de Osorno le pidieron al obispo Barros que renuncie." SoyOsorno.cl*, February 19, 2015. *www.soychile.cl/Osorno/Sociedad/2015/02/19/305960/Ahora-sacerdotes-y-diaconos-de-Osorno-envian-carta-al-nuncio-pidiendo-la-renuncia-de-Barros-como-obispo.aspx.*

———. *"Destacado sacerdote envía carta al Papa por caso Barros: 'Su figura contrasta con la de nuestro primer obispo.'" SoyOsorno.cl*, March 18, 2015. *www.soychile.cl/Osorno/Sociedad/2015/03/18/311020/Destacado-sacerdote-envia-carta-al-Papa-por-caso-Barros-Su-figura-contrasta-con-la-de-nuestro-primer-obispo.aspx.*

REDAZIONE EFE, *"El cardenal O'Malley critica los comentarios del papa sobre el obispo chileno Barros." Agencia EFE*, January 21, 2018. *www.efe.com/efe/america/sociedad/el-cardenal-o-malley-critica-los-comentarios-del-papa-sobre-obispo-chileno-barros/20000013-3498841.*

REDAZIONE IL SISMOGRAFO. *Francia Laetitia Calmeyn: "Se fossi stato un uomo, la questione dell'amicizia con il vescovo Aupetit non sarebbe sorta."* December 12, 2021. *ilsismografo.blogspot.com/2021/12/francia-laetitia-calmeyn-se-fossi-stato.html.*

REDZIOCH, W. *"Polonia: colpire la Chiesa con le false accuse sulla questione degli abusi." Acistampa*, January 19, 2019. *www.acistampa.com/story/polonia-colpire-la-chiesa-con-le-false-acuse-sulla-questione-degli-abusi-11699.*

REGLERO CAMPOS, L.F., J.M. BUSTO LAGO, eds. *Trattato sulla responsabilità civile.* Cizur Menor, Navarra: Thomson Reuters Aranzadi, 2014.

REGOLI, R. "Pope Benedict, Sex Abuse and the Catholic Church's Future." *Wall Street Journal*, February 17, 2022. *www.wsj.com/ articles/pope-benedict-xvi-sex-abuse-catholic-church-meeting-ratzinger-archbishop-munich-german-synodal-path-sauve-commission-hullerman-11645132639.*

REY-GARCIA, M., K. LIKET, L.I. ÁLVAREZ-GONZÁLEZ, K. MAAS. "Back to Basics. Revisiting the Relevance of Beneficiaries for Evaluation and Accountability in Non-Profits." *Nonprofit Management and Leadership* 27, no. 4 (2017).

RHODE, U. "*Trasparenza e segreto nel Diritto Canonico.*" *Periodica* 107, no. 3 (2018).

RÍOS, A. "*La comunicazione interna al servizio del Chiesa diocesana.*" Licentiate thesis in *Institutional Communication*, pro manuscripto. Rome: PUSC, 2014.

RIVELLA, M. "*Trasparenza nella Curia Romana.*" *Trasparenza. Una sfida per la Chiesa*, edited by M. MERLINI. Rome: Studium, 2020.

RODRÍGUEZ, S., M.J. NAVARRETE. "*Scicluna asegura que su informe no será entregado a la fiscalía.*" *La Tercera*, April 4, 2019. *www. latercera.com/nacional/noticia/scicluna-asegura-informe-no-sera-entregado-la-fiscalia/601429/.*

RODRÍGUEZ, Y., C. BERBELL. "*Auctoritas y Potestas, en la antigua Roma.*" *Confilegale*, January 5, 2016. *confilegal.com/20160105-auctoritas-potestas-antigua-roma/amp/.*

RONSON, J. *So You've Been Publicly Shamed*. London: Picador, 2015.

ROSENBERG, J. "The Meaning of Open." *Google: Official Blog*, December 21, 2009. *googleblog.blogspot.com/2009/12/ meaning-of-open.html.*

———. "The Future Is Open." *Think Open*, October 2012. *www. thinkwithgoogle.com/_qs/documents/157/the-future-is-open_ articles.pdf.*

ROYAL COMMISSION. *Institutional Responses to Child Sexual Abuse: The Final Report*, vol. 16, Book 1, 77 (2017), *www. childabuseroyalcommission.gov.au/final-report.*

SACKS, J. *Morality: Restoring the Common Good in Divided Times*. New York: Hodder & Stoughton, 2020.

SANDERS, K. "British Government Communication during the 2020 COVID-19 Pandemic: Learning from High Reliability Organizations." *Church, Communication & Culture* 5, no. 3 (2020).

———. "Communicating Effectively in High-Risk Organizations: Learning from High Reliability Organizations." In *Inspiring Trust Church Communications and Organizational Vulnerability*, edited by J. PUJOL, J. NARBONA, J.M. DÍAZ. Rome: EDUSC, 2021.

SAYÉS, J.A. *La Iglesia de Cristo. Curso de Eclesiología*. Madrid: Palabra, 1999.

SCICLUNA, C.J. "*Taking Responsibility for Processing Cases of Sexual Abuse Crisis and for Prevention of Abuse*." Presentation in the *Meeting "The Protection of Minors in the Church*." February 21, 2019. *www.vatican.va/resources/resources_mons-scicluna-protezioneminori_20190221_en.html*.

———. "*La ricerca della verità nei casi di abuso sessuale: un dovere morale e legale*." In *Verso la Guarigione e il Rinnovamento*, edited by C.J. SCICLUNA, H. ZOLLNER, D.J. AYOTTE. Bologna: EDB, 2012.

———. "The Rights of Victims in Canonical Penal Processes." *Periodica* 109 (2020).

———. "*Vos estis lux mundi: avances y desafíos de su recepción*." *La Revista Católica* 1207 (2020).

SCHOUPPE, J-P. "*Diritti fondamentali dei fedeli in rapporto alla partecipazione al governo dei beni temporali*." *Ius Ecclesiæ* 26 (2014).

SCHUDSON, M. *The Rise of the Right to Know. Politics and the Culture of Transparency, 1945–1975*. Cambridge, MA: Harvard University Press, 2015.

SEGARRA, A. *Desde el otro lado del escaparate*. Madrid: Espasa, 2009.

———. "*Discurso doctor honoris causa por la Universidad de Nebrija* [Madrid]," September 24, 2021. *forbes.es/nombre-del-dia/118069/hombre-del-dia-toni-segarra-doctor-honoris-causa-por-la-universidad-de-nebrija/*.

SECRETARY OF STATE. *Regolamento Generale della Curia Romana.* April 30, 1999, *www.vatican.va/roman_curia/secretariat_state/1999/documents/rc_seg-st_19990430_regolamento-curia-romana_it.html.*

SELZ, M. *Modestia.* Salamanca: Ediciones Síngueme, 2018.

SEMERARO, M. *"Discernere e formare per prevenire. Sugli abusi nella Chiesa."* La Rivista del Clero italiano 10 (2018).

SHAW, R. *Nothing To Hide: Secrecy, Communication, and Communion in the Catholic Church.* San Francisco: Ignatius Press, 2008.

———. *To Hunt, To Shoot, To Entertain: Clericalism and the Catholic Laity.* San Francisco: Ignatius Press, 1993.

———, T.L. MAMMOSER, F.J. MANISCALCO. *Dealing with Media for the Church.* Rome: EDUSC, 1999.

SOLOVE, D.J. *The Future of Reputation: Gossip, Rumor, and Privacy on the Internet.* New Haven & London: Yale University Press, 2007.

SORIA, C. *El laberinto informativo: una salida ética.* Pamplona: EUNSA, 1997.

STUMER, A. *La presunción de inocencia. Perspectiva desde el Derecho Probatorio y los derechos humanos.* Madrid: Marcial Pons Ediciones Jurídicas y Sociales, 2018.

STURLA, D. *"¿Confiar en una Iglesia vulnerable? La transparencia del Evangelio en el siglo XXI."* In *Inspiring Trust: Church Communications and Organizational Vulnerability,* edited by J. PUJOL, J. NARBONA, J.M. DÍAZ. Rome: EDUSC, 2021.

THE JOURNALISM SCHOOL. *Reporting an Explosive Truth: Boston Globe and Sexual Abuse in the Catholic Church.* Columbia University: Case Consortium, *ccnmtl.columbia.edu/projects/caseconsortium/casestudies/14/casestudy/files/global/14/Boston%20Globe%20and%20Sexual%20Abuse%20in%20the%20Catholic%20Church_wm.pdf.*

TKACZ, N. *Wikipedia and the Politics of Openness.* Chicago: University of Chicago Press, 2015.

Tornielli, A. *"Scicluna: Scelta epocale che toglie ostacoli e impedimenti." Vatican News*, December 17, 2019. *www. vaticannews.va/it/vaticano/news/2019-12/scicluna-scelta-epocale-che-toglie-ostacoli-impedimenti.html.*

Tosatti, M. *"Chiesa e informazione: Storia di un rapporto." Teoria e pratica del giornalismo religioso. Come informare sulla Chiesa Cattolica: Fonti, logiche, storie, personaggi,* edited by G. Tridente. Rome: EDUSC, 2014.

Tridente, G., B. Mastroianni, eds. *La missione digitale. Comunicazione della Chiesa e social media.* Rome: EDUSC, 2016.

United States Conference of Catholic Bishops (USCCB). *Charter for the Protection of Children and Young People* [Dallas Charter]. Washington, DC, 2002, *www.bishop-accountability. org/resources/resource-files/churchdocs/DallasCharter.pdf.*

―――. *2011 Annual Report: Findings and Recommendations.* April 2012, *www.usccb.org/issues-and-action/child-and-youth-protection/upload/2011-annual-report.pdf.*

―――. *2018 Annual Report: Findings and Recommendations.* June 2019, *www.usccb.org/issues-and-action/child-and-youth-protection/child-abuse-prevention/upload/2018-CYP-Annual-Report.pdf.*

Van Bühren, R. *"Caravaggio's 'Seven Works of Mercy' in Naples. The Relevance of Art History to Cultural Journalism." Church, Communication & Culture* 2, no. 1 (2017).

Van Schaijik, K. "We Need a New Principle to Balance 'Presumption of Innocence,'" in *The Personal Project,* September 11, 2018. *www.thepersonalistproject.org/home/comments/power-differentials-and-innocent-till-proven-guilty.*

Vatican Council II. Dogmatic Constitution on the Church *Lumen Gentium.* November 21, 1964.

―――. Pastoral Constitution on the Church in the Modern World *Gaudium et Spes.* December 7, 1965.

―――. Decree on the Media of Social Communications *Inter Mirifica.* December 4 1963.

VERDÚ, D., "'La revoca del segreto pontificio non risolverà tutti i problemi, ma non ci sarà più l'ostacolo istituzionale,' Interview with Charles J. Scicluna." El Pais, December 18, 2019.

VISIOLI, M. "Confidenzialità e segreto pontificio." Periodica 109 (2020).

———. "L'Istruzione sulla riservatezza delle cause. Considerazioni a margine del Rescriptum ex Audientia SS.mi del 6 dicembre 2019." Ius Ecclesiæ 33, no. 2 (2020).

VON BALTHASAR, H.U. Il Chicco di grano. Milan: Jaca Book, 1994.

VOSOUGHI, S., D. ROY, S. ARAL. "The Spread of True and False News Online." Science, vol. 359, no. 6380 (March 9, 2018).

WEICK, K.E., K.M. SUTCLIFFE. Managing the Unexpected: Resilient Performance in an Age of Uncertainty. San Francisco: Jossey-Bass, 2007.

———. Managing the Unexpected: Sustained Performance in a Complex World. Hoboken, NJ: John Wiley & Sons, 2015.

WOJTYŁA, K. Il rinnovamento della Chiesa e del mondo. Riflessioni sul Concilio Vaticano II. Madrid: LAC, 2016.

YOUNG, R.T. The Obligation of Transparency in the Administration of Temporal Goods of the Church in Canon 1287 § 2, doctoral thesis. PUSC, 2016.

ZABILDEA, D. La rendición de cuentas en el ordenamiento canónico: transparencia y misión. Pamplona: Eunsa, 2018.

ZUANAZZI, I. "La responsabilità dell'Amministrazione Ecclesiastica." La responsabilità giuridica degli enti ecclesiastici, edited by E. BAURA, F. PUIG. Milan: Guiffrè, 2020.

INDEX OF TITLES